TEACHER'S MANUAL
AND ACHIEVEMENT TESTS

NORTHSTAR 4
LISTENING AND SPEAKING

THIRD EDITION

AUTHORS

Tess Ferree

Kim Sanabria

SERIES EDITORS

Frances Boyd

Carol Numrich

PEARSON
Longman

NorthStar: Listening and Speaking Level 4, Third Edition
Teacher's Manual and Achievement Tests

Pearson Education, 10 Bank Street, White Plains, NY 10606

Teacher's Manual by Deborah B. Gordon. Activities for secondary schools by Ann Hilborn.

Achievement Tests developed by: Dr. Joan Jamison and Dr. Carol Chapelle.

Achievement Tests by Elizabeth Henly.

Staff credits: The people who made up the *NorthStar: Listening and Speaking Level 4, Third Edition Teacher's Manual* team, representing editorial, production, design, and manufacturing, are Dave Dickey, Christine Edmonds, Ann France, Margot Gramer, Gosia Jaros-White, Dana Klinek, Melissa Leyva, Sherry Preiss, Robert Ruvo, Debbie Sistino, Kathleen Smith, Jennifer Stem, and Paula Van Ells.

Listening selections and text credits: **Page T-2** © NPR ® 2000. The text and audio of the news report by NPR's Margot Adler was originally broadcast on National Public Radio's *Morning Edition* ® on June 6, 2000, and is used with the permission of National Public Radio, Inc. Any unauthorized duplication is strictly prohibited; **Page T-8** © NPR ® 2000. The text and audio of the news report by NPR's Bob Edwards was originally broadcast on National Public Radio's *Morning Edition* ® on March 26, 2000, and is used with the permission of National Public Radio, Inc. Any unauthorized duplication is strictly prohibited; **Page T-14** © NPR ® 2000. The text and audio of the news report by NPR's Michelle Trudeau was originally broadcast on National Public Radio's *All Things Considered* ® on September 9, 2000, and is used with the permission of National Public Radio, Inc. Any unauthorized duplication is strictly prohibited; **T-21** excerpt from *The Infinite Mind* program "Animal Intelligence" reproduced with permission of Lichtenstein Creative Media; **Page T-27** © NPR ® 2006. The text and audio of the news report by NPR's Alex Chadwick was originally broadcast on National Public Radio's *Remembrances* ® on February 21, 2006, and is used with the permission of National Public Radio, Inc. Any unauthorized duplication is strictly prohibited; **Page T-33** © American Public Media; **Page T-39** © NPR ® 2003. The text and audio of the news report by NPR's Margot Adler was originally broadcast on National Public Radio's *Morning Edition* ® on March 3, 2003, and is used with the permission of National Public Radio, Inc. Any unauthorized duplication is strictly prohibited; **Page T-45** © NPR ® 2001. The text and audio of the news report by NPR's Sarah Chayes was originally broadcast on National Public Radio's *Morning Edition* ® on May 7, 2001, and is used with the permission of National Public Radio, Inc. Any unauthorized duplication is strictly prohibited; **Page T-51** as heard on PRI's The World, a co-production of the BBC World Service, Public Radio International, and WGBH Boston; **Page T-56** "Noise in the City" from Living on Earth, 9/27/96. Copyright © 1996 by Living on Earth. Edited text used with permission of Living on Earth and World Media Foundation. www.loe.org Living on Earth is the weekly environmental news and information program distributed by Public Radio International.

Cover Art: Silvia Rojas/Getty Images
Text composition: ElectraGraphics, Inc.
Text font: 11.5/13 Minion

ISBN-10: 0-13-205678-X
ISBN-13: 978-0-13-205678-6

PEARSON LONGMAN ON THE WEB

Pearsonlongman.com offers online resources for teachers and students. Access our Companion Websites, our online catalog, and our local offices around the world.

Visit us at **www.pearsonlongman.com**.

Printed in the United States of America
4 5 6 7 8 9 10—HAM—13 12 11

CONTENTS

UNIT-BY-UNIT TEACHING SUGGESTIONS

ACHIEVEMENT TESTS

WELCOME TO NorthStar

THIRD EDITION

NorthStar, now in its third edition, motivates students to succeed in their **academic** as well as **personal** language goals.

For each of the five levels, the two strands—*Reading and Writing* and *Listening and Speaking*—provide a fully integrated approach for students and teachers.

WHAT IS SPECIAL ABOUT THE THIRD EDITION?

NEW THEMES

New themes and **updated content**—presented in a **variety of genres**, including literature and lectures, and in **authentic reading and listening selections**—challenge students intellectually.

ACADEMIC SKILLS

More purposeful **integration of critical thinking** and an enhanced focus on **academic skills** such as inferencing, synthesizing, note taking, and test taking help students develop strategies for **success** in the **classroom** and on **standardized tests**. A **culminating productive task** galvanizes content, language, and **critical thinking skills**.

➤ In the *Listening and Speaking* strand, a **structured approach** gives students opportunities for **more extended and creative oral practice**, for example, presentations, simulations, debates, case studies, and public service announcements.

➤ In the *Reading and Writing* strand, a new, **fully integrated writing section** leads students through the **writing process** with engaging writing assignments focusing on various rhetorical modes.

NEW DESIGN

Full **color pages** with more **photos**, **illustrations**, **and graphic organizers** foster student engagement and make the content and activities come alive.

MyNorthStarLab

MyNorthStarLab, an easy-to-use **online learning and assessment program**, offers:

➤ Unlimited access to reading and listening selections and DVD segments.

➤ Focused test preparation to help students succeed on international exams such as TOEFL® and IELTS®. Pre- and post-unit assessments improve results by providing individualized instruction, instant feedback, and personalized study plans.

➤ Original activities that support and extend the *NorthStar* program. These include pronunciation practice using voice recording tools, and activities to build note taking skills and academic vocabulary.

➤ Tools that save time. These include a flexible gradebook and authoring features that give teachers control of content and help them track student progress.

THE NORTHSTAR APPROACH

The *NorthStar* series is based on **current research in language acquisition** and on the **experiences of teachers and curriculum designers**. Five principles guide the *NorthStar* approach.

PRINCIPLES

1 The more profoundly students are stimulated intellectually and emotionally, the more language they will use and retain.

The thematic organization of *NorthStar* promotes intellectual and emotional stimulation. The 50 sophisticated themes in *NorthStar* present intriguing topics such as recycled fashion, restorative justice, personal carbon footprints, and microfinance. The authentic content engages students, links them to language use outside of the classroom, and encourages personal expression and critical thinking.

2 Students can learn both the form and content of the language.

Grammar, vocabulary, and culture are inextricably woven into the units, providing students with systematic and multiple exposures to language forms in a variety of contexts. As the theme is developed, students can express complex thoughts using a higher level of language.

3 Successful students are active learners.

Tasks are designed to be creative, active, and varied. Topics are interesting and up-to-date. Together these tasks and topics (1) allow teachers to bring the outside world into the classroom and (2) motivate students to apply their classroom learning in the outside world.

4 Students need feedback.

This feedback comes naturally when students work together practicing language and participating in open-ended opinion and inference tasks. Whole class activities invite teachers' feedback on the spot or via audio/video recordings or notes. The innovative new MyNorthStarLab gives students immediate feedback as they complete computer-graded language activities online; it also gives students the opportunity to submit writing or speaking assignments electronically to their instructor for feedback later.

5 The quality of relationships in the language classroom is important because students are asked to express themselves on issues and ideas.

The information and activities in *NorthStar* promote genuine interaction, acceptance of differences, and authentic communication. By building skills and exploring ideas, the exercises help students participate in discussions and write essays of an increasingly complex and sophisticated nature.

THE NORTHSTAR UNIT

① FOCUS ON THE TOPIC

This section introduces students to the unifying theme of the listening selections.

> **PREDICT** and **SHARE INFORMATION** foster interest in the unit topic and help students develop a personal connection to it.
>
> **BACKGROUND** AND **VOCABULARY** activities provide students with tools for understanding the first listening selection. Later in the unit, students review this vocabulary and learn related idioms, collocations, and word forms. This helps them explore content and expand their written and spoken language.

UNIT 9

Finding a Niche:
The Challenge for Young Immigrants

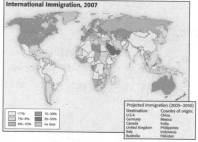
International Immigration, 2007

Projected Immigration (2005–2050)

Destination:	Country of origin:
U.S.A.	China
Germany	Mexico
Canada	India
United Kingdom	Philippines
Italy	Indonesia
Australia	Pakistan

<1%   10–20%
1%–4%   20–50%
4%–10%   no data

① FOCUS ON THE TOPIC

A PREDICT

Look at the map, the information about projected immigration, and the title of the unit. Then discuss the questions with a partner or small group.

1. Which areas of the world have the highest proportions of immigrants today? Is that likely to change in the future? Where will most immigrants probably come from in the next half century?

2. A *niche* here means a place that you fit in, or a group of people you fit in with—for example, your hometown, your family, a group of friends, a club, etc. What is a niche that you have? Why do you think it may be difficult for young immigrants to "find a niche"?

169

B SHARE INFORMATION

Work in a small group. Discuss the questions.

1. Have you ever moved to a different country? If so, describe the experience: How long did you live there? Why? What difficulties did you have? What did you learn? If you have never moved to a different country, do you know people who have? Describe their experience.

2. When teens immigrate, they face particular issues at school, and so do their teachers. Read these opinions. Decide whether you agree or disagree. Write **A** (agree) or **D** (disagree).

____ a. One of the main responsibilities of teachers is to make sure that immigrant students maintain their own language and culture, even if it means that those students learn their new language more slowly.

____ b. It is important that immigrants and non-immigrants study the same curriculum.

____ c. As immigrant teens learn their new language, they become less proficient in their first language.

____ d. Teenage immigrants should learn subjects like math and science in their first language, rather than in the language of their new country.

C BACKGROUND AND VOCABULARY

 Read and listen to the conversation between a college student and his professor. Then match the words on the left with the definitions on the right.

TRAI: Good morning, Professor. I'd like to ask your advice about an oral presentation I'm doing on international immigration. I'm trying to narrow down my topic, and I'm thinking of concentrating on language policy. I've read that in some countries, such as the Netherlands, for example, immigrants have to take a language exam.

PROFESSOR LEE: Yes, that's right. Language policy is an interesting and controversial debate worldwide, but it involves complex legal issues, too. I'd suggest that you focus more on how language learning is connected with cultural identity. That's especially fascinating in Europe and the Middle East, which have large immigrant populations.

TRAI: Yes, and I know that there are some places in the U.S. with large immigrant populations, too. I was reading about a (1) **unique** neighborhood in New York City. This article said that if you walk down the street, you hear many people speaking in their (2) **native tongue**.

170   UNIT 9

---

② FOCUS ON LISTENING

This section focuses on understanding two contrasting listening selections.

> **LISTENING ONE** is a radio report, interview, lecture, or other genre that addresses the unit topic. In levels 1 to 3, listenings are based on authentic materials. In levels 4 and 5, all the listenings are authentic.
>
> **LISTEN FOR MAIN IDEAS** and **LISTEN FOR DETAILS** are comprehension activities that lead students to an understanding and appreciation of the first selection.
>
> The **MAKE INFERENCES** activity prompts students to "listen between the lines," move beyond the literal meaning, exercise critical thinking skills, and understand the listening on a more academic level. Students follow up with pair or group work to discuss topics in the **EXPRESS OPINIONS** section.

Listen to the introduction.

Who wants to know why people donate time and money? Check (✓) the answer.

☐ Other rich people

☐ People who raise money for charities

☐ University researchers and sociologists

◀ LISTEN FOR MAIN IDEAS

Read the motivations for giving. Then listen to the interview and number the motivations in the order in which they are mentioned.

____ tax benefits

____ required by school

____ prevent something bad from happening

__1__ passion for the cause

____ family tradition

____ desire to repay someone for something

____ see the direct effects of what they're doing

◀ LISTEN FOR DETAILS

Listen to the interview again. As you listen, circle the letter of the answer that best completes each statement.

1. About ____ percent of people give money.
   a. 65   **b.** 75   **c.** 85

2. When a cause has an enemy or a threat, people tend to ____.
   a. give more   **b.** give the same as usual   **c.** give less

3. Most people seem to feel ____ about giving money than about giving time.
   a. better   **b.** worse   **c.** the same

4. ____ percent of the population say they have volunteered at some point.
   a. 50   **b.** 70   **c.** 80

(continued on next page)

◀ MAKE INFERENCES

Listen to the excerpts from the interview. Choose one or two adjectives from the box that describe the speaker's feeling. Then circle **T** (true) or **F** (false) for each statement.

aggressive	confused	playful	shocked
amused	enthusiastic	respectful	unhappy

Excerpt One

1. How does the interviewer feel? _____

2. The interviewer disagrees with Dr. Carskadon.   T   F

Excerpt Two

1. How does the interviewer feel? _____

2. The interviewer admires Dr. Dement.   T   F

Excerpt Three

1. How does the student feel? _____

2. The student knows why he is so sleepy.   T   F

Excerpt Four

1. How does Dr. Dement feel? _____

2. Dr. Dement thinks 10 minutes is a reasonable amount of time.   T   F

◀ EXPRESS OPINIONS

Work in a small group. Take turns reading the opinions. Then say whether you agree or disagree, and why.

1. Now that we know that teens are sleepier in the morning and less sleepy in the evening, high schools should change their schedules. They should start and finish much later in the day.

2. Sleep deprivation could have serious consequences for some workers, such as those in factories, hospitals, or airports. Managers should be able to require their workers to get enough sleep.

3. Sleep deprivation is a much more serious problem now than it was 50 or 100 years ago.

4. Different people need different amounts of sleep. Some people only need five or six hours a night, and others need as much as nine or ten hours a night.

LISTENING TWO offers another perspective on the topic and is usually another genre. Again, in levels 1 to 3, the listenings are based on authentic materials and in levels 4 and 5, they are authentic. This second listening is followed by an activity that challenges students to question ideas they formed about the first listening, and to use appropriate language skills to analyze and explain their ideas.

INTEGRATE LISTENINGS ONE AND TWO presents culminating activities. Students are challenged to take what they have learned, organize the information, and synthesize it in a meaningful way. Students practice skills that are essential for success in authentic academic settings and on standardized tests.

B **LISTENING TWO:** *Food in a Bowl*

What are the food trends in California? You will hear some comments from *Satellite Sisters*, a radio show featuring five sisters who live in different parts of the world and share their thoughts—via satellite—on everyday life. In this segment, Lian talks about life in California.

1 Listen to the report and answer the questions.

1. Why was Lian surprised in the supermarket?
   a. She found unusual food items in bowls.
   b. She thought the bowls were too expensive.

2. Why does Lian think this food-in-bowls trend is happening?
   a. People are too hurried to be careful about eating.
   b. Bowls keep food warmer than plates.

3. Lian jokes that maybe the next new eating style will be _____.
   a. eating while keeping one hand on the phone
   b. eating without using our hands

4. Lian exaggerates by using humor when she says, "just get yourself a nice *trough*, and put the lasagna in there." Why does she mention an animal food container?
   a. Many Californians are vegetarians and don't eat animal products.
   b. She thinks that people do not have good manners.

   trough

5. Lian thinks that teaching children to eat with a knife and fork _____.
   a. is a parent's responsibility
   b. won't be necessary in the future

6. Lian's sister, Julie, in Bangkok, also makes a comment. What is her attitude toward the subject?
   a. She shares Lian's feelings about food in bowls.
   b. She seems to have no problem accepting food in bowls.

7. What does Lian's sister Liz, in New York, struggle with?
   a. eating food on *skewers*
   b. finding lamb in a bowl

   skewers

2 Work in a small group. Discuss the questions.
   • Do you think it's important for families to eat meals together? Why or why not? What are some reasons that families might not eat together?
   • What factors are most important for you when choosing a meal: taste, price, convenience, or something else?

Goodbye to the Sit-Down Meal **155**

C **INTEGRATE LISTENINGS ONE AND TWO**

STEP 1: Organize

Work in groups of three. Fill in the chart with ideas from Listenings One and Two about food trends.

CATEGORIES	GOODBYE, SIT-DOWN MEAL	FOOD IN A BOWL
1. Examples of changes in eating habits (diet and style of eating)	• French bakeries are serving sandwiches now	
2. Reasons our eating habits are changing		
3. Speakers' attitudes toward these changes		
4. Speakers' tone		

STEP 2: Synthesize

Continue working with the same group and perform a role play. Student A is a reporter asking Student B (Fishlere) and Student C (Satellite Sister) questions from the categories on the left of the chart. The reporter also asks for examples and explanations. Use a tone similar to that of the speakers you heard.

Example

A: Most people seem to agree that our eating habits are changing in many ways. Can you give me some examples?
B: Yes, that's true. In France, for example . . .
C: Well, where I live . . .

156 UNIT 8

---

③ FOCUS ON SPEAKING

This section emphasizes development of productive skills for speaking. It includes sections on vocabulary, grammar, pronunciation, functional language, and an extended speaking task.

> The **VOCABULARY** section leads students from reviewing the unit vocabulary, to practicing and expanding their use of it, and then working with it—using it creatively in both this section and in the final speaking task.
>
> Students learn useful structures for speaking in the **GRAMMAR** section, which offers a concise presentation and targeted practice. Vocabulary items are recycled here, providing multiple exposures leading to mastery. For additional practice with the grammar presented, students and teachers can consult the GRAMMAR BOOK REFERENCES at the end of the book for corresponding material in the *Focus on Grammar* and Azar series.

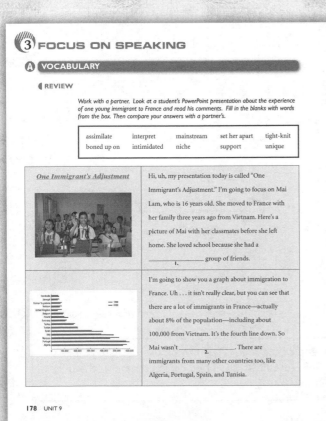

③ FOCUS ON SPEAKING

A VOCABULARY

❮ REVIEW

Work with a partner. Look at a student's PowerPoint presentation about the experience of one young immigrant to France and read his comments. Fill in the blanks with words from the box. Then compare your answers with a partner's.

assimilate	interpret	mainstream	set her apart	tight-knit
boned up on	intimidated	niche	support	unique

One Immigrant's Adjustment

Hi, uh, my presentation today is called "One Immigrant's Adjustment." I'm going to focus on Mai Lam, who is 16 years old. She moved to France with her family three years ago from Vietnam. Here's a picture of Mai with her classmates before she left home. She loved school because she had a _____1._____ group of friends.

I'm going to show you a graph about immigration to France. Uh . . . it isn't really clear, but you can see that there are a lot of immigrants in France—actually about 8% of the population—including about 100,000 from Vietnam. It's the fourth line down. So Mai wasn't _____2._____. There are immigrants from many other countries too, like Algeria, Portugal, Spain, and Tunisia.

178 UNIT 9

B GRAMMAR: Reported Speech

1 *Work with a partner. Read the conversation and answer the questions.*

A: I just did the assignment about animal communication. The article reported that some parrots could recognize themselves in a mirror.

B: Yeah, and it said they **were able to** string three or four words together, too. Actually, my professor told us that he **had just written** a paper on how parrots learn language. He said he **was going to** publish it next month.

A: What did the paper say?

B: Well, apparently it warned that researchers **had to** study animal intelligence more carefully before drawing conclusions.

1. Do we know the exact words of the article and the professor?

2. Why do you think speaker B chose not to quote the article and the professor directly?

REPORTED SPEECH

Reported speech (also called indirect speech) reports what a speaker said without using his or her exact words.

Use words like *said (that), told, indicated, mentioned, reported*, etc., to show that you are reporting information that someone else said.

When you are reporting what a speaker or article said, "backshift" the verb in the indirect speech statement.

Original: "We **are conducting** some interesting research with chimps."
Reported: The scientist explained that she **was conducting** some interesting research with chimps.

The verb in the reported speech has shifted back in time, in this case from the present continuous to the past continuous. See more examples in the chart below.

NOTE: If you are reporting a person's unchanging beliefs or a general truth, rather than an event, it is not necessary to change the tense of the original verb.

Original: "Many animals **are** remarkably intelligent."
Reported: The zoologist **told her students** that many animals **are / were** remarkably intelligent.

Animal Intelligence **73**

The **PRONUNCIATION** section presents both controlled and freer, communicative practice of the sounds and patterns of English. Models from the listening selections reinforce content and vocabulary. This is followed by the **FUNCTION** section where students are exposed to functional language that prepares them to express ideas on a higher level. Examples have been chosen based on frequency, variety, and usefulness for the final speaking task.

The **PRODUCTION** section gives students an opportunity to integrate the ideas, vocabulary, grammar, pronunciation, and function presented in the unit. This final speaking task is the culminating activity of the unit and gets students to exchange ideas and express opinions in sustained speaking contexts. Activities are presented in a sequence that builds confidence and fluency, and allows for more than one "try" at expression. When appropriate, students practice some presentation skills: audience analysis, organization, eye contact, or use of visuals.

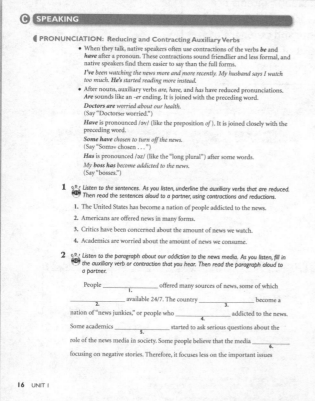

C SPEAKING

◀ PRONUNCIATION: Reducing and Contracting Auxiliary Verbs

- When they talk, native speakers often use contractions of the verbs *be* and *have* after a pronoun. These contractions sound friendlier and less formal, and native speakers find them easier to say than the full forms.

  I've been watching the news more and more recently. My husband says I watch too much. He's started reading more instead.

- After nouns, auxiliary verbs *are, have,* and *has* have reduced pronunciations. *Are* sounds like an *-er* ending. It is joined with the preceding word.

  Doctors are worried about our health.
  (Say "Doctorser worried.")

  Have is pronounced /əv/ (like the preposition *of*). It is joined closely with the preceding word.

  Some have chosen to turn off the news.
  (Say "Soməv chosen . . .")

  Has is pronounced /əz/ (like the "long plural") after some words.

  My boss has become addicted to the news.
  (Say "bosses.")

1 *Listen to the sentences. As you listen, underline the auxiliary verbs that are reduced. Then read the sentences aloud to a partner, using contractions and reductions.*

1. The United States has become a nation of people addicted to the news.
2. Americans are offered news in many forms.
3. Critics have been concerned about the amount of news we watch.
4. Academics are worried about the amount of news we consume.

2 *Listen to the paragraph about our addiction to the news media. As you listen, fill in the auxiliary verb or contraction that you hear. Then read the paragraph aloud to a partner.*

People _____ offered many sources of news, some of which
              1.
_____ available 24/7. The country _____ become a
        2.   3.
nation of "news junkies," or people who _____ addicted to the news.
                                          4.
Some academics _____ started to ask serious questions about the
                 5.
role of the news media in society. Some people believe that the media _____
                                                                        6.
focusing on negative stories. Therefore, it focuses less on the important issues

16 UNIT 1

◀ PRODUCTION: A Class Presentation

In this activity, you will work with a group to *identify arguments for and against a position related to animals and their relationship to people.* You will then present the issue to the class. Try to use the vocabulary, grammar, pronunciation, and language for giving and asking for examples that you learned in the unit.*

Step 1: Divide the class into enough groups so that each one can choose a different topic. Then each group selects its topic from the list or proposes a new one. Consider the question in terms of whether animals are intelligent or not.

1. Should animals be kept in zoos?
2. Should people eat animals?
3. Should people conduct experiments on animals?
4. Should people be allowed to hunt animals?
5. Should people pass stricter laws to protect endangered species?

Step 2: Study the example outline. Then organize your ideas in the outline on page 81. Be sure to think of reasons and examples for both sides of the argument.

Topic: Should people wear fur or leather?	
I. People should not wear fur or leather.	II. People should be allowed to wear fur or leather.
A: Killing animals for fur is cruel.	
1. Animals raised for fur are kept in inhumane conditions.	A: Animals are raised specifically for fur.
2. They are killed before they reach old age.	1. Many rabbits wouldn't be alive unless people bred them for their fur. They weren't wild animals that were shot.
B: Fur is not necessary for people.	
1. They can wear other materials.	2. Example:
2. Example:	B: Reason:
	1. Example:
	2. Example:

*For Alternative Speaking Topics, see page 81.

80 UNIT 4

ALTERNATIVE SPEAKING TOPICS are provided at the end of the unit. They can be used as *alternatives* to the final speaking task, or as *additional* assignments. RESEARCH TOPICS tied to the theme of the unit are organized in a special section at the back of the book.

MyNorthStarLab

MyNorthStarLab supports students with **individualized instruction, feedback**, and **extra help**. A wide array of resources, including a flexible **gradebook**, helps teachers manage student progress.

The MyNorthStarLab **WELCOME** page **organizes assignments and grades**, and **facilitates communication** between students and teachers.

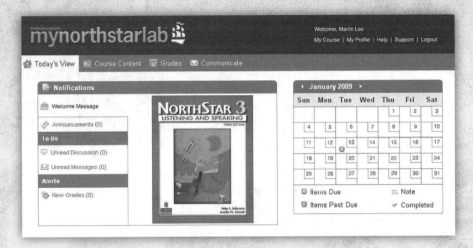

For each unit, MyNorthStarLab provides a **READINESS CHECK**.

➤ Activities **assess** student knowledge **before** beginning the unit and **follow up** with individualized instruction.

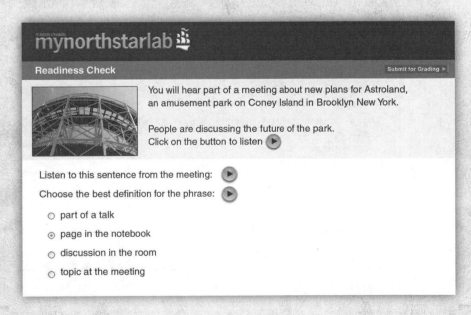

Student book material and **new** practice activities are available to students online.

➤ Students benefit from virtually unlimited **practice anywhere, anytime**.

Interaction with **Internet** and **video** materials will:

➤ Expand students' knowledge of the topic.

➤ Help students practice new vocabulary and grammar.

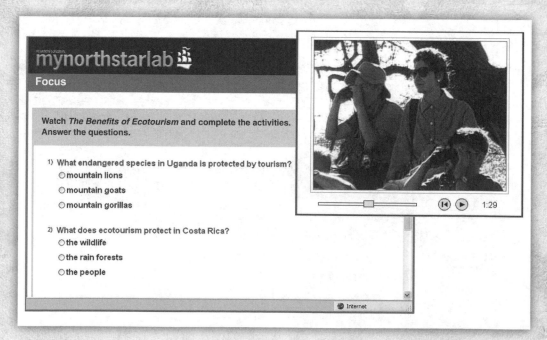

INTEGRATED SKILL ACTIVITIES in MyNorthStarLab challenge students to bring together the **language skills** and **critical thinking skills** that they have practiced throughout the unit.

The MyNorthStarLab **ASSESSMENT** tools allow instructors to customize and deliver achievement tests online.

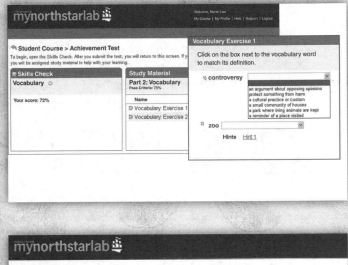

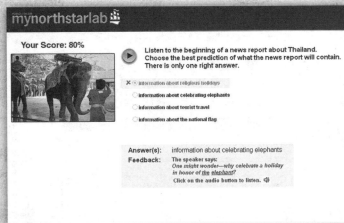

OVERVIEW OF THE TEACHER'S MANUAL AND ACHIEVEMENT TESTS

The **NorthStar Teacher's Manual** includes:

➤ Specific suggestions for teaching each unit

➤ Student Book Answer Key

➤ An alphabetized-by-unit word list of the key vocabulary items practiced in each unit

➤ Reproducible Achievement Tests with Answer Keys—including the test audioscript and test audio CD

UNIT-BY-UNIT TEACHING SUGGESTIONS

Unit-by-unit overview (scope and sequence), list of skills practiced in each section of the student book, suggested teaching times, teaching suggestions, suggestions on how to use *NorthStar* in secondary classes, Expansion/Homework activities, cross-references to the companion strand, techniques and instructions for using MyNorthStarLab

---

UNIT 7 — What's the Use of Homework?

OVERVIEW

Theme: Education
This unit examines the value and the negative effects of the amount of homework assigned to students, and the resulting involvement of the parents in their children's education. Students think about and discuss their own experiences with homework.

Listening One: *Effects of Homework on Family Life* is a radio interview with a student, parents, and experts on the issue of students spending so much time doing homework.

Listening Two: *A Duty to Family, Heritage, and Country: Another Perspective on Homework* is a radio report on another culture's view of education, homework, and grades. A young Chinese student describes her conflicting feelings about fulfilling the expectations of her family and her country instead of following her own dreams.

Critical Thinking

Interpret a cartoon	Connect opinions to specific people
Identify and evaluate assumptions	Evaluate own opinions concerning others'
Hypothesize another's point of view	thoughts

Listening

Predict content	Relate listenings to personal experiences
Listen for main ideas	Organize and synthesize information from the
Listen for details	listenings
Support answers with details	

Speaking

Express opinions	Restate statements
Use opening gambits to restate information for	Perform a role play
clarification	Conduct a town meeting

Vocabulary	Grammar
Use context clues to find meaning	*Make, let, help, and get*
Find and use synonyms	
Use idiomatic expressions	**Pronunciation**
	Stressed and unstressed vowels

📁 **MyNorthStarLab**	🔊 **NorthStar: Reading and Writing 4**
Readiness Check, Background and Vocabulary, Listenings One and Two, Notetaking and Academic Skills Practice, Vocabulary and Grammar, Achievement Test	Unit 7 deals with the advantages and disadvantages of homeschooling.

66

---

ooo A LISTENING ONE: News Resisters

📁 Go to www.mynorthstarlab.com to listen to *News Resisters.*

Suggested Time: 10 minutes

In Listening One, students listen to a radio program on "consuming" less news. The audio program should get students thinking about their own news listening, watching, or reading habits.

1. Ask students to read the title and the background information on the news report they are about to listen to. Ask them what they think a "news resister" might be.

2. Play the audio and have students answer the questions individually. Put students in pairs or small groups to compare answers. You may want to let them listen again to check their answers.

3. Go over the students' answers to both questions as a class.

LISTENING STRATEGY: Interview Your Partner

1. To prepare students for this group of interviews, have them interview their partner and take notes on their partner's responses. Have them ask the following questions: Do you watch news on TV? Do you read the newspaper each day? If not, do you think you will ever watch/read the news every day? Is it important to spend an hour a day learning about the news? What do you think about the news generally? If I gave you a story and a newspaper, which one would you prefer to read?

2. Have students meet in small groups and read their interview to the group. Then ask for volunteers to share their interview with the class.

ooo LISTEN FOR MAIN IDEAS   Suggested Time: 15 minutes

1. Have students read through the names and the opinions. Check that students understand the task. Have them draw a line between Andrew Weil and his opinion which the students should be able to do because they heard Andrew Weil's opinion in the introduction. Then check the answer as a class.

2. Tell students to listen for the people's opinions while you play the interview. Play the interview once without stopping. Have students compare their answers with a partner's before going over them as a class.

Expansion/Homework
For homework, have students keep a journal of the times that they are aware of being informed of the news. Then, have them compare their journals in the next class.

4   UNIT 1

USING *NORTHSTAR* IN SECONDARY CLASSES

Each unit of the *Teacher's Manual* offers a set of strategies that provide opportunities for greater differentiation in a typical mixed classroom to meet the needs of multi-level secondary students. These strategies are equally beneficial in academic and adult classes. The scaffolded instruction enables teachers to facilitate student mastery of complex skills and ideas. Repeated exposure to concepts helps accelerate English language learning.

Reading/Listening Strategies give teachers additional support to guide students who have limited experience with basic reading/listening skills as they learn to explore and understand academic content. Suggestions are given to help students understand how to predict, determine main idea and supporting details, navigate and comprehend a text, monitor their understanding, and organize information.

Reaching All Students are activity suggestions for two levels of language proficiency, intended to assist less proficient students and challenge students with higher proficiencies. These are generally included in the Reading/Listening section to help teachers to modify reading/listening activities.

Critical Thinking suggestions focus on a hierarchy of questions using Bloom's taxonomy. These are designed specifically to scaffold questions to move students from knowledge-based questions to higher order thinking.

Vocabulary Expansion builds upon vocabulary introduced in each unit to help students further integrate vocabulary. They are offered as word analysis or as vocabulary strategies to reinforce vocabulary skills and provide opportunities for review.

COURSE PLANNERS

Each unit contains approximately eight hours of classroom material, plus expansion, homework, and support material, including MyNorthStarLab. Teachers can customize the units by assigning some exercises for homework and/or eliminating others. To help teachers customize the units for their specific teaching situation, the unit-by-unit teaching suggestions in the *Teacher's Manual* include 1, 2, or 3 stars to indicate the relative importance of each section or exercise as follows:

✪✪✪ **Essential:** Predict, Background and Vocabulary, Listening One, Listen for Main Ideas, Listen for Details, Make Inferences, Express Opinions, Listening Two, Integrate Listenings One and Two, Production

✪✪ **Recommended:** Share Information, Expand, Grammar, Pronunciation, Function

✪ **Optional:** Review, Create, Speaking Topics, Research Topics

Class time available per unit	Sections to complete
8 hours or more	Essential (✪✪✪), Recommended (✪✪), Optional (✪)
6 hours	Essential (✪✪✪), Recommended (✪✪)
4 hours	Essential (✪✪✪) only

For more detailed, downloadable unit-by-unit course planners, visit www.mynorthstarlab.com or www.longman.com/northstar.

ACHIEVEMENT TESTS

The reproducible Achievement Tests allow teachers to evaluate students' progress and to identify areas where the students might have problems developing their listening and speaking skills. The Achievement Tests should be given upon completion of the corresponding unit.

Description

There are four parts for every test:

Parts 1 and **2** test students' receptive skills. Part 1 assesses students' mastery of listening comprehension. **Part 2** assesses the knowledge of the vocabulary introduced in the unit. **Parts 3** and **4** test students' productive skills. Part 3 assesses students' knowledge of the grammar, pronunciation, and functions introduced in the unit. Part 4 is a speaking test related to the content of the unit.

Administration

All parts of each test should be taken in class and students should not be allowed access to any *NorthStar* materials or to their dictionaries. Students should be able to complete Parts 1–3 within 40 minutes and Part 4 within 10 minutes.

Teachers can decide how to incorporate Part 4 (the speaking task) into their testing situations. Some teachers will assign each speaking task immediately after students complete Parts 1–3; others may decide to set aside another time to complete it.

Scoring the Parts

Parts 1–3: Individual test items are worth one point, for a maximum total of 30 points per test. A student's raw score can be obtained by adding together the number of correct items, or by subtracting the total number of incorrect items from 30. To convert the raw score to a percentage score, multiply it by 3.33.

Part 4: The speaking tasks are evaluated based on speaking skills and function. There are two shorter test items in this part, each worth one point. These should be scored according to the suggestions provided in the answer key for each test. The extended speaking tasks are evaluated holistically using scoring rubrics. The scale ranges from 0–4 and includes information from the listening and fluency/pronunciation, connectedness, structures and vocabulary from the unit, and errors.

Combining scores from Parts 1–3 and Part 4: To get a total Achievement Test score, multiply the extended speaking task score by 2. Add the score for the shorter speaking items to this score for the extended speaking task. Then, add the score in Parts 1–3. Multiply this new score by 2.5 to get a percentage score.

Example 1

Score on Test Parts 1–3 = 30
Score on Part 4 (extended task) = 4
Multiply 4 x 2
Score on Part 4 (shorter items) = 2
Add 10 to 30
Multiply 40 x 2.5
Total score = 100%

Example 2

Score on Parts 1–3 = 25
Score on Part 4 (extended task) = 2
Multiply 2 x 2
Score on Part 4 (shorter items) = 1
Add 5 to 25
Multiply 30 by 2.5
Total score = 72.5%

Using the Scoring Rubrics

The *NorthStar Listening and Speaking* rubrics are adapted from the integrated speaking rubric of TOEFL iBT. Whereas the TOEFL iBT scoring rubric is intended to distinguish levels of English proficiency among candidates to colleges and universities, the *NorthStar* scoring rubrics are intended to show progress in students' speaking at each of the five *NorthStar* levels. Therefore, *NorthStar* scoring bands make finer distinctions than TOEFL iBT's scoring band. In this way, students at each level will be able to both see improvement in their scores and receive high marks. The detailed scoring rubric is included in the Achievement Tests Answer Key.

Relationship between TOEFL iBT Rubric and *NorthStar 4* Integrated Speaking Rubric		
TOEFL iBT	⬅➡	*NorthStar 4*
4	⬅➡	4
3	⬅➡	3
3	⬅➡	2
2–3	⬅➡	1
1–2	⬅➡	0
0	⬅➡	

OTHER NORTHSTAR COMPONENTS

EXAMVIEW

NorthStar ExamView is a stand-alone CD-ROM that allows teachers to **create and customize** their own *NorthStar* tests.

DVD

The *NorthStar* DVD has **engaging, authentic video clips**, including animation, documentaries, interviews, and biographies, that correspond to the themes in *NorthStar*. Each theme contains a three- to five-minute segment that can be used with either the *Reading and Writing* strand or the *Listening and Speaking* strand. The video clips can also be viewed in MyNorthStarLab.

COMPANION WEBSITE

The companion website, www.longman.com/northstar, includes resources for teachers, such as the scope and sequence, correlations to other Longman products and to state standards, and podcasts from the *NorthStar* authors and series editors.

UNIT 1

Information Overload

OVERVIEW

Theme: Media

This unit focuses on the different ways we get information today and how the news influences individuals and society. Students think about the places and the ways in which they get information most often.

Listening One: *News Resisters* is a radio report about people who don't believe there is value in knowing as much news as we do or in getting the news as often as we do.

Listening Two: *Does the Media Overwhelm Our Lives?* is an interview with Todd Gitlin, author of the book, *Media Unlimited,* who believes that having so much access to news can be harmful.

Critical Thinking

Compare sources of news	Hypothesize another's point of view
Recognize assumptions about media	Analyze goals of news reporting
Interpret graphs	Analyze effects of news reporting styles
Infer information not explicit in the interview	Reflect on the role news has in individuals' lives

Listening

Make predictions	Relate listenings to personal values
Listen for main ideas	Organize and synthesize information from the
Listen for details	listenings
Provide evidence to support answers	Listen to student broadcasts and analyze them

Speaking

Summarize points	Give a newscast
Act out a scripted conversation	Express and defend opinions

Vocabulary

Use context clues to find meaning
Find and use synonyms
Use idiomatic expressions
Use descriptive adjectives

Grammar

Passive voice

Pronunciation

Reducing and contracting auxiliary verbs

 MyNorthStarLab
Readiness Check, Background and Vocabulary, Listenings One and Two, Notetaking and Academic Skills Practice, Vocabulary and Grammar, Achievement Test

 NorthStar: Reading and Writing 4
Unit 1 deals with the effects of tabloid journalism and the news media's intrusion into people's private lives.

Go to www.mynorthstarlab.com for the MyNorthStarLab *Readiness Check*.

FOCUS ON THE TOPIC

◀ SKILLS

Predict the content of the unit based on a cartoon and the title of the unit; activate prior knowledge; express opinions; infer the meaning of new vocabulary from context.

✿✿✿ A PREDICT

Suggested Time: 10 minutes

1. Write the unit title on the board and have students read it. Ask students to identify whether or not "overload" is a negative or positive term. Ask them why having information could be a bad or negative thing. Then have them reflect on what the title means and what the unit might be about.

2. Have students work in pairs or small groups (of different language backgrounds or language levels, if possible) to look at the cartoon. Have them say what they see happening in the cartoon, and how the cartoon relates to the title.

3. Have the pairs or groups discuss the questions. As a class, elicit answers to the questions

✿✿ B SHARE INFORMATION

Suggested Time: 20 minutes

1. Have students read the instructions. Check students' comprehension of the term *news media* (singular: *medium*). You might want to go through each news medium and type of information listed in the chart together.

2. Have students complete the chart individually. Then, put students into small groups to compare and discuss their charts.

Expansion/Homework
Ask students to copy the chart onto a piece of paper and interview a select number of people outside of class, filling in the chart for them as they answer. In class, have students speculate on the collected data.

✱✱✱ C BACKGROUND AND VOCABULARY

 Go to www.mynorthstarlab.com for *Background and Vocabulary*.

Suggested Time: 25 minutes

1. Have students read the instructions for **Exercise 1**. Then have them read the three categories of news consumers, checking their comprehension of each. You might want to have them check the one they think applies to them before doing the survey.

2. Play the recording of the survey and have students listen as they read. Then have them check their responses.

3. Go over the key in **Exercise 2** with the students, checking that they know how to score the surveys. You might also want to go over the characteristics of the three different categories before putting students into pairs to exchange books and use the key to score each other's surveys. Have students tell their partners which category they fell into and then have them discuss their reactions to that.

4. Have students read the instructions for **Exercise 3**. Tell them to check the contexts in the survey if they aren't clear on the meaning of some of the words. Then have them complete the exercise.

5. Go over the answers as a class, checking their comprehension of the vocabulary words. You might want to elicit other sentences for the words that cause particular difficulties.

Expansion/Homework

It can be very useful to have students highlight or underline the parts of the text, for example, the contexts, which helped them to understand the meaning of the boldfaced words. You might want to do this with students at first.

Link to *NorthStar: Reading and Writing 4*

If students are also using the companion text, you may want to list vocabulary from Background and Vocabulary in Unit 1 on the board and see if students can find synonyms for those words in the list of words they just worked on.

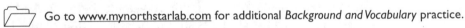 Go to www.mynorthstarlab.com for additional *Background and Vocabulary* practice.

②FOCUS ON LISTENING

◖ SKILLS

Make predictions about the content of the radio report; listen for main ideas; listen for details; make inferences and support them with evidence from the report; express opinions; listen to an interview.

Go to www.mynorthstarlab.com to listen to *News Resisters*.

Suggested Time: 10 minutes

In Listening One, students listen to a radio program on "consuming" less news. The audio program should get students thinking about their own news listening, watching, or reading habits.

1. Ask students to read the title and the background information on the news report they are about to listen to. Ask them what they think a "news resister" might be.

2. Play the audio and have students answer the questions individually. Put students in pairs or small groups to compare answers. You may want to let them listen again to check their answers.

3. Go over the students' answers to both questions as a class.

LISTENING STRATEGY: Interview Your Partner

1. To prepare students for this group of interviews, have them interview their partner and take notes on their partner's responses. Have them ask the following questions: Do you watch news on TV? Do you read the newspaper each day? If not, do you think you will ever watch/read the news every day? Is it important to spend an hour a day learning about the news? What do you think about the news generally? If I gave you a story and a newspaper, which one would you prefer to read?

2. Have students meet in small groups and read their interview to the group. Then ask for volunteers to share their interview with the class.

✪✪✪ LISTEN FOR MAIN IDEAS

Suggested Time: 15 minutes

1. Have students read through the names and the opinions. Check that students understand the task. Have them draw a line between Andrew Weil and his opinion which the students should be able to do because they heard Andrew Weil's opinion in the introduction. Then check the answer as a class.

2. Tell students to listen for the people's opinions while you play the interview. Play the interview once without stopping. Have students compare their answers with a partner's before going over them as a class.

Expansion/Homework

For homework, have students keep a journal of the times that they are aware of being informed of the news. Then, have them compare their journals in the next class.

- **Less Proficient:** Have students complete a web to record ideas before answering the Main Idea questions.

- **More Proficient:** After completing the activity, have students provide reasons to support the list of main ideas.

✪✪✪ LISTEN FOR DETAILS   Suggested Time: 15 minutes

Have students read the items and answer the questions they think they know. You might want to have them do that in pencil. Play the report again, and have students complete the exercise. If students seem to be having trouble, play the report one more time, and allow them to compare their answers with a partner's.

✪✪✪ MAKE INFERENCES   Suggested Time: 15 minutes

1. Have students read the instructions. Go over the different ways of choosing an answer listed, giving examples of your own to illustrate different tones of voice.

2. Play the audio and have students complete the exercise. Replay the excerpts as needed so students can write down the language used by the speaker. Emphasize that it is possible for students to draw varying inferences, as long as their reasoning is sound.

3. Go over the answers as a class. Encourage discussion.

Expansion/Homework
To teach students how to make inferences based on what they hear, you may want to do Excerpt One as a class. After playing the excerpt, elicit students' answers to question 1. Then ask them to explain why they chose that answer. Write the information they provide as support on the board. It might be useful to show why this is an inference as opposed to a stated fact.

✪✪✪ EXPRESS OPINIONS   Suggested Time: 10 minutes

1. Have students read the discussion questions. You might want to give them a few minutes to formulate their own thoughts.

2. Put students in small groups to discuss the questions. Encourage them to use the new vocabulary and support their ideas with reasons and information based on the listening.

Link to NorthStar: Reading and Writing 4
If students are also using the companion text, you can ask them to speculate about how the interviewees would react to the "Peeping Tom Journalism" described in Reading One.

CRITICAL THINKING

Give students the following questions for discussion in small groups before discussing as a whole class:

1. According to the report, what is a news resister?

   Answer: A person who limits their daily attention to news.

2. Tupton Shudrun suggests that the news creates despair. Do you agree or disagree with her?

   Answers will vary, but students should support their opinions with specific reasons and examples.

3. Do you agree that reading or watching the news every day is excessive?

   Answers will vary, but students should support their opinions from the text and their own knowledge and experience.

4. How can someone stay informed, but avoid getting too much news?

   Students should be encouraged to offer a variety of explanations, using information from the text and from their own knowledge and experience.

✸✸✸ B LISTENING TWO: Does the Media Overwhelm Our Lives?

Go to www.mynorthstarlab.com to listen to *Does the Media Overwhelm Our Lives?*

Suggested Time: 20 minutes

In Listening Two, students listen to an interview with a person who believes that the way the news is presented to us can distract and overwhelm us. The purpose of this interview is to further challenge students to consider the problems of being inundated with the news at all times or any time.

1. Read the segment title and the background information with the class. Check students' comprehension of *overwhelm* and if they ever feel this way. Ask them what they think of Todd Gitlin's claim, and to imagine why he might think that.

2. Read through the questions in **Exercise 1** with students. Then play the interview, having students circle their answers to the questions. Replay the audio as needed stopping at appropriate places. For problematic questions, you might ask students to raise their hands when they hear the relevant information on the audio, stopping only when you see raised hands.

3. Have students read the discussion questions in **Exercise 2**. Put students in small groups to discuss the questions. Encourage students to give specific examples to support their opinions.

◀ **SKILLS**

Organize information from the listening in a chart; synthesize the information from the listenings in a role play.

STEP 1: Organize   Suggested Time: 15 minutes

1. Have students read the instructions and then look at the chart. Have students fill in the chart from what they remember. Then put them in pairs to compare and add each other's information to their own charts.

2. Have pairs or groups compare answers with another pair's before going over the answers with the entire class.

STEP 2: Synthesize   Suggested Time: 15 minutes

1. Read the instructions with the class. Check students' comprehension of *commentator*. To discuss the meaning, it could be useful to divide the word into its root and suffix. Discuss the idea that the reporter will probably want to defend the way news is presented today as that is his/her job.

2. Put students in pairs and tell them to choose a role. You might want to have the reporters and commentators get into groups before having them do their role plays to work together to come up with questions and possible comments. Then, have the pairs practice their role plays while you circulate to help with individual questions.

3. If time allows, have a few pairs perform their role plays for the class.

 Link to *NorthStar: Reading and Writing 4*

If students are also using the companion text, you can list the relevant vocabulary from Unit 1 on the board and suggest students try to use the vocabulary in their role play.

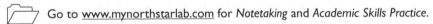 Go to www.mynorthstarlab.com for *Notetaking* and *Academic Skills Practice*.

3 FOCUS ON SPEAKING

A VOCABULARY

◀ SKILLS

Review vocabulary from Listenings One and Two; apply vocabulary learned in the unit to a new context—a conversation; categorize words; use new vocabulary creatively in a speaking activity.

✪ REVIEW   Suggested Time: 15 minutes

 Go to www.mynorthstarlab.com for *Review*.

1. Have students read the instructions for **Exercise 1** and review the meanings of the words together as a class. You might want to go over the word forms of each vocabulary item, reviewing with students the function of each word form. Review the pronunciation of the words and have students practice repeating them.

2. Have students fill in the blanks individually. Then, put them in pairs to first check their answers, and then practice the conversation.

3. Check students' comprehension of *connotation*. Model **Exercise 2** with a pair of words that are similar in meaning but have positive and negative connotations (for example, assertive/aggressive or determined/stubborn).

4. Have students complete the exercise individually before working with partners to compare their answers.

✪✪ EXPAND   Suggested Time: 15 minutes

1. Have students look at the descriptions briefly. Ask them where they would see these descriptions, eliciting a listing of TV shows. Read the instructions with the class. Go over the titles of each news program with students.

2. Have students complete the exercise individually. Put students into pairs or small groups to compare their answers when they are finished. Encourage them to say whether the words have a positive, negative, or neutral connotation.

Expansion/Homework
Both the Review and Expand exercises could be done for homework and then discussed in class, if desired. You may want to have students say which of the news programs they would prefer to watch and why.

VOCABULARY EXPANSION: Dictation

1. Dictation provides focused listening while presenting vocabulary in context and helping to prepare students for notetaking. For more effective dictation, and to help students with punctuation and spelling, provide copies of the sentences so that students can correct their work. Allow time for dictation each week, beginning with sentences and progressing to paragraphs.

2. Dictate sentences using each word in the vocabulary list, reminding students to write what they hear. An important step is to provide a handout of the dictation or display it on an overhead and give students time to complete and correct their work. You might also wish to have student pairs read their sentences to each other before having students complete the correction process.

✪ CREATE

Suggested Time: 20 minutes

Put students in pairs or small groups to discuss the news programs. Remind them to use as many of the vocabulary words as they can. You might want to throw out a few questions for students to think about prior to putting them in pairs or groups such as: What kind of people do you think watch each program? Why do you think *Regional Recap* is on Friday mornings? Why would people want to be able to laugh about the news?

 Go to www.mynorthstarlab.com for additional *Vocabulary* practice.

✪✪ B GRAMMAR: Passive Voice

 Go to www.mynorthstarlab.com for *Grammar Chart* and *Exercise 2*.

◖ SKILLS

Practice the passive voice in form and meaning.

Suggested Time: 25 minutes

1. Have students practice the conversation in **Exercise 1** with a partner. Then discover students' existing knowledge of the passive voice by having them underline the examples of the passive in the conversation. Alternatively, put them on the board and ask students to say what they are, and how they are different.

2. Go over each section in the grammar chart with the class providing more examples, or eliciting more examples from students.

3. Read the instructions for **Exercise 2** with students. Then put students in pairs to complete the exercise and check their answers. Go over the answers with the class. Make sure students understand why the different verb tenses were used.

4. Read the instructions for **Exercise 3**. Then put students in pairs to practice the conversations. Check the answers by asking each pair to perform a line of dialogue while other students listen and correct the verb forms. Then review the answers and address questions and problems as a class.

Expansion/Homework

(**1**) Exercise 2 could be done for homework and then discussed in class, if desired. Have students refer back to the three reasons for using the passive voice in the grammar explanation and discuss the reasons as a class. (**2**) For further practice, offer exercises from *Focus on Grammar 4, 3rd Edition,* and Azar's *Understanding and Using English Grammar, 3rd Edition.* See the Grammar Book References on page 225 of the student book for specific units and chapters.

 Go to www.mynorthstarlab.com for additional *Grammar* practice.

C SPEAKING

SKILLS

Practice using the reduced form of *be* and *have;* practice stating opinions; integrate the concepts, vocabulary, grammar, pronunciation, and function from the unit in a presentation of a news broadcast.

PRONUNCIATION: Reducing and Contracting Auxiliary Verbs

Suggested Time: 15 minutes

1. Read the example sentences in both unreduced and uncontracted and reduced and contracted forms. Help students to see that the reduced forms sound "friendlier" and are used commonly in conversation. Have students practice repeating the sentences using the reduced and contracted forms.

2. Have students listen to the sentences in **Exercise 1** and underline the words that contain reduced sounds. Play the audio again to let students check their answers before going over the answers as a class. Then have students take turns practicing reading the sentences with a partner while you circulate to offer individual assistance.

3. Read the instructions for **Exercise 2**. You might want to have students read the paragraph first, trying to imagine the various possibilities. Then play the audio and have students fill in the missing words while they listen. Check answers as a class, and then have students practice reading the paragraph aloud with a partner.

✪✪ FUNCTION: Stating an Opinion

Suggested Time: 25 minutes

1. With books closed, ask students what they would say to express an opinion. Write the responses on the board. Ask what they would say to express a strong opinion and an opinion they are unsure about. Again, write the responses on the board. Then have students open their books and read the introductory explanation and list of expressions.

2. Put students in pairs to take turns being Student A and Student B. Remind students to use the phrases in the box. You might want to have them check each phrase that they use. Encourage students to expand on the discussions by explaining the reasons for their opinions.

3. Have a few pairs perform their conversations for the class. Be sure to elicit a variety of answers for each one.

✪✪✪ PRODUCTION: A News Broadcast

Suggested Time: 50 minutes

If you wish to assign a different speaking task than the one in this section, see page 20. The alternative topics relate to the theme of the unit, but may not target the same grammar, pronunciation, or function taught in the unit.

1. Go over the instructions in the task box and the four steps. Put students in pairs to write their news stories and commentator's opinions.

2. Have students practice their news reports and commentators' comments before having them perform them for the class. Before they perform, make sure everyone knows that when they aren't performing, they will be grading their fellow students' broadcasts.

3. Have students present their news broadcasts to the class while the class grades them.

4. Have students rank the presentations. Go over all the rankings as a class after all the presentations are finished.

Expansion/Homework

You can also do this activity as an opinion poll. Assign one question to each student. Have students move freely around the room, getting an answer from each of their classmates. Then have each student report on the class's answers, again using the expressions for stating an opinion.

✪ ALTERNATIVE SPEAKING TOPICS

These topics give students an alternative opportunity to explore and discuss issues related to the unit theme.

✪ RESEARCH TOPICS

Suggested Time: 30 minutes in class

1. Have students turn to page 218. Review the instructions for the activity with the class. Tell students that they will be completing a chart after listening to or watching the news for one or more days.

2. Have students complete their charts. You may want to review the discussion on what makes good and bad news with the class.

3. Have students present the results of their charts to the class or in small groups. If possible, tally the results and make comparisons of them to share with the class.

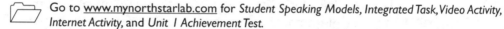 Go to www.mynorthstarlab.com for *Student Speaking Models, Integrated Task, Video Activity, Internet Activity,* and *Unit 1 Achievement Test.*

UNIT 2 The Achilles Heel

<table>
<tr><td colspan="2" align="center">**OVERVIEW**</td></tr>
</table>

Theme: Overcoming obstacles

This unit focuses on people with disabilities and how they have overcome obstacles in their lives. Students think about their own personal challenges and the challenges of others, and what is needed to overcome personal challenges in general.

Listening One: *Dreams of Flying and Overcoming Obstacles* is a radio broadcast of a student's college application essay in which he outlines his own physical challenges and his path to overcoming them.

Listening Two: *The Achilles Track Club Climbs Mount Kilimanjaro* is a television news broadcast about a group of disabled athletes who overcame their own challenges to climb Mount Kilimanjaro.

Critical Thinking

Identify personal obstacles
Rank the value of personal qualities
Analyze narrative techniques in an essay
Hypothesize another's point of view

Analyze sensitive language referring to disabilities
Infer meaning not explicit in the listening
Compare and contrast two life histories
Frame contrasting points of view

Listening

Make predictions
Summarize main ideas
Listen for details
Relate listenings to knowledge of the world

Identify connecting themes between two listenings
Identify thought groups in speech
Listen to classmates' reports and pose questions

Speaking

Share experiences
Construct and tell a story from provided notes
Conduct an interview

Practice storytelling
Plan and give a three-minute speech

Vocabulary	Grammar
Use context clues to find meaning	Gerunds and infinitives
Define words	**Pronunciation**
Differentiate between literal versus figurative language	Thought groups

 MyNorthStarLab
Readiness Check, Background and Vocabulary, Listenings One and Two, Notetaking and Academic Skills Practice, Vocabulary and Grammar, Achievement Test

 NorthStar: Reading and Writing 4
Unit 2 deals with a writer and a jazz singer who have had to overcome adversity in their lives.

Go to www.mynorthstarlab.com for the MyNorthStarLab *Readiness Check*.

①FOCUS ON THE TOPIC

◖SKILLS

Predict the content of the unit based on a photograph and the title of the unit; activate prior knowledge; express opinions; infer the meaning of new vocabulary from context.

✸✸✸ Ⓐ PREDICT

Suggested Time: 10 minutes

1. Have students look at the photograph and the title. Ask students if any of them know who Achilles was, explaining if necessary that he was a hero in Greek mythology. Have students look down at the footnote on the page. Ask them to think about how the picture and the unit title might be related.

2. Put students in pairs or small groups to discuss the questions. As a class, elicit answers to the questions from several of the students, trying to get a variety of opinions. For question 1, write a few of the suggested obstacles on the board to encourage brainstorming.

✸✸ Ⓑ SHARE INFORMATION

Suggested Time: 15 minutes

1. After reading the instructions, review the list of obstacles as a class, explaining terms that may be unfamiliar. Elicit examples of each type of obstacle, if desired.

2. Put students in small groups to discuss the questions. Then have the groups report on their discussions to the class.

✸✸✸ Ⓒ BACKGROUND AND VOCABULARY

📁 Go to www.mynorthstarlab.com for *Background and Vocabulary*.

Suggested Time: 20 minutes

1. Explain that overcoming obstacles is an American value. Then have students read the introductory paragraph individually.

2. Have students read the instructions for **Exercise 1**. Go over the list of vocabulary items with the class, taking time to pronounce each word. Have students complete the exercise individually before checking their answers in pairs.

3. Play the audio in **Exercise 2** and have students listen as they read.

Expansion/Homework
You can assign Exercise 1 as homework and use class time to check answers and to work on pronunciation.

 Link to *NorthStar: Reading and Writing 4*
If students are also using the companion text, you may want to list vocabulary from Background and Vocabulary in Unit 2 on the board and see if students can find synonyms for those words in the list of words in this section.

FOCUS ON LISTENING

◖ SKILLS

Make predictions about the content of the radio report; listen for main ideas; identify details; make inferences and support them with evidence from the report; express opinions; listen to an interview.

 **LISTENING ONE: Dreams of Flying and Overcoming Obstacles**

⌂ Go to www.mynorthstarlab.com to listen to *Dreams of Flying and Overcoming Obstacles*.

Suggested Time: 10 minutes

In Listening One, students listen to a radio program about one student's college application essay about overcoming obstacles. The segment should get students thinking about their own obstacles and ways to overcome them.

1. Ask students to read the segment title and the introductory paragraph and look at the photograph. Then play the excerpt from the interview and have them answer the question and check off the predictions.

2. Go over students' answers to both questions as a class. Affirm each prediction as a possibility.

Expansion/Homework
Have students write predictions, share them with a partner, and then discuss them with the class.

LISTENING STRATEGY: Freewrite

To prepare students to listen to the essay, have them freewrite on this topic: A personal obstacle I have to overcome is _____. Tell students to name the obstacle and offer a few examples to clarify. Then tell them to write for five minutes without lifting their pen from the paper. If they run out of ideas, tell them to make circles or lines as they review what they've written until another idea comes to them (and it will). Remind students that the secret to this process is keeping their pen on the paper and moving.

✪✪✪ LISTEN FOR MAIN IDEAS

Suggested Time: 15 minutes

Have students read through the questions. Play the interview once without stopping while students answer the questions. Have students compare their answers with a partner's. Replay the segment for students to check their answers.

Expansion/Homework

After students have listened to the complete interview, have them look back at their predictions and say whether or not their predictions were correct. Remind students that it doesn't matter whether or not their predictions are correct. The value of making predictions is that it gives students an additional reason to listen, and hypotheses to confirm or change as they listen.

✪✪✪ LISTEN FOR DETAILS

Suggested Time: 15 minutes

Have students read the items and answer the questions they already know in pencil. Then play the segment, and have students write *T* or *F*. You might want to suggest that students correct the false statements after listening. If students seem to be having trouble, play the report one more time and allow students to check their answers. Then go over the answers as a class.

REACHING ALL STUDENTS: Listen for Details

- **Less Proficient:** Reduce demands on listening recall by having students listen and complete items 1–4. Then, have students listen again to complete items 5–8.

- **More Proficient:** Have students answer the questions based on their recall from the first listening, and then listen a second time to confirm or correct their answers.

✪✪✪ MAKE INFERENCES

Suggested Time: 10 minutes

1. Have students read the instructions. Then ask them to look at the question and options for each excerpt. Play each excerpt and then stop the audio, allowing students time to choose their answers.

2. After listening to all of the excerpts, go over the answers as a class, replaying excerpts as needed.

Link to *NorthStar: Reading and Writing 4*

If students are also using the companion text, you can ask them to speculate what experiences Frank McCourt might have chosen to highlight in his college application essay.

✪✪✪ **EXPRESS OPINIONS**   **Suggested Time: 15 minutes**

1. Have students read the discussion questions. Give them a few minutes to formulate their own thoughts. Tell them to refer back to the previous exercises to help them support their answers.

2. Put students in small groups to discuss the questions. Encourage them to support their ideas with reasons and information based on the listening. Encourage them to use the new vocabulary.

CRITICAL THINKING

Give students the following questions for discussion in small groups before discussing as a whole class:

1. Do you agree with Richard when he says that, "if we recognize our talents and make the best of them, we've got a fighting chance to overcome our obstacles and succeed in life"?

   Answers will vary, but students should support their opinion from experience and the information in the text.

2. What information tells you that Richard Van Ornum had overcome his first obstacle?

   Answer: He says, "I was proof of that, walking."

3. Why do you think Richard dreamed of flying after he realized that his gifts helped him?

   Answers will vary, but might include thoughts related to the idea that his realization frees him from limitation.

4. What gifts do you have that help you to overcome obstacles?

   Answers will vary. Encourage students to be generous in exploring their gifts and offering some examples in support.

✪✪✪ **B**   **LISTENING TWO: The Achilles Track Club Climbs Mount Kilimanjaro**

   Go to www.mynorthstarlab.com to listen to *The Achilles Track Club Climbs Mount Kilimanjaro.*

Suggested Time: 20 minutes

In Listening Two, students listen to various physically challenged people talk about their experiences climbing a mountain. The purpose of this interview is to further challenge students to consider the perceived limitations of the physically challenged and the feelings of overcoming those limitations as well as the different terms used to describe people with disabilities.

1. Read through the background information with the class and ask students to try to imagine climbing a mountain blind or with some other physical challenge. Ask students to think about which physical disabilities would prevent someone from climbing a mountain.

2. Read the questions in **Exercise 1** with the class. Then play the interview while students answer the questions. Then play the interview again to allow students to check their answers. Replay the audio as needed. Discuss their answers as a class.

3. Have students read the questions in **Exercise 2**. Check their comprehension of *inspirational*. Put them in small groups to discuss the questions. After sufficient time, have the groups report on their discussions to the class. You may want to make a list on the board of the terms students came up with for the word *disabled*.

Expansion/Homework
You could introduce additional terms for referring to people who are blind (for example, visually impaired) and deaf (for example, hearing impaired), and discuss feelings people might associate with the different terms.

 Link to *NorthStar: Reading and Writing 4*
If students are using the companion text, you can have them skim the article by Diane Schuur, and discuss what term Diane might prefer to use to describe herself (rather than "handicapped").

C INTEGRATE LISTENINGS ONE AND TWO

◖SKILLS

Organize information from the listenings in a Venn diagram; synthesize the information from the listenings in a role play.

STEP 1: Organize   Suggested Time: 15 minutes

1. Have students read the instructions and then look at the Venn diagram. You may want to fill out a simple Venn diagram on the board to make sure students are familiar with it. To do this, draw the diagram and fill it in with the clothing of two students in the class who are wearing some different things and some similar ones.

2. Have students fill in the diagram from what they remember individually or in pairs. Remind them that they can look back at the previous exercises to refresh their memories. Then have them compare their diagrams with other students' before going over the answers with the entire class.

Link to *NorthStar: Reading and Writing 4*
If students are also using the companion text, have them add information to this chart for Frank McCourt and Diane Schuur, and compare their challenges to those of Richard Van Ornum and the Achilles Track Club.

STEP 2: Synthesize

Suggested Time: 20 minutes

1. Read the instructions with the class. You may want to have students formulate some questions for the interviewer together as a class or in groups.

2. Put students in groups and tell them to choose an interviewer, a representative of the Achilles Track Club, and Richard Van Ornum. You might want to have the students of each role get into groups again before having them do their role plays to practice what they might say. Then, have the groups practice their role plays while you circulate to help with individual questions.

3. If time allows, have a few groups perform their role plays for the class. You might want to make a note of errors or language issues that come up to present to the class later.

 Go to www.mynorthstarlab.com for *Notetaking* and *Academic Skills Practice*.

③ FOCUS ON SPEAKING

Ⓐ VOCABULARY

◖ SKILLS

Review vocabulary from Listenings One and Two; apply vocabulary learned in the unit to a new context—an online journal; understand the difference between literal and figurative meanings; use new vocabulary creatively in a speaking activity.

✪ REVIEW

Suggested Time: 15 minutes

 Go to www.mynorthstarlab.com for *Review*.

1. Have students read the instructions and review the meanings of the vocabulary items together as a class. You might want to go over the word forms of each vocabulary item, reviewing with the students the function of each word form to help them complete the exercise.

2. Have students fill in the blanks individually. Then put them in pairs to check their answers.

Expansion/Homework
This exercise could be assigned for homework. You could also have students role-play being the person who wrote the journal entries and a friend or family member.

The journal writer is telling the friend or family member all about his/her experiences based on the entries. The friend or family member should ask questions that will elicit answers from the journal entries.

✪✪ EXPAND

Suggested Time: 15 minutes

1. Have students read the background information on literal and figurative meanings of words. Look at the example together, and if possible, elicit additional examples of words or phrases students know that have both literal and figurative meanings.

2. Have students work with partners to identify the literal and figurative use of words in the sentences. Compare answers as a class.

VOCABULARY EXPANSION: Personal Dictionary (Verbs)

Have students create a page in their personal dictionaries for new verbs, organized alphabetically or thematically. Remind them to create visual boxes to record the information instead of simply writing definitions. Divide a rectangle into four sections. Top left = write the word (present, past, and past participle forms), top right = draw an illustration, bottom left = write the definition, bottom right = write a sentence or synonym.

✪ CREATE

Suggested Time: 20 minutes

1. Read the instructions with the class and go over the boldfaced words. Give students some time to jot down some notes to help them, but tell them not to write out the answers.

2. Put students in pairs to take turns asking and answering the questions, using the boldfaced vocabulary in their answers.

Expansion/Homework

You may want to ask several students to ask and answer the questions in front of the class, as an interview role play.

📁 Go to www.mynorthstarlab.com for additional *Vocabulary* practice.

✪✪ B GRAMMAR: Gerunds and Infinitives

📁 Go to www.mynorthstarlab.com for *Grammar Chart and Exercise 1*.

◗ SKILLS

Practice the form and usage of gerunds and infinitives.

Suggested Time: 25 minutes

1. Read the instructions in **Exercise 1** and then have students read the segment. You may want to see what students know about the way gerunds and infinitives

are used by attempting to elicit a list of rules to put on the board before having students look through the grammar chart.

2. Go over each section in the chart with students, providing more examples, or eliciting more examples from students.

3. Have students look at the flyer in **Exercise 2** and talk about the uses of the different devices shown. Then have students look at the boxed descriptions and the phrases below the box. Put students in pairs to discuss the uses of the devices.

4. Read the instructions for **Exercise 3** and the background information with students. Put students in pairs to complete the chart based on the town or city you are in. Put pairs together with other pairs to compare their charts.

Expansion/Homework

(1) You may want to have students role-play the situation of a sales person and people who need to adapt their homes for people with differing types of disabilities or physical challenges. (2) For further practice, offer exercises from *Focus on Grammar 4, 3rd Edition,* and Azar's *Understanding and Using English Grammar, 3rd Edition.* See the Grammar Book References on page 225 of the student book for specific units and chapters.

 Go to www.mynorthstarlab.com for additional *Grammar* practice.

C SPEAKING

◖ SKILLS

Recognize thought groups; practice sharing personal stories; integrate the concepts, vocabulary, grammar, pronunciation, and function from the unit in a personal speech.

◌◌ PRONUNCIATION: Thought Groups

Suggested Time: 15 minutes

1. Read the explanation and play examples of thought groups. Help students see that speaking in thought groups makes conversation sound more natural and will help them to be more fluent. Have students practice repeating the sentences.

2. Have students listen to the sentences in **Exercise 1** and mark the thought groups. Check answers as a class, and then have students practice reading the sentences with a partner.

3. Look at the instructions and the charts in **Exercise 2** with the class. Make an untrue sentence as an example, eliciting from students that it is untrue. Then have students complete the exercise.

Expansion/Homework

Have students write each completed sentence from Exercise 2 on a separate sheet of paper (or on the board) and have them try to read the sentences without pausing between thought groups (after completing this section, they should find it difficult). Then read the sentences with the correct pauses, and discuss how the thought groups aid comprehension.

✪✪ FUNCTION: Sharing a Personal Story

Suggested Time: 25 minutes

1. You may want to elicit from students the basic elements of a narrative or personal story before having them complete this section. You could do this by discussing the different elements of Richard Van Ornum's story, eliciting the background, challenge, and accomplishment or life lesson. Then have students read the introductory explanations and boxed elements of personal stories.

2. Read the instructions for **Exercise 1** and have students look at the photos of the three disabled people. If possible, group students by the person they are most interested in. You may have to arbitrarily group students if you don't have enough interested in all three people. Then have students discuss their person's situation and limitations and determine a greater meaning for other people.

3. Regroup students so each group has one or two students representing each of the photographed people. Read the instructions for **Exercise 2** together, and then give them time to retell their stories. You might suggest that the listeners in each group think of at least one question they can ask while they are listening.

Link to *NorthStar: Reading and Writing 4*

If students are also using the companion text, you can have them examine the paragraph about Greg Barton in Unit 2. Have students identify the narrative techniques used by the writer, and decide if the paragraph might be made more vivid by increased use of the elements of a personal story studied.

✪✪✪ PRODUCTION: A Personal Speech

Suggested Time: 50 minutes

If you wish to assign a different speaking task than the one in this section, see page 40. The alternative topics relate to the theme of the unit, but may not target the same grammar, pronunciation, or function taught in the unit.

1. Go over the instructions in the task box and the three steps. You may want to circulate while students are filling in the chart to help with individual language questions.

2. Have students practice their personal speeches either in class or at home before having them perform them for the class. Before they perform, make sure everyone knows that when they aren't performing, they will be listening and formulating at least one question to ask.

3. Have students present their personal speeches to the class or, in the case of very large classes, large groups. You may want to model the types of questions to ask by asking one yourself to the first few speech givers.

 Link to *NorthStar: Reading and Writing 4*
If students are also using the companion text, encourage them to include points made by any of the people mentioned in their speeches on overcoming challenges.

✪ ALTERNATIVE SPEAKING TOPICS

These topics give students an alternative opportunity to explore and discuss issues related to the unit theme.

✪ RESEARCH TOPICS

Suggested Time: 30 minutes in class

1. Have students turn to page 219. Review the instructions for the activity with the class. Tell students that they choose either to watch a movie about a person or research a famous person who has overcome a disability.

2. If students watch a movie, have them take notes while watching it. They then should write a summary of what the obstacle was and how the character overcame it. If students research a famous person, have them find out as much as they can by researching on the Internet. Have students write about the obstacle and how the famous person overcame it. Encourage students to include additional information they find.

3. Have students present their reports to the class or in small groups.

 Go to www.mynorthstarlab.com for *Student Speaking Models, Integrated Task, Video Activity, Internet Activity,* and *Unit 2 Achievement Test.*

UNIT 3 Early to Bed, Early to Rise . . .

OVERVIEW

Theme: Medicine

This unit focuses on sleep habits and on the effects of sleep deprivation. Students are encouraged to think about and discuss their own sleep habits.

Listening One: *Teen Sleep Needs* is a radio news report regarding teenagers' sleep needs according to researchers who have studied the problem and teens who have experienced it.

Listening Two: *Get Back in Bed* is an interview with a doctor and a sleep deprived mother.

Critical Thinking

Interpret a cartoon
Interpret a proverb
Compare and contrast sleep habits
Hypothesize scenarios

Draw conclusions about sleep deprivation
Propose solutions to problems
Analyze a case of sleep deprivation and its
    consequences

Listening

Make predictions
Take notes
Summarize main ideas
Listen for details

Interpret speakers' tone and emotions
Relate listenings to personal experiences
Compare information from two listenings
Identify emphasis in speech and its meaning

Speaking

Use new vocabulary in a guided conversation
Make contrastive statements
Act out scripted dialogues
Form and express opinions

Interrupt politely to clarify or confirm
    information
Role-play asking for and giving advice
Role-play a meeting situation

Vocabulary

Use context clues to find meaning
Define words
Use idiomatic expressions

Grammar

Present unreal conditionals

Pronunciation

Contrastive stress

 MyNorthStarLab
Readiness Check, Background and
Vocabulary, Listenings One and Two,
Notetaking and Academic Skills Practice,
Vocabulary and Grammar, Achievement Test

 NorthStar: Reading and Writing 4
Unit 3 deals with nonmedical ways of
curing illness, including prayer and "laugh
therapy."

FOCUS ON THE TOPIC

◖SKILLS

Predict the content of the unit based on a cartoon and the title of the unit; activate prior knowledge; express opinions; infer the meaning of new vocabulary from context.

✪✪✪Ⓐ PREDICT

Suggested Time: 10 minutes

1. Have students keep their books closed. Write the unit title on the board and have students read it. Explain that this is the first part of a proverb or expression and ask students to try and complete it in pairs or small groups. Write some of their answers on the board, and then have them open their books and look at question 2 to compare their answers to the complete proverb.

2. Have students look at the cartoon and describe what they see happening. Then put them in pairs or small groups to discuss the questions. Then, as a class, elicit answers to the questions from several of the students, trying to get a variety of responses.

✪✪Ⓑ SHARE INFORMATION

Suggested Time: 20 minutes

1. Read the instructions and go over the questions in the chart with the class. Give students a few minutes to complete the chart for themselves before putting them in pairs to find out about each other's sleep habits. Tell students to take turns asking each other the questions in the chart.

2. Have students review their charts in preparation for sharing something of interest with the class. You might want to put some phrases on the board to use such as: "One thing I found particularly interesting was that . . ." or "One difference between my partner and me is that . . ." Then have students share with the class one or two interesting things they found out.

✪✪✪ C BACKGROUND AND VOCABULARY

📁 Go to www.mynorthstarlab.com for *Background and Vocabulary*.

Suggested Time: 20 minutes

1. Explain that school counselors are school employees who give advice and guidance to students. Have students read the instructions and look at the form of the e-mails. Tell students to pay attention to the boldfaced words as they read and try to guess their meaning from context. Play the recording of the e-mails and have students listen as they read.

2. Have students match the number of the boldfaced words with their meanings or synonyms. Go over the answers as a class. For disputed words, have students use the context to defend or explain their choice.

📁 Go to www.mynorthstarlab.com for additional *Background and Vocabulary* practice.

②FOCUS ON LISTENING

◖ SKILLS

Make predictions about the content of the listening; differentiate between main ideas and details; make inferences about speakers' feelings based on tone of voice and word choice; express opinions; listen to an interview.

✪✪✪ A LISTENING ONE: Teen Sleep Needs

📁 Go to www.mynorthstarlab.com to listen to *Teen Sleep Needs*.

Suggested Time: 10 minutes

In Listening One, students listen to a radio program on the unique sleep patterns and sleep needs of teens. The segment should get students thinking about their own teen experiences or about teens they know and about realistic solutions to the problem of sleep deprivation.

1. Ask students to read the segment title and the background information on the news report they are about to listen to. Play the audio and have students answer the questions.

2. Go over students' answers to the questions as a class. Elicit predictions for question number 3 from several students. Affirm each prediction as a possibility.

1. Remind students that prediction is an important listening strategy. It will help them to focus on the subject, and it will bring vocabulary to mind that they might need to help them comprehend. Have students read the title "Teen Sleep Needs" and predict what this report will be about.

2. Suggest that they discuss the title with their partner and come up with several possible ideas and explanations. Then have them share how much vocabulary was brought into play as they thought about this three-word title.

✪✪✪ LISTEN FOR MAIN IDEAS   Suggested Time: 15 minutes

1. Have students read the introductory information and the five questions. Play the report while students answer the questions. Then give them sufficient time to complete their answers. If students seem to have trouble, play the report one more time.

2. Go over the answers. If disagreements arise, replay those segments rather than simply giving the answer.

Expansion/Homework
Have students look again at their predictions to see whether or not they accurately predicted the topics in the segment.

✪✪✪ LISTEN FOR DETAILS   Suggested Time: 15 minutes

Have students read the questions and answer those that they can. You might want to have them do that in pencil. Then have students listen to the radio report and circle the correct answers. Play the audio once more for students to check their answers. Go over the answers as a class.

Expansion/Homework
Have students research one of the people interviewed on the Internet. Tell them to note down a relevant piece of information that they find online regarding this person and the news, or possibly anything else, and bring that information back to class to share.

✪✪✪ MAKE INFERENCES   Suggested Time: 10 minutes

1. Have students read the instructions. Check students' comprehension of all the feeling words in the box. Then elicit examples to illustrate the different tones of voice corresponding to the different feeling words.

2. Play the excerpts, and have students complete the exercise. Tell students to discuss their answers with a partner and use actual language to support their answers. Then ask the pairs to share their answers with the class.

• **Less Proficient:** Use TPR to ensure that students understand the adjectives. Have them draw a smiley face next to the word to help them remember.	• **More Proficient:** Have students give specific evidence to support their choice of adjectives for each statement.

✪✪✪ EXPRESS OPINIONS   Suggested Time: 10 minutes

1. Have students read the instructions. Then have them read the statements and decide whether they agree or disagree individually. You might want to give them a few minutes to formulate their own thoughts.

2. Put students in small groups to discuss their opinions. Encourage them to support their ideas with reasons and information based on the listening.

3. If time allows, have groups share their thoughts on one or more of the statements with the class.

Expansion/Homework
For homework, or in class, have students choose one of the statements to write a paragraph about. Encourage students to draw comparisons from their own experiences as students.

CRITICAL THINKING

Give students the following questions for discussion in small groups before discussing as a whole class:

1. Review the Share Information section and summarize your daily experience with sleep. How much and when do you sleep?

   Answers will vary.

2. How does this compare with explanations in the report?

   Answers will vary, but students should offer a clear comparison with the research in the interview and specific examples from their personal experience.

3. How can teachers use this information to improve teaching?

   Students should be encouraged to offer a variety of suggestions, which might include planning of activities, classroom environment, and teacher expectations.

4. How can you use this information in your life?

   Answers will vary, but students should use information from the text and their experiences, especially regarding sleep deprivation.

📁 Go to www.mynorthstarlab.com to listen to *Get Back in Bed*.

Suggested Time: 20 minutes

In Listening Two, students listen to a conversation with a doctor about how common sleep deprivation is and what the negative results of sleep deprivation are. The purpose of this interview is to further challenge students to think about the issues involved in sleep for all age groups.

1. Have students read the segment title and look at the picture and describe what they see. Ask students if any of them have personal experience with what they see in the picture or know someone who has small children and has sleep problems.

2. Have students read the background information. Ask them who they think might need to go to a sleep disorder center.

3. Play the interview, and then have students complete **Exercise 1**. Play the interview again if needed to allow students to check their answers.

4. Put students in small groups to discuss the questions in **Exercise 2**. Encourage students to give specific examples to support their opinions.

Expansion/Homework
Have students research online some information supporting the theory that too much sleep is not good for you.

✪✪✪ **C** **INTEGRATE LISTENINGS ONE AND TWO**

◀ **SKILLS**

Organize information from the listenings in a chart; synthesize the information from the listenings in a role play.

STEP 1: Organize　　　　　　　　　　　　**Suggested Time: 10 minutes**

1. Read through the directions for the exercise and look at the chart with students. Have students work in small groups to complete the chart with information from Listenings One and Two.

2. Have groups compare answers with another group's before going over the answers with the entire class.

STEP 2: Synthesize　　　　　　　　　　　　**Suggested Time: 20 minutes**

1. Read the instructions with the class. Put students in groups of three and tell them to choose roles, or choose for them. You might want to have the "parents" and "teens" get into groups before having them do their role plays to work together to come up with what they'd like to say.

2. Have the groups practice their role plays while you move around the room to help with individual problems. Then, if time allows, have a few groups perform their role plays for the class.

Expansion/Homework

In pairs, have students discuss which of the dangers of sleep deprivation seem the most serious and why, and/or which of the recommendations they think they should or could follow themselves.

Link to *NorthStar: Reading and Writing 4*

If students are also using the companion text, you can ask them to skim Reading Two and imagine that Norman Cousins is a guest on the Satellite Sisters radio show. What sorts of questions do you think the sisters would ask? Would they support his approach to treatment? Why?

Go to www.mynorthstarlab.com for *Notetaking* and *Academic Skills Practice*.

③ FOCUS ON SPEAKING

Ⓐ VOCABULARY

◖ SKILLS

Review vocabulary from Listenings One and Two; expand vocabulary by identifying idiomatic expressions; use vocabulary creatively in a speaking activity.

✪ REVIEW   Suggested Time: 15 minutes

Go to www.mynorthstarlab.com for *Review*.

Have students read the instructions and look at the picture and the title of the magazine article. Then have students read the article and complete the exercise. Go over the answers as a class.

✪✪ EXPAND   Suggested Time: 15 minutes

1. Have students look at the photo of a MetroNaps sleep pod and comment on it. Ask them where they think these pods might be in use.

2. Read the instructions with the class. Go over the phrases and words with students and then have them complete the exercise by filling in the blanks in the two conversations individually.

3. Put students into pairs to compare their answers and then practice saying the conversations. Have selected pairs read parts of the dialogues for the class.

Expansion/Homework

Both the Review and Expand exercises could be done for homework and then discussed in class, if desired. Students could also research MetroNaps online and prepare a brief presentation for the next class.

VOCABULARY EXPANSION: Antonym Mirrors

Remind students that one way to learn a new word is to identify an antonym for the word. Have students draw a horizontal line on a piece of paper and write these words above the line: *alert, captivated, chronically, dim, irritable.* Below the line, have them write a word which is the opposite of the word used in the text.

alert	captivated	chronically	dim	irritable
inattentive	bored	temporarily	bright	good-humored

Then ask students to work with their partner to write a contrast sentence using both words (for example, Maria was alert, but John was inattentive).

✪ CREATE   Suggested Time: 20 minutes

1. Read the instructions. Read through the questions with students and give them time to think of some answers. Also, go through the boxed vocabulary items with students, making sure they can pronounce them correctly.

2. Put students into pairs. Have Student A ask Student B question 1. While Student B answers the question using some of the vocabulary items listed, Student A checks the words used. Then have students switch roles.

 Go to www.mynorthstarlab.com for additional *Vocabulary* practice.

✪✪ B GRAMMAR: Present Unreal Conditionals

 Go to www.mynorthstarlab.com for *Grammar Chart* and *Exercise 2.*

◖ SKILLS

Practice the form and meaning of present unreal conditionals.

Suggested Time: 30 minutes

1. Have students practice the conversation with a partner. Then, discover students' existing knowledge of the present unreal conditional by having them answer the questions in **Exercise 1**.

2. Go over each section in the grammar chart with students providing more examples, or eliciting more examples.

3. Read the instructions for **Exercise 2** with the class. Have students fill in the blanks individually and compare answers with a partner's. Go over the answers with the class.

4. Read the instructions for **Exercise 3**. Then put students in pairs to take turns role-playing the situation and asking and answering the questions. Monitor the discussions, making grammatical and other corrections as necessary.

Expansion/Homework

(**1**) To check students' grammar individually, you can ask them to write short responses to one of the problems in Exercise 3 for homework, using the present unreal conditional to give advice. Collect the responses and correct the grammar usage. (**2**) For further practice, offer exercises from *Focus on Grammar 4, 3rd Edition,* and Azar's *Understanding and Using English Grammar, 3rd Edition.* See the Grammar Book References on page 225 of the student book for specific units and chapters.

 Link to *NorthStar: Reading and Writing 4*

If students are also using the companion text, have them use the grammar guidelines in Unit 3 and change the present unreal conditionals in their exercises to past unreal conditionals, where appropriate.

 Go to www.mynorthstarlab.com for additional *Grammar* practice.

C SPEAKING

◀ SKILLS

Recognize and use contrastive stress; practice interrupting politely to ask for clarification; integrate the concepts, vocabulary, grammar, pronunciation, and function from the unit in a hospital role play.

✪ PRONUNCIATION: Contrastive Stress

Suggested Time: 20 minutes

1. Read the explanation with the class. Have students repeat the example sentence with the correct stress and pitch patterns.

2. Have students listen to the recorded sentences in **Exercise 1** and underline the contrasted words. Play the audio again to let students check their answers before going over the answers as a class. Then have students take turns reading the sentences with a partner while you move around the room to offer individual assistance.

3. Go over the examples in **Exercise 2** as a class. Then, in pairs, have students make sentences using contrastive stress to compare the information in the columns. Go over answers as a class.

4. Read the instructions for **Exercise 3** with the class. Have students complete the chart about themselves individually first. Then put students into pairs to take

turns asking and answering the questions in the sleep quiz and complete the charts about their partners. Have them report their findings to the class, using contrastive stress to compare their answers.

Expansion/Homework
For Exercise 1, you may want to have students change the contrasting stress to see if their partners can figure out what they are stressing. For example, in number 1, students could repeat the sentence a second time stressing *I* in both parts of the sentence to show contrast with someone else.

Link to *NorthStar: Reading and Writing 4*
If students are also using the companion text, you can give them more practice using contrastive stress to communicate meaning by asking them to choose one paragraph from Reading One. Ask them to read the paragraph aloud three times— one time using stress to show that they support the parents' choice, one time as a neutral reporter, and one time using stress to show they disagree with the parents' choice.

✪✪ FUNCTION: Interrupting to Ask for Clarification

Suggested Time: 20 minutes

1. With books closed, ask students what they would say to interrupt someone in order to ask a question. Write down students' responses on the board. Then have them open the books and read the introductory explanation and the example expressions used to make a polite interruption. Ask students to compare the list with the expressions on the board and discuss any differences between them.

2. Read the instructions for the pair work and go over the example. Put students in pairs to complete the exercise. Monitor the pairs, listening for usage of the polite phrases to make interruptions.

Expansion/Homework
Have a few pairs perform their conversation exchanges for the class. Alternatively, have pairs write new exchanges to perform.

✪✪✪ PRODUCTION: A Hospital Role Play

Suggested Time: 45 minutes

If you wish to assign a different speaking task than the one in this section, see page 62. The alternative topics relate to the theme of the unit, but may not target the same grammar, pronunciation, or function taught in the unit.

1. Go over the information in the task box. Then read the instructions. Have students read the situation and then divide the class into three groups and assign each group a role (hospital administrators, interns, and patients' rights group). Allow students some time to clarify their points of view for Step 1, and to brainstorm what they will say in the role play for Step 2 in their groups.

2. For Step 2, divide the class into new groups of three, with each student playing one of the roles. Have the groups role-play a meeting to discuss the situation, with instructions to reach a compromise that will satisfy everyone.

3. For Step 3, have groups summarize their meetings, giving their recommendations.

4. Have a discussion with the class to answer the additional questions. Alternatively, put students back in their groups to discuss the questions.

 Link to *NorthStar: Reading and Writing 4*

If students are also using the companion text, encourage them to include several questions in their survey about the ailments mentioned in Unit 3 to see if they find any correlation between attitudes toward sleep and attitudes toward treatment of illness.

✪ ALTERNATIVE SPEAKING TOPICS

These topics give students an alternative opportunity to explore and discuss issues related to the unit theme.

✪ RESEARCH TOPICS

Suggested Time: 30 minutes in class

1. Have students turn to page 219. Review the instructions for the activity and the questions with the class. Tell students that they can use a search engine to search for information on sleep deprivation or jet lag.

2. Have students prepare their reports. Emphasize that they should include answers to the questions listed in the book. Encourage students to include additional information they find.

3. Have students present their reports to the class or in small groups.

 Go to www.mynorthstarlab.com for *Student Speaking Models, Integrated Task, Video Activity, Internet Activity,* and *Unit 3 Achievement Test.*

UNIT 4

Animal Intelligence

OVERVIEW

Theme: Animal intelligence
This unit focuses on animal intelligence and emotions. Students think about their ideas about animal intelligence and how similar or dissimilar they are to humans in that regard. Students also prepare a presentation using the information from the unit.

Listening One: *The Infinite Mind: Animal Intelligence* is a radio interview with three professors regarding their research with three different types of animals.

Listening Two: *What Motivates Animals?* is an interview with a science newswriter about animal cognition.

Critical Thinking

Recognize speakers' attitudes
Support opinions with information from the reports

Make judgments
Support generalizations with examples
Infer information not explicit in the interview

Listening

Make predictions
Relate previous knowledge to the listenings
Identify main ideas
Listen for details

Infer word meaning from context
Listen for specific information
Infer speakers' attitudes

Speaking

Give and ask for examples
Form and express opinions
Report on research

Construct and perform a presentation
Evaluate the opinions of others

Vocabulary	Grammar
Use context clues to find meaning	Reported speech
Define words	**Pronunciation**
Find and use synonyms	Questions with *or*

 MyNorthStarLab
Readiness Check, Background and Vocabulary, Listenings One and Two, Notetaking and Academic Skills Practice, Vocabulary and Grammar, Achievement Test

 NorthStar: Reading and Writing 4
Unit 4 deals with animal intelligence and perception.

Go to www.mynorthstarlab.com for the MyNorthStarLab *Readiness Check.*

FOCUS ON THE TOPIC

◀ SKILLS

Predict the content of the unit; activate prior knowledge; express opinions; infer the meaning of new vocabulary from context.

✪✪✪ A PREDICT

Suggested Time: 10 minutes

1. Before opening the book, you might want to ask your students if anyone in the class has a pet and if they do, if they've ever wondered how much their pet understands or been surprised by an unexpected show of intelligence.

2. Have students identify the animals and label the pictures. Then have students read the unit title and the two questions. Check students' comprehension of *reason.* Have students discuss the questions with a partner, sharing summaries of their discussions with the class.

Expansion/Homework

Have students think of a specific animal experiment they would like to conduct complete with hypothesis and procedure.

✪✪ B SHARE INFORMATION

Suggested Time: 20 minutes

1. Have students read the questions in **Exercise 1**. Then discuss with the class.

2. Have students take the quiz in **Exercise 2** and then check their answers. Put them in pairs to compare their answers and discuss any information that surprised them.

✪✪✪ C BACKGROUND AND VOCABULARY

Go to www.mynorthstarlab.com for *Background and Vocabulary.*

Suggested Time: 25 minutes

1. Have students read the instructions and the text. Play the recording of the lecture and have students listen as they read.

2. Have students match the number of the boldfaced words with their meanings or synonyms. Go over the answers as a class. For disputed words, have students use the context to defend or explain their choice.

 Go to www.mynorthstarlab.com for additional *Background and Vocabulary* practice.

2 FOCUS ON LISTENING

(SKILLS

Make predictions about the content of the segment; identify main ideas; listen for details; make inferences about speakers' attitudes based on tone of voice and word choice; express opinions; listen to a conversation about animal research.

✿✿✿A LISTENING ONE: The Infinite Mind: Animal Intelligence

 Go to www.mynorthstarlab.com to listen to *The Infinite Mind: Animal Intelligence*.

Suggested Time: 10 minutes

In Listening One, students listen to a radio interview with three professors on research they have done on animal intelligence. The segment should get students thinking about their own perceptions of animal intelligence and the different ways to study it.

1. Ask students to read the segment title, the background information, and the titles and affiliations of the three professors. Ask them what an "infinite mind" might be.

2. Play the audio and have students listen for the names of the animals, and write them down while they are listening. Then go over students' answers as a class.

Expansion/Homework
Elicit predictions about what the professors are going to say about the intelligence of these three animals. Affirm each prediction as a possibility. Make a list on the board.

LISTENING STRATEGY: 5Ws and an H

To provide a focus for listening, have students create a simple 5W chart for each experiment, listing *who, what, where, when, why,* and *how.* As they listen to information about an experiment, have them complete the chart. Have student pairs compare their information, adding and revising where necessary, and then use their chart to summarize the experiments.

✪✪✪ LISTEN FOR MAIN IDEAS

1. Have students look at the pictures and say what they see the animals doing in each one. You might want to ask students what each picture indicates about animal intelligence.

2. Play the segment while students check the correct pictures. Go over the answers. If disagreements arise, replay those segments rather than simply giving the answer.

3. If you had students make predictions, have students see how close their predictions were to what they heard.

Expansion/Homework

You might want to have students discuss each checked picture to decide which one they think indicates a higher level of intelligence. Remind them to give reasons for their answers.

✪✪✪ LISTEN FOR DETAILS

1. Have students read the statements and write *T* or *F* for those that they can. You might want to have them do that in pencil.

2. Have students listen to the segment again, and complete the exercise. Then have them correct the false statements individually.

3. Put students in pairs to compare their answers and their corrected false statements. Go over the answers as a class eliciting all the possible variations on the corrected false statements.

REACHING ALL STUDENTS: Listen for Details	
• **Less Proficient:** Suggest that students make their own illustrations to retell the story or abilities of each animal before answering the questions.	• **More Proficient:** Have student pairs expand the true and corrected false statements by adding an imaginary anecdote.

✪✪✪ MAKE INFERENCES

1. Have students read the questions and the possible answers before listening to each excerpt. You might want to have them choose their answers if they think they can.

2. Play each excerpt going over the answers after each one, or allow students to discuss their answers with a partner, encouraging them to give reasons for their answers. Tell students to use actual language to support their answers. Replay the excerpts as needed while the pairs are discussing them. Then ask the pairs to share their answers with the class.

✪✪✪ EXPRESS OPINIONS   Suggested Time: 15 minutes

1. Have students read the instructions. Then have them look back at the Predict questions again and decide if they've changed their minds.

2. Put them into small groups to explain their opinions and discuss question 2. Encourage them to support their ideas with reasons and information based on the listening.

3. If time allows, have groups share their thoughts on one or both of the questions with the class.

Expansion/Homework

For homework, or in class, have students choose one of the statements to write a paragraph about.

Link to *NorthStar: Reading and Writing 4*

If students are also using the companion text, you can ask them to speculate about how Oskar Pfungst in Reading One would react to the acts of intelligence and emotions described in Listening One.

CRITICAL THINKING

Give students the following questions for discussion in small groups before discussing as a whole class:

1. What animals are discussed in this article?

   Answer: Sara, the chimpanzee; Alex, the parrot, and killer whales.

2. What is your opinion of Sara's behavior with Abigail? Support your opinion with convincing reasons.

   Opinions will vary, from students believing that Sara's behavior is unexceptional to those who believe that Sara's behavior is extraordinary. Students should be prepared to offer support with information from their knowledge and from the listening.

3. What can you conclude about parrots from Alex's communication?

   Answers will vary, but conclusions might include that parrots can talk, think, understand, and learn. Students should be able to support their conclusions with specifics from the report.

4. What is your opinion about animal intelligence after listening to these interviews?

   Answers will vary, but students should be able to give reasons and examples to support their opinions.

✪✪✪ B LISTENING TWO: What Motivates Animals?

📁 Go to www.mynorthstarlab.com to listen to *What Motivates Animals?*

Suggested Time: 20 minutes

In Listening Two, students listen to a conversation with a science newswriter on recent research on animal cognition. The purpose of this interview is to further challenge students to think about the issues involved in researching animal intelligence and cognition and the similarities between animal and human intelligence.

1. Have students read the segment title and the background information. Ask students what they think motivates most animals to do things. Also ask them if any of them know of any research with large apes or birds. Check students' comprehension of *cognition.* Play the interview and have students complete **Exercise 1**. Go over the answers as a class.

2. Have students read the discussion question in **Exercise 2**. Put them in small groups to discuss it. Encourage students to give specific examples to support their opinions.

✪✪✪ C INTEGRATE LISTENINGS ONE AND TWO

◖ SKILLS

Organize the information from the listenings in a chart; synthesize the information in a role play.

STEP 1: Organize   Suggested Time: 10 minutes

Read through the instructions for the exercise and look at the chart with students. Have them work individually or in pairs to complete the chart with information from Listenings One and Two. Have students compare answers, before going over the answers with the entire class.

STEP 2: Synthesize   Suggested Time: 20 minutes

1. Read the instructions with the class. Put students in groups of three and tell them to choose an animal. You might want to have students get into groups by animal choice to talk about what they are going to say prior to doing the role play.

2. Have the groups practice their role plays while you circulate to help with individual problems. Have select groups perform their role plays for the class.

Link to NorthStar: Reading and Writing 4
You can ask students to say what Oskar Pfungst might think about the experiments and theories discussed in the listenings.

📁 Go to www.mynorthstarlab.com for *Notetaking* and *Academic Skills Practice.*

3 FOCUS ON SPEAKING

A VOCABULARY

❙ SKILLS

Review vocabulary from Listenings One and Two; define new words; use new vocabulary creatively in a speaking activity.

✪ REVIEW   Suggested Time: 10 minutes

📁 Go to www.mynorthstarlab.com for *Review*.

Have students read the instructions and the example and then complete the exercise individually. Go over the answers as a class. You might want to go over the word forms of each vocabulary item, reviewing with students the function of each word form.

Expansion/Homework
This exercise could be done for homework and then discussed in class.

✪✪ EXPAND   Suggested Time: 15 minutes

Have students read the instructions and then the script in **Exercise 1**. Then have pairs discuss the meanings of the boldfaced words and phrases using the contexts to help them. Finally, have students complete **Exercise 2**. Go over the answers as a class.

VOCABULARY EXPANSION: Suffixes

1. Remind students that a suffix can change the meaning of a word and / or it can change the part of speech of a word. Give students these three vocabulary words, *socialize*, *categorize*, and *vocalize*. Have students locate -ize in a dictionary to learn the meaning of the suffix.

2. Tell students that words ending in -ize often can add, -ation. Have students write the base word, the word with -ize added, and the word with -ation added (social – socialize – socialization). Then ask them to identify the part of speech for each word. They should conclude that the base word can be a noun or an adjective, -ize creates a verb, and -ation creates a noun. Have them list other words which follow this pattern.

✪ CREATE   Suggested Time: 20 minutes

1. Read the instructions. Give students a few minutes to take some notes on each question. Remind them to attempt to use the vocabulary from Review and Expand in their answers where possible.

2. Make sure students understand that they are to actually take turns asking each other the questions. Put them in pairs to complete the exercise. Have select pairs perform sets of two questions and answers each for the class.

📁 Go to www.mynorthstarlab.com for additional *Vocabulary* practice.

✪✪ B GRAMMAR: Reported Speech

📁 Go to www.mynorthstarlab.com for *Grammar Chart* and *Exercise 1*.

◖ SKILLS

Practice the form and meaning of reported speech.

Suggested Time: 30 minutes

1. Have students practice the conversation in **Exercise 1** with a partner and answer the questions. Ask students if they see any pattern in the verb tense changes.

2. Go over each section in the grammar chart with the class providing more examples, or eliciting more examples from students.

3. Read the instructions for **Exercise 2** and the example with the class. Have students complete the exercise in pairs. Move around the room and offer assistance if necessary.

4. Read the instructions for **Exercise 3** with students. Then put students in pairs to take turns role-playing the situation. Remind students to use vocabulary from the unit and reported speech from the grammar box and Exercise 2. Monitor the discussions, making grammatical and other corrections as necessary. Then choose a few pairs to perform their role plays for the class.

Expansion/Homework
(1) To check students' grammar individually, have them write their responses to the situation. Collect the responses and correct the grammar usage. (2) Write several sentences on the board using direct speech (you may want to include sentences with the verb tenses and modals included in the grammar chart). Have students restate the sentences in reported speech for homework. Collect the papers, and either make corrections or turn their examples into an exercise for class correction. (3) For further practice, offer exercises from *Focus on Grammar 4, 3rd Edition,* and Azar's *Understanding and Using English Grammar, 3rd Edition.* See the Grammar Book References on page 225 of the student book for specific units and chapters.

📁 Go to www.mynorthstarlab.com for additional *Grammar* practice.

❨ SKILLS

Practice the pronunciation of questions with *or;* practice giving and asking for examples; integrate the concepts, vocabulary, grammar, pronunciation, and function from the unit in a class presentation.

✪✪ PRONUNCIATION: Questions with *or*

Suggested Time: 15 minutes

1. Read the explanation together, making clear that some questions that contain an *or* are not really *or* questions, but rather *yes/no* questions. Have students repeat the example questions with the correct intonation.

2. Have students listen to the recorded sentences in **Exercise 1** and repeat them with the correct intonation. Circulate to offer individual help with intonation.

3. Go over the instructions for **Exercise 2** as a class. Point out to students that the difference here is that the speaker has more information before asking the question than he/she did in Exercise 1. For example, the questioner this time knows in item number 1 that the person has a pet, just not what kind of pet.

4. Have students listen again, and repeat using *or*-question intonation. Circulate to offer individual help with intonation. You might want to have students say what the information is that the questioner has prior to asking the question.

5. Read the instructions for **Exercise 3** with the class. Have them read the questions deciding first whether they would be better as *or*-questions, *yes/no* questions or either. Then put students in pairs to take turns asking and answering the questions with the correct intonation.

Expansion/Homework
For homework, you could have students come up with original *or* or *yes/no* questions to ask each other when they return to class.

✪✪ FUNCTION: Giving and Asking for Examples

Suggested Time: 25 minutes

1. Read the introductory conversation in **Exercise 1** and the phrases in the chart. Put students in pairs to read the conversation. You might want to have them reread the conversation using other phrases from the chart.

2. Read the instructions for **Exercise 2** and go over the example. Put students in pairs to complete the exercise.

3. Read the instructions for **Exercise 3** and put students in groups of four. Have them select a square and read the information. Circulate to answer individual questions while they are reading. Have the groups share their information. Remind students who are listening to ask for an example and tell students who are talking to stop until they are asked for an example.

✪✪✪ PRODUCTION: A Class Presentation

Suggested Time: 50 minutes

If you wish to assign a different speaking task than the one in this section, see pages 81–82. The alternative topics relate to the theme of the unit, but may not target the same grammar, pronunciation, or function taught in the unit.

1. Go over the instructions and the topics. Put students in groups to choose their topics or propose a new one.

2. Have groups study the outline and then use it as a guideline to formulate their own ideas and arguments.

3. Have groups give their presentations and conduct a class vote.

✪ ALTERNATIVE SPEAKING TOPICS

These topics give students an alternative opportunity to explore and discuss issues related to the unit theme.

✪ RESEARCH TOPICS

Suggested Time: 30 minutes in class

1. Have students turn to page 220. Review the instructions for the activity with the class. Have them choose which activity they will be doing. If students choose to research an animal, have them use a search engine to find information on the animal.

2. Have students prepare their reports. Remind students who are doing research that they need to also include their opinions on the results of the research.

3. Have students present their reports to the class or in small groups.

Go to www.mynorthstarlab.com for *Student Speaking Models, Integrated Task, Video Activity, Internet Activity*, and *Unit 4 Achievement Test.*

UNIT 5

Long vity: Refusing to Be Invisible

<table>
<tr><td colspan="2" align="center">**OVERVIEW**</td></tr>
</table>

Theme: Longevity

This unit focuses on the changing attitudes concerning aging and how society views older people. Students share and discuss their views on aging using the information and vocabulary from the unit.

Listening One: *The Red Hat Society* is a radio interview with members of the Red Hat Society, a "club" for women over 50 years old, dedicated to having fun.

Listening Two: *On Vinegar and Living to the Ripe Old Age of 115* is an interview with the granddaughter of a remarkable woman who recently died at age 115.

Critical Thinking

Recognize feelings from tone of voice	Support opinions with information from the reports
Draw conclusions from graphs	Create graphs from opinions

Listening

Make predictions	Listen for specific information
Relate previous knowledge to the listenings	Infer information not explicit in the interview
Identify main ideas	Identify speakers' feelings

Speaking

Make suggestions	Ask and answer questions
Form and express opinions	Role-play a family meeting
Call in to a radio talk show	

Vocabulary	Grammar
Use context clues to find meaning	Tag questions
Define words	**Pronunciation**
Find and use synonyms	Recognizing word blends with *you*

MyNorthStarLab	**NorthStar: Reading and Writing 4**
Readiness Check, Background and Vocabulary, Listenings One and Two, Notetaking and Academic Skills Practice, Vocabulary and Grammar, Achievement Test	Unit 5 deals with longevity and the effects of aging on society.

Go to www.mynorthstarlab.com for the MyNorthStarLab *Readiness Check.*

FOCUS ON THE TOPIC

◀ SKILLS

Predict the content of the unit from pictures; activate prior knowledge; express opinions; infer the meaning of new vocabulary from context.

✦✦✦ Ⓐ PREDICT

Suggested Time: 10 minutes

1. Before opening the book, you might ask your students if anyone in the class has a family member over 50 who has recently changed their priorities, and if so, how. For example, do they know of any older people who have recently changed professions, taken up new hobbies, joined new clubs, or somehow changed their behavior to focus more on enjoying life?

2. Have students open the book and read the unit title. Ask them to discuss why anyone would need to refuse to be invisible. Then have them look at the photographs and the questions. Have students discuss the questions, sharing summaries of their discussions with the class.

✦✦ Ⓑ SHARE INFORMATION

Suggested Time: 20 minutes

1. Put students in pairs and have each student choose one of the graphs.

2. Read the instructions for **Exercise 1** and have students read their graph and fill in the blanks in the paragraph following their graph. You might want to group the students working on the same graph together to compare their answers and their added statements.

3. Have pairs describe their graphs to each other while you move around the room to offer individual assistance.

4. Put pairs together to form groups of four to discuss the questions in **Exercise 2**. Have groups practice what they want to report to the class, and then have them share their reports with the class.

Expansion/Homework
Have students research selected countries' life spans to report back to the class. They could then return to class and get into groups with the others who researched their countries to compare their findings. You might also have them make hypotheses about why the countries they researched have those life spans.

BACKGROUND AND VOCABULARY

📁 Go to www.mynorthstarlab.com for *Background and Vocabulary*.

Suggested Time: 20 minutes

1. Have students read the instructions. Check students' comprehension of *publications* and *seniors*. Ask students at what age a person becomes a senior in their countries.

2. Read the instructions for the exercise. Ask students what the title of the publication is. Point out to students that they should try to understand the meaning of the boldfaced words from the contexts. You may want to move around the room to help point out relevant contexts.

3. Have students match the number of the boldfaced words in the exercise with their meanings or synonyms. Put them in pairs to check their answers. For disputed words, have students use the context to defend or explain their choice. Go over the answers as a class.

Expansion/Homework
You can assign this exercise as homework. Also, it can be very useful to have students highlight or underline the parts of the text, for example, the contexts, which helped them to understand the meaning of the boldfaced or underlined words.

📁 Go to www.mynorthstarlab.com for additional *Background and Vocabulary* practice.

FOCUS ON LISTENING

◀ SKILLS

Make predictions about the content of the listening; differentiate between main ideas and details; make inferences about speakers' attitudes based on tone of voice and word choice; express opinions; listen to an interview.

✦✦✦ A **LISTENING ONE: The Red Hat Society**

📁 Go to www.mynorthstarlab.com to listen to *The Red Hat Society*.

Suggested Time: 10 minutes

In Listening One, students listen to a radio report about the Red Hat Society. The segment should get students thinking about their own perceptions of aging and hearing the perceptions of aging from the voices of elderly people themselves.

1. Read the segment title and the instructions and have students read the two questions. Tell them to make some notes on the answers to the questions while they are listening.

2. Play the report. Then give students time to construct their answers. Go over the answers to the questions as a class, or let students compare their answers in pairs or small groups.

LISTENING STRATEGY: Visualize

1. Tell students to create pictures in their mind as they listen to the radio report. Then have them discuss their pictures in small groups. What did they see? What do these women look like? Suggest that each student in the group offer specific sensory details.

2. Have each group select a recorder to jot down their ideas so they can share their descriptions with the class. Ask students if they can imagine anyone in their family joining such a group. Can they visualize a grandparent wearing those clothes and participating in a parade?

✪✪✪ LISTEN FOR MAIN IDEAS   Suggested Time: 15 minutes

Have students read the questions. Then play the report while students answer the questions. If students seem to have trouble, play the audio one more time before going over the answers. Then go over the answers as a class. If disagreements arise, replay those segments rather than simply giving the answers.

Expansion/Homework
Have students turn to their answers in the previous section to see if their predictions were correct. Ask them what other topics they had predicted.

REACHING ALL STUDENTS: Listen for Main Ideas

- **Less Proficient:** To help students understand symbols, elicit obvious examples (heart–love, flag–country, ring–marriage, dove–peace).

- **More Proficient:** Brainstorm various things that are associated with colors. Then have students work in small groups to connect with symbols (for example, purple robes of royalty, red heart on Valentine's Day).

✪✪✪ LISTEN FOR DETAILS   Suggested Time: 15 minutes

1. Have students read the statements and choose the answers for those that they can. You might want to have them do that in pencil.

2. Have students listen to the segment again, completing the exercise. Then put students in pairs to compare their answers.

✪✪✪ MAKE INFERENCES

Suggested Time: 10 minutes

1. Have students read the instructions and the boxed adjectives. You might want to elicit example sentences that could be read in the appropriate tones of voices for each adjective in the box.

2. Have students read the statement for each excerpt. Play the excerpts and give students time to complete the task. Then go over the answers, or allow students to discuss their answers with a partner, encouraging them to give reasons for their answers. Tell students to use actual language to support their answers. Replay the excerpts as needed while the pairs are discussing them. Then ask the pairs to share their answers with the class.

✪✪✪ EXPRESS OPINIONS

Suggested Time: 15 minutes

1. Have students read the questions. Check that students understand the graph and the task in question 4. Put students in groups to discuss questions 1, 2, and 3 and complete their graphs for question 4. Encourage them to support their ideas with reasons and information based on the listening.

2. If time allows, have groups share their thoughts on one or all of the questions and their graphs with the class.

CRITICAL THINKING

Give students the following questions for discussion in small groups before discussing as a whole class:

1. What do the women in this report wear?

   Answer: Red hats and purple clothing

2. In the poem, why does the author want to wear something which "doesn't go and doesn't suit me"?

   Answers will vary, but might include a need for individuality, for freedom, for self-expression, and for personal pleasure.

3. What is your opinion of the Red Hat Society?

   Answers will vary, but students should support their opinions with clear reasons.

4. Why are groups like the Red Hat Society important for people?

   Answers will vary, but might include that they provide support, a sense of belonging, identification with others of like mind.

 Link to *NorthStar: Reading and Writing 4*

If students are also using the companion text, you can ask them to speculate about how the Red Hat Society members might react to the information in Reading Two.

B LISTENING TWO: On Vinegar and Living to the Ripe Old Age of 115

📁 Go to www.mynorthstarlab.com to listen to *On Vinegar and Living to the Ripe Old Age of 115*.

Suggested Time: 20 minutes

In Listening Two, students listen to an interview with the granddaughter of a woman who lived to the age of 115. The purpose of this interview is to challenge students to think about the issues of health and happiness as it relates to aging.

1. Have students read the segment title and say what vinegar might have to do with living longer. Then have them read the background information. Ask students to think about older people that they know. Ask them if they've learned anything from these people, and if so, what? Also, ask them to think of some questions they think would be interesting to ask their older relatives or friends.

2. Play Listening Two, and then have students complete **Exercise 1**. Play the segment again to allow students to check their answers stopping as needed. Go over the answers as a class.

3. Have students discuss the questions in **Exercise 2**. Encourage students to give specific examples to support their opinions.

C INTEGRATE LISTENINGS ONE AND TWO

◗ SKILLS

Organize information from the listenings in a chart; synthesize the information in a role play.

STEP 1: Organize   Suggested Time: 10 minutes

1. Read through the directions for the exercise and look at the chart with students. Have them work individually to complete the chart with information from Listenings One and Two.

2. Have students compare answers with a partner's before going over the answers with the entire class.

STEP 2: Synthesize   Suggested Time: 15 minutes

1. Read the instructions with the class. Put students in pairs and tell them to choose roles. You might want to have students get into groups by role choice to talk about what they are going to say prior to doing the role play.

2. Have the pairs practice their role plays while you move around the room to help with individual problems. If time allows, have select pairs perform their role plays for the class.

Link to *NorthStar: Reading and Writing 4*

If students are also using the companion text, you can list relevant vocabulary from Background and Vocabulary in Unit 5 on the board and encourage students to use it in their role plays.

Go to www.mynorthstarlab.com for *Notetaking* and *Academic Skills Practice*.

FOCUS ON SPEAKING

A VOCABULARY

◖ SKILLS

Review vocabulary from Listenings One and Two; expand understanding of vocabulary items by seeing them in additional contexts; use new vocabulary creatively in a speaking activity.

✪ REVIEW   Suggested Time: 10 minutes

Go to www.mynorthstarlab.com for *Review*.

Have students read the instructions and the example. You may want to review the pronunciation and word forms of each word. Then have students complete the exercise individually before going over the answers as a class.

Expansion/Homework
This exercise could be done for homework and then discussed in class, if desired. Additionally, you could have students write a call-in question using the unit vocabulary for homework.

✪✪ EXPAND   Suggested Time: 15 minutes

1. Have students read the instructions for **Exercise 1**. Check students' comprehension of all the words and phrases in the box. Then have students read the doctor's advice and fill in the blanks with correct words.

2. Read the instructions for **Exercise 2**. Put students in pairs and have them choose their roles and perform the role play.

3. Have students change roles and continue their role play. You might want to have students work together first to come up with ideas for the doctor's reply to the second caller's question before role-playing the situation.

VOCABULARY EXPANSION: Words with Multiple Meaning

1. Tell students that many words have several meanings, but often those meanings have some relationship to each other.

2. Give students these vocabulary words and have them investigate the multiple meanings for each: *bitter, bold, chapter, face,* and *senior.* Provide dictionaries and have students work in small groups to determine what idea the meanings of each word have in common.

✪ CREATE

Suggested Time: 20 minutes

1. Read the instructions for **Exercise 1**. Give students a few minutes to choose their problems and take some notes, or to brainstorm in pairs or groups. Then have students read the example role play in **Exercise 2**.

2. Put students in groups of three to role-play the radio show. Make sure students understand that they are to actually take turns asking and answering questions. Have a few groups perform their role plays for the class.

 Go to www.mynorthstarlab.com for additional *Vocabulary* practice.

✪✪ B GRAMMAR: Tag Questions

 Go to www.mynorthstarlab.com for *Grammar Chart* and *Exercise 2*.

◀ SKILLS

Practice the form and meaning of tag questions.

Suggested Time: 30 minutes

1. Have students read the two lines in **Exercise 1**. Ask them if they see any pattern in the tag question verbs as related to the verbs in the statements. Also ask them what the difference between the intonation patterns is and if they can say why.

2. Go over each section in the chart with students, providing more examples, or eliciting more examples from them.

3. Read the instructions to Step 1 of **Exercise 2** and the example with the class. Have students complete the exercise in pairs. Then read the instructions to Step 2 and play the audio segment for students while they mark the intonation patterns. Then have them take turns reading the conversation using the correct intonation patterns.

4. Read the instructions to Step 1 of **Exercise 3**. Have students circle their choices individually. Tell them not to worry about whether they are right or wrong, but to make a mark next to the ones they are sure about and a different mark next to the ones they aren't sure about. Then read the instructions to Step 2 and the

example with the class. Put students in pairs to take turns asking and answering the questions. Choose a few pairs, or ask for volunteers, to perform some or one of their questions and answers for the class.

Expansion/Homework
For further practice, offer exercises from *Focus on Grammar 4, 3rd Edition,* and Azar's *Understanding and Using English Grammar, 3rd Edition.* See the Grammar Book References on page 225 of the student book for specific units and chapters.

 Link to *NorthStar: Reading and Writing 4*
If students are also using the companion text, you can have them change the sentences from Grammar, Exercise 3 into tag questions.

 Go to www.mynorthstarlab.com for additional *Grammar* practice.

C SPEAKING

◀ SKILLS

Recognize word blend; practice making suggestions; integrate the concepts, vocabulary, grammar, pronunciation, and function from the unit to role-play a family meeting.

✪ PRONUNCIATION: Recognizing Word Blends with *You*

Suggested Time: 15 minutes

1. Read the explanation together. Have students listen to the sample sentences and read the boxed explanation of the blending of words with *you.*

2. Have students listen to the sentences in **Exercise 1** and repeat them with the correct blending pronunciation. Move around the room and offer individual help.

3. Go over the instructions for **Exercise 2.** Play the segment and pause to give students time to repeat.

4. Play the segment again while students fill in the blanks with options from Column 2. You might want to put students in pairs and have them take turns saying the questions and statements with the correctly blended sounds. Move around the room and offer individual help with pronunciation.

✪ FUNCTION: Making Suggestions

Suggested Time: 25 minutes

1. Read the instructions for **Exercise 1** and have students complete the exercise individually. Then go over the boxed suggestions with the class, paying special attention to the form of the verbs that follow each suggestion.

Longevity: Refusing to Be Invisible **53**

2. Read the instructions for **Exercise 2** and have students complete the exercise individually. Put them in pairs to compare answers before going over the answers as a class.

3. Read the instructions for **Exercise 3** and have students read all the situations, thinking of some suggestions for each one. Put students in pairs and have them talk about the situations and give suggestions.

✪✪✪ PRODUCTION: A Family Meeting

Suggested Time: 45 minutes

If you wish to assign a different speaking task than the one in this section, see page 102. The alternative topics relate to the theme of the unit, but may not target the same grammar, pronunciation, or function taught in the unit.

1. Go over the instructions and the situation. Put students into groups of three and have them choose their roles and read the relevant boxes of information as specified in Step 1.

2. Have students read Step 2 and then role-play the situation coming to a consensus about the solution.

3. Have groups tell the class what their solution is and why. You might want to list the solutions with noted reasons on the board and have the class conduct a vote as to the best solution.

✪ ALTERNATIVE SPEAKING TOPICS

These topics give students an alternative opportunity to explore and discuss issues related to the unit theme.

✪ RESEARCH TOPICS

Suggested Time: 30 minutes in class

1. Have students turn to page 220. Review the questions about the topics with the class. Tell students that after they choose a topic, they can use a search engine to search for information.

2. Have students do their research either individually or in small groups. Emphasize that they should include answers to the questions listed in the book. Encourage students to include additional information they find.

3. Have students present the results of their research to the class.

Go to www.mynorthstarlab.com for *Student Speaking Models, Integrated Task, Video Activity, Internet Activity,* and *Unit 5 Achievement Test.*

UNIT 6

Giving to Others: Why Do We Do It?

OVERVIEW

Theme: Philanthropy

This unit examines the motivations of people who give money to charity. Students reflect on their own and their culture's philosophies concerning philanthropy and create a public service announcement using information from the unit.

Listening One: *Why We Give* is a radio interview with an editor of a publication about philanthropy, detailing the reasons and ways people in the U.S. volunteer or give money to charities.

Listening Two: *The Mystery Donor* is a radio report about an anonymous donor, what her motivation is, and how she decides to whom to donate.

Critical Thinking

Read and interpret graphs
Make judgments about motivations for philanthropy
Identify personal assumptions

Hypothesize rationales for philanthropic actions
Compare and contrast information
Rank desirable employee qualities

Listening Tasks

Make predictions
Identify main ideas
Listen for details
Listen and take notes using a graphic organizer

Organize and synthesize information from the listenings
Listen to and evaluate students' presentations

Speaking Tasks

Express opinions about philanthropy
Discuss examples of charitable efforts
Prioritize and rank ideas

Practice correct intonation
Develop and perform a public service announcement

Vocabulary

Use context clues to find meaning
Find and use synonyms
Identify correct word forms

Grammar

Adjective clauses

Pronunciation

Intonation in lists

 MyNorthStarLab
Readiness Check, Background and Vocabulary, Listenings One and Two, Notetaking and Academic Skills Practice, Vocabulary and Grammar, Achievement Test

 NorthStar: Reading and Writing 4
Unit 6 deals with the benefits that volunteers receive from donating their time and energy to a charity.

Go to www.mynorthstarlab.com for the MyNorthStarLab *Readiness Check*.

①FOCUS ON THE TOPIC

◖SKILLS

Predict the content of the unit; activate prior knowledge; express opinions; infer the meaning of new vocabulary from context.

✲✲✲Ⓐ PREDICT

Suggested Time: 10 minutes

1. Have students look at the cartoon and describe what they see happening. Then have them look at the unit title. Put them in pairs or small groups to discuss the questions.

2. As a class, elicit answers to the questions from several of the students, trying to get a variety of responses. Then ask students if they think giving to charities is only for rich people and why.

✲✲Ⓑ SHARE INFORMATION

Suggested Time: 20 minutes

1. Read the background information on philanthropy and charity, and the instructions for **Exercise 1** with the class. Go over the word forms in the chart, checking that students can pronounce the different forms. Then put students in pairs to read the words to each other while you circulate.

2. Read the instructions for **Exercise 2** and have students look at the two graphs. Then divide the class into small groups and have them discuss the graphs and the questions and prepare a summary of their discussion.

3. Have the groups report their summaries to the class. You may want to ask students if anything in the graphs surprised them at all.

✲✲✲Ⓒ BACKGROUND AND VOCABULARY

 Go to www.mynorthstarlab.com for *Background and Vocabulary*.

Suggested Time: 25 minutes

1. Have students read the instructions for **Exercise 1** and look at the magazine section. Point out to students that the words in bold are new vocabulary words

and that they should try to understand the meaning of them from the contexts. Then have them read the article paying attention to the boldfaced words.

2. Have students read the words and the definitions in **Exercise 2**, checking their comprehension of the definitions. Put students in pairs to complete the exercise. You might want to have students complete the exercise individually first and then compare answers in pairs. When students are discussing their answers, encourage them to use the context to defend or explain their choice. Go over the answers as a class.

Expansion/Homework
You can assign these exercises as homework and use class time to check answers.

 Link to *NorthStar: Reading and Writing 4*
If students are also using the companion text, you can write the vocabulary from Background and Vocabulary in Unit 6 on the board and see if students can find synonyms for those words in the list of words they just worked on.

 Go to www.mynorthstarlab.com for additional *Background and Vocabulary* practice.

2 FOCUS ON LISTENING

◀ SKILLS

Make predictions about the content of the listening; differentiate between main ideas and details; make inferences about speakers' feelings; express opinions.

❋❋❋ Ⓐ LISTENING ONE: Why We Give

 Go to www.mynorthstarlab.com to listen to *Why We Give.*

Suggested Time: 10 minutes

In Listening One, students listen to a radio program on the ways and reasons people give time or money to charities. The segment should get students thinking in more depth about the issue of giving money or time to those in need.

1. Ask students to read the segment title and the background information. Then have them read the question and the options.

2. Play the introduction and have students answer the question. Then discuss the answers as a class. Encourage discussion.

1. Remind students that we listen differently according to our purpose, and identifying a purpose for listening changes the way we listen and helps us to concentrate. First, have students listen once to get the gist of the information. Then have them listen a second time for specific details.

2. Prior to the first listening, tell students they will listen to see what the listening is about. Before the second listening, tell students they will listen for the answers to questions (provide three specific questions). Then ask students to debrief in small groups to compare how the listening was different each time. How was the first listening different from the second? What did they do differently the second time? Invite volunteers to share their experience with the class.

✪✪✪ LISTEN FOR MAIN IDEAS
Suggested Time: 15 minutes

Have students read the instructions and the list of seven motivations. Play the report while students number the motivations. If students seem to have trouble, play the audio one more time, having students raise their hands to indicate they've heard another motivation and then pausing the segment to allow students to discuss what they heard.

Expansion/Homework
You might want to have students discuss which of these reasons they think might motivate them if they had enough time or money.

 ### Link to *NorthStar: Reading and Writing 4*
If students are also using the companion text, you can ask them to compare the reasons for volunteering and donating money given here to the ones outlined in the readings in Unit 6. Ask students to decide whether any of the reasons in Listening One would apply to Justin's volunteer work.

✪✪✪ LISTEN FOR DETAILS
Suggested Time: 15 minutes

Have students read the questions and possible answers and answer those that they can. You might want to have them do that in pencil. Then have students listen to the radio report again and circle the correct answers. Play the audio once more for students to check their answers.

✪✪✪ MAKE INFERENCES
Suggested Time: 10 minutes

1. Have students read the instructions and the statement for each excerpt before listening to it. You might want to have them attempt to say whether it is true or false and then check their answers.

2. Play each excerpt, and then allow students to discuss their answers with a partner, or with the class. Tell students to use actual language to support their answers. Replay the excerpts as needed while discussing them. It might be useful to show why these are inferences as opposed to stated facts.

REACHING ALL STUDENTS: Make Inferences

- **Less Proficient:** Have students underline specific information in the script on pages 236–237 from which they can infer an answer.

- **More Proficient:** Have students write a paragraph to explain each choice.

✪✪✪ **EXPRESS OPINIONS**   **Suggested Time:** 15 minutes

1. Have students read the comments and think about whether or not they agree or disagree while they are reading.

2. Have students discuss the questions in small groups. Encourage them to support their ideas with reasons and information based on the listening.

CRITICAL THINKING

Give students the following questions for discussion in small groups before discussing as a whole class:

1. According to the interview, why do people give time and/or money to charity?

   Answer: The biggest motive is that people care about what they are giving to or involved in.

2. What conclusions can you draw about the giving of wealthy and less wealthy people?

   Answers will vary, but should include specific information from the interview. (The wealthy give more often, like black tie affairs, like to have their name attached; the less wealthy give anonymously and give more proportionately.)

3. Would you support a mandatory community service requirement in your school if elective credit were given?

   Answers will vary, but students should support their opinions with clear reasons and examples.

4. What might you gain/learn personally from a community service requirement?

   Answers will vary, but students should be able to give specific gains and how they might occur from participating in community service.

✪✪✪ **B** **LISTENING TWO: The Mystery Donor**

Go to www.mynorthstarlab.com to listen to *The Mystery Donor*.

Suggested Time: 20 minutes

In Listening Two, students listen to a radio report about a person who donates money anonymously. The woman and a charity she donates to are interviewed. The purpose of this interview is to further challenge students to think about the reasons motivating people to donate money or time, and what they themselves get out of it.

1. Have students read the title of the listening. Ask students what they think a "mystery donor" might be. Then have students read the background information and check their comprehension of *anonymously.*

2. Play Listening Two, and then have students complete **Exercise 1**. Play the interview again to allow students to check their answers, stopping as needed.

3. Have students read the instructions for **Exercise 2** and the list of causes and discuss the questions in small groups. Encourage students to give specific examples and reasons to support their opinions. You may want to ask the groups to try and convince one another and come to a consensus about the top three most important causes.

Expansion/Homework

In groups, have students discuss what the mystery donor means by statement in item 3 in Exercise 1. How do you think she thinks her relationship with the recipient of her donation might change?

✪✪✪ C INTEGRATE LISTENINGS ONE AND TWO

◖ SKILLS

Organize the information from the listenings in a chart; synthesize the information by role-playing a relevant situation.

STEP 1: Organize   Suggested Time: 15 minutes

1. Read through the directions for the exercise and look at the chart with students. Have students work with a partner or in small groups to complete the chart with information from Listenings One and Two.

2. Have pairs or groups compare answers with those of another pair or group before going over the answers with the entire class.

STEP 2: Synthesize   Suggested Time: 15 minutes

1. Read the instructions and the boxed phrases with the class. Put students into pairs and tell them to choose roles, or choose for them. You might want to have the different roles get into groups before having them do their role plays to work together to come up with what they'd like to say.

2. Have the pairs practice their role plays while you move around the room to help with individual problems. Have the partners switch roles after the first three points, or after they've completed the role play.

3. If time allows, have select pairs perform their role plays for the class.

Link to *NorthStar: Reading and Writing 4*

If students are also using the companion text, you can ask them to look again at Reading One to find similarities and differences between the motivations for giving money or time outlined in both listening segments, and Justin Lebo's philanthropic work.

 Go to www.mynorthstarlab.com for *Notetaking* and *Academic Skills Practice*.

③ FOCUS ON SPEAKING

Ⓐ VOCABULARY

◀ SKILLS

Review vocabulary from Listenings One and Two; expand students' understanding of vocabulary items by seeing them in additional contexts; use new vocabulary creatively in a speaking activity.

✪ REVIEW   Suggested Time: 10 minutes

 Go to www.mynorthstarlab.com for *Review*.

Have students read the instructions and look at the chart. Point out that not all the boxes can be filled in. Have them use a dictionary for words they are not sure about. When done, go over the answers as a class.

✪✪ EXPAND   Suggested Time: 10 minutes

1. Have students look at the background information and the instructions for **Exercise 1**. Point out that students need to change the form of the words in the box, so you might want to look at each sentence with them, eliciting from them what kind of word form (part of speech) would fit in each sentence. Have students complete the exercise. Then go over the answers as a class.

2. Read the instructions for **Exercise 2** and the boxed words and phrases with the class. Then have students read the e-mail and fill in the blanks with words from the box. Go over the answers with the class.

VOCABULARY EXPANSION: Roots and Affixes Illustration

1. Have students work in small groups to create an illustration showing roots, prefixes, and suffixes on large chart paper. Students might draw items like a plant (roots, stem, flowers, leaves), a train (engine, cars, caboose), etc. on which to

(continued on next page)

---

write roots and affixes. Or they might put roots/base words on the roots and trunk of a tree, with prefixes and suffixes on branches and leaves.

2. Have students begin by drawing from these vocabulary words: *anonymously, charitable, contribute, donation, fund-raiser, generosity, motivated,* and *philanthropist.* Allow time for them to research a variety of sources for other roots and affixes.

✪ CREATE
Suggested Time: 20 minutes

1. Read the instructions and the boxed words with students, checking their pronunciation of each word. Then have students take some time to read the information and decide how they'd like to donate the $1 million.

2. Put students in pairs or groups to discuss donating their money. Remind them to use as much of the vocabulary items listed as possible. Then have each pair or group share with the class how they divided up the money.

Expansion/Homework
Have students choose one of the charities to research online. They could be given different questions to research such as the age of the organization, the countries it operates in, the amount of money it raises each year, the number of employees it has, any controversy surrounding it, etc. Then have students get into groups to discuss what they found.

 Go to www.mynorthstarlab.com for additional *Vocabulary* practice.

✪✪ B GRAMMAR: Relative Pronouns in Adjective Clauses

 Go to www.mynorthstarlab.com for *Grammar Chart* and *Exercise 2.*

◖ SKILLS

Practice the form and meaning of adjective clauses.

Suggested Time: 30 minutes

1. For **Exercise 1**, have students read the segment and answer the questions with a partner.

2. Go over each section in the chart with the class providing more examples, or eliciting more examples from students.

3. Read the instructions for **Exercise 2** with the class. Have students fill in the blanks individually. Then put students in pairs to compare answers and read the paragraphs aloud with their partners.

4. For **Exercise 3**, divide the class into two groups, group A and group B. Have the groups read their own set of instructions.

5. Have students complete the sentences. Then put them into A-B pairs to take turns reading their sentences and identifying the noun described or identified.

6. Review the answers, and address questions and problems as a class. Remind students to use vocabulary from the unit and adjective clauses from the grammar box and the previous exercises.

Expansion/Homework

For further practice, offer exercises from *Focus on Grammar 4, 3rd Edition,* and Azar's *Understanding and Using English Grammar, 3rd Edition.* See the Grammar Book References on page 225 of the student book for specific units and chapters.

 Go to www.mynorthstarlab.com for additional *Grammar* practice.

C SPEAKING

SKILLS

Practice the intonation in lists; practice prioritizing and ranking ideas; integrate the concepts, vocabulary, grammar, pronunciation, and function from the unit in a presentation of a public service announcement for a not-for-profit organization.

✪✪ PRONUNCIATION: Intonation in Lists

Suggested Time: 20 minutes

1. Read the explanation together. Have students listen to the conversation and answer the questions as a class. Then read the explanation in the chart with students.

2. Read the instructions for **Exercise 1**. Play the audio and have students decide whether the list is finished or unfinished. Play the audio again to let students check their answers before going over the answers as a class.

3. For **Exercise 2**, have students take turns reading the sentences with a partner while you move around the room to offer individual assistance.

4. Read the instructions for **Exercise 3** with students. Make sure they understand that there are two tasks. You might want to have them underline the lists first, and then listen to the segment, deciding whether the lists are finished or not while they listen. Then, in pairs, have students practice the conversation. Have select pairs read the conversation for the class.

5. Read the instructions for **Exercise 4** with the class. Have students spend some time thinking of three helpful things they could do while you move around the room to help with individual questions. Then put students in groups to tell each other their three ideas. You might suggest that the groups make a list of the three things and then share them with the class. You could make a list on the board of all the ways students thought of to be of help.

✪✪ FUNCTION: Prioritizing or Ranking Ideas

Suggested Time: 25 minutes

1. Put students in pairs to read the conversation. Then have them read the information on prioritizing or ranking.

2. Have students read the phrases in the box. Then elicit additional phrases from students and write them on the board.

3. Have students read the ads for volunteer jobs. Move around the room to answer individual questions, or check students' comprehension together as a class.

4. Put students in pairs to complete the exercise. Have students read the personal qualities listed in Step 2 and discuss them using the boxed phrases. Monitor students' discussions for usage of the target phrases. Have selected pairs share their ranked qualities with the class.

✪✪✪ PRODUCTION: A Public Service Announcement

Suggested Time: 50 minutes

If you wish to assign a different speaking task than the one in this section, see page 126. The alternative topics relate to the theme of the unit, but may not target the same grammar, pronunciation, or function taught in the unit.

1. Read the directions with the class. Ask students if they have ever seen or heard PSAs (Public Service Announcements) on TV or the radio. If so, ask what they were for. Explain that PSAs are short radio or television reports that send educational messages to the public. They give important information about specific issues, such as health or encourage people to donate time or money to a cause.

2. Read the instructions for Step 1 with students. Have them read the questions. Then play the PSA and have students discuss the questions in pairs.

3. Read the instructions for Step 2 with the class. Have the pairs choose a not-for-profit organization and a target audience. Move around the room to help each group as needed.

4. Have pairs fill out the chart in Step 3 while you move around the room to help. Emphasize that everyone should have a speaking part and that students should be creative—using humor, sound effects, and anything else they can think of to make their PSA catchy and interesting.

5. Have the pairs write their PSAs. Encourage them to use the unit vocabulary, grammar, and intonation. They may need to practice and then rewrite once they see how long their announcement is. You may want to circulate to help them time their PSAs.

6. Help the pairs record their PSAs or have them perform their PSAs for the class. Have the groups vote to select the most interesting and most convincing PSA.

Expansion/Homework

If possible, students can perform their PSAs on videotape, which would allow the use of costumes or other visuals, or they can perform them in class. To encourage students' creativity, you can have two simple prizes, which you can award for the best PSAs.

 Link to *NorthStar: Reading and Writing 4*

If students are also using the companion text, you can make a connection to the readings by asking at least one group to choose high school students as their target audience, and asking another group to write a PSA to encourage people to donate old bicycles for Justin Lebo's bicycle rebuilding project.

✪ ALTERNATIVE SPEAKING TOPICS

These topics give students an alternative opportunity to explore and discuss issues related to the unit theme.

✪ RESEARCH TOPICS

Suggested Time: 25 minutes in class

1. Have students turn to page 221. Review the instructions for the activity with the class. Tell students that they first need to choose a person or an organization to research. Discuss with the class other organizations, perhaps ones active in your area.

2. Tell students that they should use a search engine to search for information on the person or organization they are researching.

3. Have students prepare their reports. Emphasize that they should include answers to the questions listed in the book. Encourage students to include additional information they find.

4. Have students present their reports to the class or in small groups.

 Go to www.mynorthstarlab.com for *Student Speaking Models, Integrated Task, Video Activity, Internet Activity*, and *Unit 6 Achievement Test.*

UNIT 7 Wh t's the Us of Homework?

OVERVIEW

Theme: Education
This unit examines the value and the negative effects of the amount of homework assigned to students, and the resulting involvement of the parents in their children's education. Students think about and discuss their own experiences with homework.

Listening One: *Effects of Homework on Family Life* is a radio interview with a student, parents, and experts on the issue of students spending so much time doing homework.

Listening Two: *A Duty to Family, Heritage, and Country: Another Perspective on Homework* is a radio report on another culture's view of education, homework, and grades. A young Chinese student describes her conflicting feelings about fulfilling the expectations of her family and her country instead of following her own dreams.

Critical Thinking

Interpret a cartoon
Identify and evaluate assumptions
Hypothesize another's point of view

Connect opinions to specific people
Evaluate own opinions concerning others' thoughts

Listening

Predict content
Listen for main ideas
Listen for details
Support answers with details

Relate listenings to personal experiences
Organize and synthesize information from the listenings

Speaking

Express opinions
Restate information for clarification
Restate statements

Perform a role play
Conduct a town meeting

Vocabulary

Use context clues to find meaning
Find and use synonyms
Use idiomatic expressions

Grammar

Make, let, help, and *get*

Pronunciation

Stressed and unstressed vowels

 MyNorthStarLab
Readiness Check, Background and Vocabulary, Listenings One and Two, Notetaking and Academic Skills Practice, Vocabulary and Grammar, Achievement Test

 NorthStar: Reading and Writing 4
Unit 7 deals with the advantages and disadvantages of homeschooling.

66

Go to www.mynorthstarlab.com for the MyNorthStarLab *Readiness Check*.

1 FOCUS ON THE TOPIC

◖ SKILLS

Predict the content of the unit; activate prior knowledge; express opinions; infer the meaning of new vocabulary from context.

✦✦✦ A PREDICT

Suggested Time: 10 minutes

1. Before opening the book, you might want to ask students to remember how much homework they had each night at different ages. Put them in groups to compare and make a list of the amounts of time they needed to do their homework at three different ages, 10, 13, and 17. Then ask them to discuss whether or not they thought the homework was too little, enough, or too much, and how they felt about it. Also, ask them if their parents helped them with their homework.

2. Have students open their books and look at the cartoon and describe what they see happening. Then have them look at the unit title. Put them in pairs or small groups to discuss the questions.

✦✦ B SHARE INFORMATION

Suggested Time: 20 minutes

1. Read the instructions for **Exercise 1** and have students read the descriptions of the assignments. Answer any vocabulary or comprehension questions. Then put students in pairs to complete the exercise.

2. Regroup students for **Exercise 2**, and have them compare and discuss their answers. Encourage students to give reasons for their answers.

✦✦✦ C BACKGROUND AND VOCABULARY

 Go to www.mynorthstarlab.com for *Background and Vocabulary*.

Suggested Time: 25 minutes

1. Read the instructions for **Exercise 1** with the class. Divide the class into groups A, B, and C to read the assigned paragraphs and choose the correct definitions of the vocabulary words.

2. Form new groups of three with an A, B, and C student in each group to complete **Exercise 2**. You might suggest that when each student is talking, the others close their books, or cover the paragraphs and relevant lists of words.

3. For **Exercise 3**, have the groups use the information they exchanged with one another to cooperatively complete the graph. Go over the completed graphs with the class to see how similar or different they are.

 Link to *NorthStar: Reading and Writing 4*
If students are also using the companion text, you can write the vocabulary from Background and Vocabulary in Unit 7 on the board and see if students can find synonyms for those words in the list of words they just worked on.

 Go to www.mynorthstarlab.com for additional *Background and Vocabulary* practice.

2 FOCUS ON LISTENING

◖ SKILLS

Make predictions about the content of the listening; listen for main ideas; identify supporting details; make inferences about speakers' feelings; express opinions.

✿✿✿ A LISTENING ONE: Effects of Homework on Family Life

 Go to www.mynorthstarlab.com to listen to *Effects of Homework on Family Life*.

Suggested Time: 10 minutes

In Listening One, students listen to a radio program on the history of the present homework situation in U.S. schools, and different people's opinions of the benefits and disadvantages of having so much homework to do. The segment should get students thinking in more depth about the issue of the value of homework and how much parents should be involved in their children's education.

1. Ask students to read the segment title and say what they think the effects of homework on family life might be. Then have them read the two questions.

2. Play the segment and have students answer the questions. You might want to ask students if they understand the meaning of *alien* (in this case, something new or different) or *over the top* (beyond what is expected or should be done).

3. Put students in pairs or small groups to compare answers and make their predictions. Call on individual students to share their predictions with the class. Affirm each prediction as a possibility.

1. Remind students that we often listen to information that we agree or disagree with. The stronger our agreement or disagreement, the more likely we are to interject our own thoughts into the process and distract ourselves from listening. A topic like homework, with which students have ample experience, is likely to be a subject for which there is disagreement. Suggest that students take this as an opportunity to monitor their thoughts.

2. To help students attend to the report, have them draw a two-column chart and label one side Agree and the other Disagree. Making notes of those items will help them to attend to the discussion. If they strongly agree or disagree, have them add an exclamation point to their note.

✪✪✪ LISTEN FOR MAIN IDEAS   Suggested Time: 15 minutes

1. Have students read the instructions and the list of people and ideas. Tell students that the ideas are not always the exact words they will hear in the segment. Also, you might want to tell students that the list of people is in the same order that they are in the recording.

2. Play the report while students match the people to their comments. If students seem to have trouble, play the audio one more time, having students raise their hand to indicate they've heard another comment and then pausing the segment to allow students to discuss what they heard. When done, go over the answers with the class.

REACHING ALL STUDENTS: Listen for Main Ideas

- **Less Proficient:** To help students attend to the information, have pairs listen a second time, focusing on speakers. Have them write the names of each speaker in a six-column chart and then add notes in one- or two-word phrases under each name as they listen.

- **More Proficient:** Suggest that pairs of students summarize the arguments. Have students make a two-column chart, entitled Pros and Cons, and list the arguments for and against homework.

✪✪✪ LISTEN FOR DETAILS   Suggested Time: 15 minutes

Have students read the questions and possible answers, and answer those that they can. You might want to have them do that in pencil. Then have students listen to the report again and circle the correct answers. Play the audio once more for students to check their answers. Then go over the answers as a class.

Link to *NorthStar: Reading and Writing 4*

If students are also using the companion text, you can ask them to compare the amount of homework schooled students get with the amount the homeschoolers in Reading One might get.

✪✪✪ MAKE INFERENCES   Suggested Time: 15 minutes

1. Have students read the instructions, the statement, and possible answers for each excerpt. You might want to have them attempt to say which they think is the correct answer, and then listen and check their answers.

2. Play each excerpt, and then allow students to discuss their answers with a partner, or with the class. Tell students to use actual language to support their answers and replay the excerpt as needed while discussing it. It might be useful to show why these are inferences as opposed to stated facts.

✪✪✪ EXPRESS OPINIONS   Suggested Time: 15 minutes

Have students read the instructions and the quotations. Tell them to rate their level of agreement individually, and then put them in small groups to compare and discuss their opinions. Encourage them to support their ideas with reasons and information based on the listening.

CRITICAL THINKING

Give students the following questions for discussion in small groups before discussing as a whole class:

1. What evidence does the article give to support having homework?

   Answer: Students do better on standardized tests; homework teaches responsibility; it keeps students off the streets; and it involves parents.

2. According to the people in the report, what are the problems with homework?

   Answer: The amount of homework can be excessive; parents are too involved; it impacts family life.

3. Taking answers from questions 1 and 2 into account, what is your opinion of homework? Explain.

   Answers will vary, but students should offer convincing reasons and examples to support or refute the evidence in item 1 and item 2.

4. Propose a solution to the problem of homework—to give enough to improve achievement, but not so much that it affects family life.

   Solutions will vary, but students should support their solutions with convincing reasons.

B   LISTENING TWO: A Duty to Family, Heritage, and Country: Another Perspective on Homework

📁   Go to www.mynorthstarlab.com to listen to *A Duty to Family, Heritage, and Country: Another Perspective on Homework*.

Suggested Time: 20 minutes

In Listening Two, students listen to a recorded account of a young Chinese girl's thoughts on her feelings about homework. The purpose of this interview is to further challenge students to think about the reasons for homework, the benefits of homework, and how the culture affects a student's ideas and performance in school.

1. Have students read the title of the listening. Ask students what they think *heritage* (legacy, tradition) might be. You might want to check their comprehension of *duty* (obligation, responsibility), as well.

2. Have students read the background information and the statements in **Exercise 1**. Then play the audio and have students cross out the false information, correcting it where possible. You may need to replay the segment to give students time to hear the corrections they need to make and write them in. Then go over the answers as a class.

3. Have students read the instructions for **Exercise 2** and the questions. Put students in groups to discuss the questions. Encourage students to give specific examples and reasons to support their opinions.

Expansion/Homework
Students could do an online research for homework requirements in Chinese schools at different ages and report back to the class.

 Link to *NorthStar: Reading and Writing 4*
If students are also using the companion text, you can ask them to consider what Ying Ying Yu might think about the homeschooling options in Reading One.

C   INTEGRATE LISTENINGS ONE AND TWO

◀ SKILLS

Organize the information from the listenings in a chart; synthesize the information in a role play.

STEP 1: Organize   **Suggested Time: 15 minutes**

1. Have students read the instructions for Step 1, and then look at the chart and read the list of the effects of homework column. Have students work with a partner or in small groups to complete the chart.

2. Have pairs or groups compare answers with those of another pair or group before going over the answers with the entire class.

STEP 2: Synthesize   **Suggested Time: 15 minutes**

1. Read the instructions with the class. Put students in pairs and tell them to choose roles, or choose for them. You might want to have the different roles get into groups before having them do their role plays to work together to come up with what they'd like to say.

2. Have the pairs practice their role plays while you move around the room to help with individual problems. Have the partners switch roles after they've completed the role play once. Remind students to use the vocabulary from the unit where possible. If time allows, have a few pairs perform their role plays for the class.

📁 Go to www.mynorthstarlab.com for *Notetaking* and *Academic Skills Practice*.

3 FOCUS ON SPEAKING

A VOCABULARY

◖ SKILLS

Review vocabulary from Listenings One and Two; expand students' understanding of vocabulary items by seeing them in additional contexts; use new vocabulary creatively in a speaking activity.

✪ REVIEW   **Suggested Time: 10 minutes**

📁 Go to www.mynorthstarlab.com for *Review*.

Have students read the instructions. Point out that there are two tasks to do. Then put students in pairs to complete the exercise. You might want to have students do the exercise individually and then compare and discuss their answers with a partner. Then go over the answers as a class.

✪✪ EXPAND   **Suggested Time: 20 minutes**

1. Have students look at the background information and the instructions. Have them read the abstract and the chart. You might check that students know where each country is. Then have students read the phrases and their meanings. Make sure students can pronounce the phrases.

2. Have students complete the exercise individually. Then put students in groups of three to compare and discuss their answers and to read the conversation together.

VOCABULARY EXPANSION: Password

1. To review vocabulary studied thus far, have students play the game *Password*. Students should first copy vocabulary words onto index cards and organize at least ten categories (for example, positive words that describe people, negative words that describe people, words associated with the elderly, things we do, ways that we feel, words that deal with charities, etc.). Or, you can supply the categories and students can select words that fit into each of them.

2. To play the game, divide the class into groups. Select a card for the clue-givers (one or two students from the group). Give them a few moments to think about the clues, and then return to their group. They should give one-word, short phrases, or sentences as clues to help the group guess the word (for example, ritual = something we do regularly, they do these in church, saying a prayer before meals is one of these, saying the Pledge of Allegiance every morning at school is one of these, etc.). Students may not use the word in their clues, and the team to guess the word in the shortest time will win the point.

✪ CREATE
Suggested Time: 20 minutes

1. Read the instructions and put students in groups of three. Have them discuss the study results again. Then have students complete their graphs and compare them in groups.

2. Finally, have groups of three role-play a conversation between the three students based on their thoughts about the information in Figure 2. Tell them to discuss their ideas and make notes in the chart. Give the groups time to practice their role plays while you move around the room to comment on their charts and offer individual help as needed.

 Link to *NorthStar: Reading and Writing 4*
If students are also using the companion text, you can write the vocabulary from the Vocabulary section in Unit 7 on the board and ask students to use those words in their discussion as well.

 Go to www.mynorthstarlab.com for additional *Vocabulary* practice.

✪✪ B GRAMMAR: *Make, Let, Help, and Get*

 Go to www.mynorthstarlab.com for *Grammar Chart* and *Exercise 2*.

◖ SKILLS

Practice the use of verbs *make*, *let*, *help*, and *get*.

Suggested Time: 25 minutes

1. Have students read the conversation in **Exercise 1**. Then discover students' existing knowledge of the verbs by having them say what they think the

differences are between *make, let, help,* and *get* both in meaning and grammatically.

2. Present the grammar. You may want to review the meaning of *objects* with students first. Go over each section in the chart with the class providing more examples, or eliciting more examples from students.

3. Read the instructions for **Exercise 2** with the class. Have students fill in the blanks individually. Put students in pairs to compare answers. Then call on two students to read the completed conversation aloud to the class.

4. Read the instructions for **Exercise 3** with students. You may want to explain the role of a school counselor if students aren't familiar with it. Then have students read the three steps, and get into groups to complete the exercise. Move around the room to offer individual assistance or help with vocabulary problems.

5. Once students are finished, have the groups share the suggestions they chose as the best for each problem with the class. Put the suggestions on the board and have students vote on the best one for each problem.

Expansion/Homework

For further practice, offer exercises from *Focus on Grammar 4, 3rd Edition,* and Azar's *Understanding and Using English Grammar, 3rd Edition.* See the Grammar Book References on page 226 of the student book for specific units and chapters.

⒞ SPEAKING

◀ SKILLS

Practice pronunciation of stressed and unstressed vowels; practice restating ideas for clarity; integrate the concepts, vocabulary, grammar, pronunciation, and function from the unit in a role play of a town meeting with the Board of Education.

✪ PRONUNCIATION: Stressed and Unstressed Vowels

Suggested Time: 15 minutes

1. Write the example words on the board. Introduce the schwa sound, helping students to pick out the syllables that are unstressed and modeling the pronunciation. Then have students listen to the list of words. Discuss the different sounds in stressed and unstressed vowels in the words they heard. Have students answer the questions as a class. Read the boxed explanation together, giving them a chance to repeat the words with the correct pronunciation.

2. Read the instructions for **Exercise 1**. Have students listen to the recorded words and decide which vowels are the stressed ones. Play the audio again and have students check their answers before going over the answers as a class.

3. Read the instructions for **Exercise 2** and go over the example with the class. Then play the audio and let students repeat the words before having them write the words out correctly.

4. Play the audio in **Exercise 3** and have students repeat the questions. Then put them in pairs to take turns asking the questions and discussing the answers.

✪✪ FUNCTION: Restating for Clarity

Suggested Time: 20 minutes

1. Have students read the explanation and the restating phrases. Then have students read the instructions. Divide the class into two groups and have each group read their own statements and reword them. You might want to have students find synonyms by looking in a thesaurus.

2. Put students in pairs to take turns reading their statements and asking each other for restatement or further clarity. You might want to review ways for students to ask for clarity, for example, "Could you say that in another way?" or "I'm not sure I understand what you mean." You might want to move around the room to offer pairs individual assistance and monitor students to make sure they are using the introductory phrases.

Expansion/Homework

To give individual feedback, you can ask students to write restatements of one or two of their statements as homework.

✪✪✪ PRODUCTION: A Town Meeting with the Board of Education

Suggested Time: 45 minutes

If you wish to assign a different speaking task than the one in this section, see page 147. The alternative topics relate to the theme of the unit, but may not target the same grammar, pronunciation, or function taught in the unit.

1. Read the background information with the class. Ask students if they are familiar with town meetings and if they know what a Board of Education is, explaining that it is very similar to a local version of the Ministries of Education in many of their countries.

2. Have students read the situation in Step 1. Check their comprehension.

3. Read the instructions for Step 2 with the class. Divide students into three groups—School Board members, anti-homework group, and pro-homework group.

4. Go over the chart in Step 3 with students and have the groups work together to make notes on what they want to say. Move around the room to help each group as needed. Emphasize that everyone should have a speaking part.

5. Set up the chairs in the class so students can simulate a town meeting. Put the Board of Education in chairs at the front of the class, and the other groups either on different sides of the room or all together. You may want to put one

chair in front of the others and tell students it is the podium from where they will speak. For very large classes, you may choose to split the class in two and do it twice. The listening group could observe and say whether they thought the Board of Education's decision was fair or not based on the arguments of the two groups.

6. After all the students have been called on to speak, give the Board of Education students some time to make their decision. Then have the Board of Education deliver their decision. You may want to give the class a chance to reflect on the decision saying why they thought the Board of Education arrived at that decision.

 Link to *NorthStar: Reading and Writing 4*
If students are also using the companion text, you could have students redo the town meeting to be about whether or not they think homeschooling should be better monitored, and whether there should be any monitoring of the amount of homework given by the parents.

✪ ALTERNATIVE SPEAKING TOPICS

These topics give students an alternative opportunity to explore and discuss issues related to the unit theme.

✪ RESEARCH TOPICS

Suggested Time: 30 minutes in class

1. Have students turn to page 222. Review the instructions for the activity with the class. Tell students that they will be doing a survey. They need to interview two or three people for this survey. Go over the questions and categories in the questionnaire.

2. Have students prepare their questionnaires. Encourage students to include an additional question or two.

3. After students have completed their surveys, have them present the results to the class or in small groups.

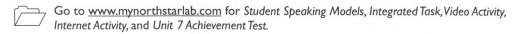 Go to www.mynorthstarlab.com for *Student Speaking Models, Integrated Task, Video Activity, Internet Activity*, and *Unit 7 Achievement Test.*

Goodbye to the Sit-Down Meal

OVERVIEW

Theme: Food

This unit focuses on changing trends in eating habits. Students think about their own eating habits and the changing food trends in their own countries. As a culminating activity, students prepare and present a cooking show using the information from the unit.

Listening One: *French Sandwiches* is a radio report on changing eating habits in France.

Listening Two: *Food in a Bowl* is a radio report on a fast food trend in California and how it affects family life.

Critical Thinking

Identify and analyze food trends
Relate general factors to specific behaviors
Compare food practices

Interpret meaning from text
Infer situational context
Infer word meaning from context

Listening

Make predictions
Summarize main ideas
Listen for details
Interpret speakers' tone and attitude
Relate the listening to local food trends

Compare and contrast two restaurants
Classify vowel sounds
Listen to and evaluate student food shows using a rubric

Speaking

Share ideas on food trends
Use tone of voice to indicate attitude
Use new vocabulary in free conversation
Compose and perform a dialogue

Practice gambits which call attention to a particular item
Explain how to use a tool
Develop and perform a food show

Vocabulary

Use context clues to find meaning
Find and use synonyms
Analyze figurative meanings of words
Use idiomatic expressions

Grammar

Phrasal verbs

Pronunciation

Spelling and sounds—*oo* and *o*

 MyNorthStarLab
Readiness Check, Background and Vocabulary, Listenings One and Two, Notetaking and Academic Skills Practice, Vocabulary and Grammar, Achievement Test

 NorthStar: Reading and Writing 4
Unit 8 deals with cooking processes, traditions, superstitions, and religious beliefs involved with eating.

FOCUS ON THE TOPIC

❮ SKILLS

Predict the content of the unit; activate prior knowledge; express opinions; infer the meaning of new vocabulary from context.

✪✪✪ Ⓐ PREDICT

Suggested Time: 10 minutes

Have students look at the cartoon and describe what they see happening. Then have them look at the unit title. Put them in pairs or small groups to discuss the questions. Then have volunteer groups share summaries of their discussions with the class.

Expansion/Homework
You could make a chart on the board with columns for time spent on meals, frequency of restaurant meals eaten, and frequency of take-out food eaten, and then tally up students' experiences in the chart. Ask students to make generalizations from the completed chart.

✪✪ Ⓑ SHARE INFORMATION

Suggested Time: 20 minutes

1. Ask students to say how they think food preparation and eating habits have changed since their parents' day before having them study the pictures and questions.

2. Have students look at the pictures, and be sure everyone is familiar with the factors identified. Have students read and answer the questions individually, and then discuss their answers in small groups. Then have groups report back to the class on the results of their discussions.

✪✪✪ Ⓒ BACKGROUND AND VOCABULARY

Go to www.mynorthstarlab.com for *Background and Vocabulary*.

Suggested Time: 20 minutes

1. Have students read the instructions and then listen to the interview on changing food trends while they read along.

2. Give students time to reread the passage focusing on the boldfaced words and their contexts, and then circling the correct meanings. Put students in pairs to compare and discuss their answers. For disputed words, have students use the context to defend or explain their choice. Go over the answers as a class.

 Go to www.mynorthstarlab.com for additional *Background and Vocabulary* practice.

2 FOCUS ON LISTENING

◀ SKILLS

Make predictions about the content of the listening; differentiate between main ideas and details; make inferences about speaker's meaning based on word choice; express opinions; listen to a radio report.

✪✪✪ Ⓐ LISTENING ONE: French Sandwiches

 Go to www.mynorthstarlab.com to listen to *French Sandwiches*.

Suggested Time: 10 minutes

In Listening One, students listen to a radio interview about changing food habits in France and how these changes reflect other changes in current French society and culture. The segment should get students thinking in more depth about their own eating habits and where these habits come from.

1. Have students read the title of the listening, and ask if they know what French sandwiches are.

2. Play the audio and have students answer the questions.

3. Put students in pairs or small groups to compare and discuss their answers. Have pairs share their answers with the class. Affirm all predictions as possibilities.

REACHING ALL STUDENTS: Listening One

• **Less Proficient:** Before listening, have students discuss changes to their diet since they came to the United States.
• **More Proficient:** Before listening, have students compare diet in the United States to diet in other countries.

✪✪✪ LISTEN FOR MAIN IDEAS   **Suggested Time: 15 minutes**

1. Have students read the instructions and the two statements and possible reasons.

2. Play the report while students check the reasons and changes. If students seem to have trouble, play the report one more time, having students raise their hands to indicate they've heard a relevant piece of information, and then pausing the segment to allow students to discuss what they heard. Finally, go over the answers as a class.

✪✪✪ LISTEN FOR DETAILS   Suggested Time: 15 minutes

Have students read the questions and possible answers, and answer those that they can. You might want to have them do that in pencil. Then have students listen to the segment again and circle the correct answers. Play the segment once more for students to check their answers. Go over the answers as a class.

 Link to *NorthStar: Reading and Writing 4*
If students are also using the companion text, you can ask them to discuss what they think Eileen Yin-Fei Lo's family in Reading One would think about the changes in French eating habits.

LISTENING STRATEGY: Add a Detail

To help students listen and recall details, have students complete this activity after they listen to the radio report: Divide students into groups of four or five, and have students draw numbers. The first student will name one of the details in the report. Student 2 will repeat that detail and add another. Student 3 will repeat what was said by Student 1 and Student 2, and add another detail until all members of the group have contributed.

✪✪✪ MAKE INFERENCES   Suggested Time: 10 minutes

1. Read the instructions together, and provide a model to demonstrate double meaning in words (for example, a person or the weather can be "cold").

2. Play the excerpts, stopping after each one to allow students to circle their answers. Replay the excerpts as needed. Then, in small groups or as a class, have students compare and check their answers.

Expansion/Homework
To focus in on the actual language used in the excerpts that students are making inferences about, replay the excerpts, stopping to ask students what words or phrases are used to describe or talk about each situation.

✪✪✪ EXPRESS OPINIONS   Suggested Time: 15 minutes

Have students read the discussion questions and put them in small groups to discuss them. Encourage students to support their ideas with reasons and information from the listening. If time allows, have groups share their thoughts on one or more of the questions with the class.

CRITICAL THINKING

Give students the following questions for discussion in small groups before discussing as a whole class:

1. According to the report, what do the changes in eating habits show about the changes in French society?

Answer: Changes in the workforce, more women, more white-collar workers

2. How do women affect this change?

Answer: They represent half of the workforce now, making their wishes known and wanting to spend less time at lunch in order to leave work earlier in the evening.

3. What is your opinion of this change from three course meals to quick sandwiches at lunch?

Answers will vary, but students should give clear reasons to support their opinions.

4. What do eating choices, like fast food, tell us about culture or a group of people?

Answers will vary, but might include eating choices reflect social changes, preferences, work habits, and socio-economic groups. Students should provide specific examples to support their ideas.

 B   LISTENING TWO: Food in a Bowl

Go to www.mynorthstarlab.com to listen to *Food in a Bowl*.

Suggested Time: 20 minutes

In Listening Two, students listen to a radio report about a new California food trend. The purpose of this report is to further challenge students to think about their own eating habits, and those of the society they live in.

1. Have students read the title of the listening. Discover what students already know about the topic by asking them if fast food in their country includes meals in which all the ingredients are in one bowl. Then read through the introductory paragraph together.

2. Play the audio, and have students circle the correct answer for each item of **Exercise 1**. Replay the report as needed. Then go over the answers as a class.

3. Have students read the instructions and the questions for **Exercise 2**. Put students in groups to discuss the questions. Encourage students to give specific examples and reasons to support their opinions.

Link to *NorthStar: Reading and Writing 4*

Ask students to discuss how Slow Food movement advocates might feel about food trends highlighted in the listenings.

◖ **SKILLS**

Organize the information from the listenings in a chart; synthesize the information in a role play.

STEP 1: Organize   Suggested Time: 15 minutes

1. Have students look at the chart and read the list of categories. Have students work in small groups to complete the chart with information from Listenings One and Two. Replay sections of the listenings, if requested.

2. Go over the answers with the entire class. You may want to have students listen for speaker's tone by replaying the relevant parts of the segments and having students attempt to repeat the speakers' tones.

STEP 2: Synthesize   Suggested Time: 15 minutes

1. Read the instructions with the class. Keeping students in the same groups of three, tell them to choose roles, or choose for them. You might want to have the different roles get into groups before having them do their role plays to work together to come up with what they'd like to say.

2. Have the groups practice their role plays while you move around the room to help with individual problems. You might want to have the groups switch roles after they've completed the role play once. Remind students to use the vocabulary from the unit where possible. If time allows, have a few groups perform their role plays for the class.

 Go to www.mynorthstarlab.com for *Notetaking* and *Academic Skills Practice*.

③ FOCUS ON SPEAKING

A ╏ **VOCABULARY**

◖ **SKILLS**

Review vocabulary from Listenings One and Two; expand students' understanding of vocabulary items by seeing them in additional contexts; use new vocabulary creatively in a speaking activity.

✪ REVIEW   Suggested Time: 10 minutes

 Go to www.mynorthstarlab.com for *Review*.

Have students read the instructions. Explain that these words and phrases are being used idiomatically. You might want to have students read through the words and phrases and elicit the literal meanings of some of them, such as *tough* meaning *hard*. Have students complete the exercise individually. Then go over answers as a class.

✪✪ EXPAND
Suggested Time: 10 minutes

1. Have students read the background information, the examples, and the instructions. You might want to have students read the sentences first, attempting to understand the meaning of each boldfaced word or phrase from the context before matching them to their meanings.

2. Have students complete the exercise individually. Then put students into pairs or groups to take turns reading the sentences aloud and compare and discuss their answers. Circulate to check that students can pronounce the phrases. Then go over the answers as a class.

VOCABULARY EXPANSION: Multiple Meaning Words

1. Remind students that the meaning of any word depends on the context in which it is used. When they consult a dictionary for the meaning of a word, they must choose the definition that appropriately fits in the sentence or paragraph. Often, that will depend on the part of speech of the word as used in the sentence.

2. Give students these vocabulary words and have them check the dictionary for multiple meanings and different parts of speech, and then select the one which will best complete the meaning in the text: *stack, shift, core, tough, hit, taste, bean,* and *chain.*

Expansion/Homework
Have students think of food idioms and phrases in their own languages. They could then attempt to translate them into English. It can be fun to collect these and write all or a sampling on the board for all the students to see.

✪ CREATE
Suggested Time: 15 minutes

Read the instructions and have students read the boxed idioms and figures of speech, checking that they know the meaning of them all. Then have students read the list of topics and the example conversation below the topics. You might want to give them a few minutes to think about one or more of the topics and how they might use the boxed phrases before putting them into groups of three to complete the exercise. Move around the room to check that the phrases are being used correctly.

Go to www.mynorthstarlab.com for additional *Vocabulary* practice.

📁 Go to www.mynorthstarlab.com for *Grammar Chart* and *Exercise 2*.

◖ SKILLS

Practice the form and meaning of phrasal verbs.

Suggested Time: 40 minutes

1. Elicit from students what a phrasal verb is, if possible, asking for examples that you put on the board. Then tell students to read the short conversation in **Exercise 1**. After students read, ask them what the boldfaced words mean.

2. Go over each section in the chart with the class providing more examples, or eliciting more examples from students.

3. Have students read the instructions for **Exercise 2**. Make sure they understand that there are three tasks to do—choose the pronoun, put it in the right place, and determine the correct verb tense. Put students in pairs to complete the exercise. Check answers as a class by having students read lines from the conversations.

4. Have students match the phrasal verbs in **Exercise 3** with their definitions individually before comparing answers in pairs or groups.

5. Read the instructions for **Exercise 4** with students and put them in groups of four to create a conversation, using phrasal verbs from the unit. After students have finished their conversations, have them perform their conversation for the class.

Expansion/Homework
For further practice, offer exercises from *Focus on Grammar 4, 3rd Edition,* and Azar's *Understanding and Using English Grammar, 3rd Edition.* See the Grammar Book References on page 226 of the student book for specific units and chapters.

📁 Go to www.mynorthstarlab.com for additional *Grammar* practice.

C SPEAKING

◖ SKILLS

Practice pronouncing words with *oo* and *o*; use language to call attention to a particular item; integrate the concepts, vocabulary, grammar, pronunciation, and function from the unit to role-play a cooking show.

✪✪ PRONUNCIATION: Spelling and Sounds—oo and o

Suggested Time: 25 minutes

1. Write some example words from the box on the board. Introduce the *oo* and *o* sounds, modeling the pronunciation. Read the boxed information with students having them repeat the examples after you.

2. Read the instructions for **Exercise 1** with the class. Have students listen to the words and decide which words have the different vowel sounds to the others. You might want to have students attempt to do this before listening, and then check their answers while listening. Play the recording again to let students check their answers before going over the answers as a class and having students take turns pronouncing the words for each other.

3. Read the instructions for **Exercise 2** with the class. Pronounce the column heads for students having them repeat after you. Then play the segment and let students repeat the words.

4. Put students into pairs to write the words from the list under the appropriate sound. Have students practice reading the words and correcting each other's pronunciation.

5. Repeat the procedure above for **Exercise 3**. Then go over students' charts as a class.

6. Read the instructions for **Exercise 4** and have students mark the correct vowel sound for each *oo* and *o* sound in the box (have students use phonetic symbols, or assign a number to each sound).

7. Put students into pairs and have them take turns asking and answering the questions using the boxed words in their answers. Move around the room to monitor students, and correct their pronunciation as necessary.

✪✪ FUNCTION: Calling Attention to a Particular Item

Suggested Time: 25 minutes

1. Introduce how to focus on something specific by demonstrating with a classroom object (for example, Do you see what I'm holding?). Ask students what word and phrases you used to focus their attention. Then look at the example and explanation in the book.

2. Have students read the list of phrases to focus attention and then choose one of the items pictured and think through how they would demonstrate that item, using the listed phrases. You might want to get students into groups by item they chose and have them work together to come up with a good explanation.

3. Regroup students so they are with students who have not chosen their item, if possible. Then, in their groups, have students take turns explaining how to use their chosen utensil or gadget. Monitor students to make sure they are using the attention-focusing phrases. If time allows, have students who are willing present their demonstration for the class.

✪✪✪ PRODUCTION: A Cooking Show

Suggested Time: 50 minutes

If you wish to assign a different speaking task than the one in this section, see page 168. The alternative topics relate to the theme of the unit, but may not target the same grammar, pronunciation, or function taught in the unit.

1. Ask students to talk about TV food shows that they are familiar with, either in the United States or in their home countries.

2. Read the instructions for Step 1 and put students in pairs. Have them decide what to demonstrate for their episode. Move around the room to offer individual assistance as needed.

3. Have students read the instructions for Step 2 and the example. Then have them write their scripts for their demonstrations. Direct students to include phrasal verbs and idioms from the unit in their demonstrations. You might want to have students look at the evaluation chart in Step 4 to use as a guideline when they are creating their script. Circulate to offer individual assistance.

4. Go over the chart in Step 4 with students. Tell students they will use the chart to evaluate each other's episodes. Use the evaluation charts to discuss each presentation.

5. Have students perform their cooking shows for the class, or videotape the demonstrations and show the class at a later time.

✪ ALTERNATIVE SPEAKING TOPICS

These topics give students an alternative opportunity to explore and discuss issues related to the unit theme.

✪ RESEARCH TOPICS

Suggested Time: 30 minutes in class

1. Have students turn to page 223. Review the instructions for the activity with the class. Read through the questions and ask students if they have any other questions that they want to find answers to.

2. Have students prepare their reports. Emphasize that they should include answers to the questions listed in the book. Encourage students to include additional information they find.

3. Have students present their reports to the class or in small groups.

📁 Go to www.mynorthstarlab.com for *Student Speaking Models, Integrated Task, Video Activity, Internet Activity,* and *Unit 8 Achievement Test.*

Finding a Niche:
The Challenge for Young Immigrants

OVERVIEW

Theme: Immigration

This unit focuses on the experiences of young immigrants and different philosophies about how immigrants should assimilate into a new culture. Students discuss their own experiences and possible expectations about living in other countries.

Listening One: *A World within a School* is a news report about teachers and students at the International High School in Queens, New York, where students and teachers are dealing with the problems of students studying in a new language.

Listening Two: *The Words Escape Me* is a song about one young person's experience coming to a new country.

Critical Thinking

Compare personal experiences
Recognize personal assumptions
Hypothesize scenarios
Infer word meaning from context

Compare and contrast two experiences
Infer meaning not explicit in the listening
Propose solutions
Interpret graphs

Listening

Make predictions
Identify main ideas and details
Interpret speakers' tone and pitch

Relate the listenings to personal values and
    interests
Understand and interpret song lyrics

Speaking

Express opinions
Practice gambits to hesitate in response to a
    question

Ask and answer questions about a chart
Simulate a town meeting
Conduct an interview

Vocabulary

Use context clues to find meaning
Find and use synonyms
Define words
Use idiomatic expressions

Grammar

Present and past—contrasting verb tenses

Pronunciation

ship /ʃ/, measure /ʒ/, cheap /tʃ/, and jazz /dʒ/

 MyNorthStarLab
Readiness Check, Background and
Vocabulary, Listenings One and Two,
Notetaking and Academic Skills Practice,
Vocabulary and Grammar, Achievement Test

 NorthStar: Reading and Writing 4
Unit 9 deals with the feelings of
homesickness and nostalgia that many
immigrants experience after moving to a
new country.

Go to www.mynorthstarlab.com for the MyNorthStarLab *Readiness Check.*

①FOCUS ON THE TOPIC

◖SKILLS

Predict the content of the unit; activate prior knowledge; express opinions; infer the meaning of new vocabulary from context.

✪✪✪ Ⓐ PREDICT

Suggested Time: 10 minutes

1. If you are teaching in an English speaking country, ask your students to think about the hardest thing they experienced in coming to the country they are in at the moment. If you are teaching in your students' country, ask if any of them have ever lived abroad or thought about emigrating to another country. Have students share their thoughts with the class.

2. Have students open their books and look at the graph and describe what the graph depicts. Then have them look at the unit title. Put them in pairs or small groups to discuss the questions. Then have volunteer groups share summaries of their discussions with the class.

✪✪ Ⓑ SHARE INFORMATION

Suggested Time: 20 minutes

1. Put students in groups to discuss the first question. Have groups share summaries of their discussions with the class. If none or very few of your students have moved to another country or know someone who has, then have them try and imagine.

2. Review with students what the teen years are. Have students read the instructions and the opinions, indicating whether or not they agree or disagree. Encourage students to support their opinions, but also to respect differing opinions.

Expansion/Homework
You could have students tally their agreements and disagreements in groups, and then share them with the class while you tally them up for the class. Then have students discuss what conclusions they can come to from the number of people who agree and disagree with the statements.

Link to *NorthStar: Reading and Writing 4*
If students are also using the companion text, you can have them refer to the chart in Share Information in Unit 9. Students can discuss how the reasons for immigrating may differ among people from different countries.

❊❊❊ C BACKGROUND AND VOCABULARY

Go to www.mynorthstarlab.com for *Background and Vocabulary*.

Suggested Time: 20 minutes

1. Have students listen and read the conversation. Suggest that they focus first on the meaning of the conversation and not the boldfaced words. Then let them reread the conversation focusing on the meaning of the boldfaced words.

2. Have students match the underlined words with their definitions individually. Put students in pairs to compare and discuss their answers. For disputed words, have students use the context to defend or explain their choice. Go over the answers as a class.

Go to www.mynorthstarlab.com for additional *Background and Vocabulary* practice.

② FOCUS ON LISTENING

◖ SKILLS

Make predictions about the content of the listening; differentiate between main ideas and details; make inferences about speaker's meaning; express opinions; listen to and interpret a song.

❊❊❊ A LISTENING ONE: A World Within a School

Go to www.mynorthstarlab.com to listen to *A World Within a School*.

Suggested Time: 10 minutes

In Listening One, students listen to a radio interview about a unique high school in New York City attended by students from many different countries. The segment should get students thinking in more depth about the difficulties confronting young immigrants studying in a new language.

1. Have students read the title of the segment, and ask what they think it refers to.

2. Ask students to read the two questions, and then play the segment. After they've listened, have them speculate about the answer to the first one, and answer the second question. Go over the answers as a class.

LISTENING STRATEGY: Structure

1. To help students know where to focus their listening, tell them that they can consider a report or a lecture to be similar to their own essays. They can expect an introduction, body, and a conclusion. The introduction will give them the main idea. The body of the report will give details that support the main idea and examples to elaborate the details. Finally, the conclusion will summarize.

2. To illustrate, have students listen to the introduction (Mary Ambrose) and identify the main idea. Then have them listen to the reporter (Richard Schiffman) to identify the first detail (students learn by doing). Then listen to the reporter and the teacher (Jennifer Shenke) for the examples. Once students are clear on a general structure, have them listen to the rest of the report to see what they can recognize (for example, a detail, an example).

✪✪✪ LISTEN FOR MAIN IDEAS   Suggested Time: 15 minutes

1. Have students read the instructions and the five statements. Check that they understand they are only to check the true statements.

2. Play the report while students check the true statements. If students seem to have trouble, play the audio one more time, having students raise their hands to indicate they've heard a relevant piece of information and then pausing the segment to allow them to discuss what they heard. Go over the answers as a class.

REACHING ALL STUDENTS: Listen for Main Ideas

- **Less Proficient:** Have pairs of students listen to the body of the report a second time and write three facts they think are interesting or important.

- **More Proficient:** As they listen, have student teams write questions and answers which they will use to ask other teams.

✪✪✪ LISTEN FOR DETAILS   Suggested Time: 15 minutes

First, have students look at the chart. Then play the report again, and have students fill in the chart and then compare their answer with a partner's. If needed, play the report again. Go over the answers as a class. If disagreements arise, replay the segments rather than simply giving the answers.

 Link to *NorthStar: Reading and Writing 4*
If students are also using the companion text, you can ask them to discuss what they think Lucy in Reading One would think about this school.

✪✪✪ MAKE INFERENCES

Suggested Time: 10 minutes

1. Read the instructions together. Play the excerpts, stopping after each one to allow students to choose their answers. Replay the excerpts as needed.

2. In small groups or as a class, have students compare and check their answers. Encourage students to say what it is about the excerpt that makes them think the speaker would agree or disagree.

✪✪✪ EXPRESS OPINIONS

Suggested Time: 15 minutes

1. Have students read the instructions and the statements. Give students some time to decide which of the beliefs is closest to their own, and then put them in groups to compare and discuss their choices. Encourage them to support their choices with reasons and information from the listening.

2. If time allows, have groups share their thoughts on one or more of the questions with the class.

CRITICAL THINKING

Give students the following questions for discussion in small groups before discussing as a whole class:

1. What experiences have you had with students being punished or criticized for using their first language in class?

Answers will vary, but students should describe specific experiences.

2. According to the report, what are the advantages of students' being able to use their first language in classes?

Answer: Students help each other, retain their first language, and feel more comfortable.

3. How does the International High School compare to your school?

Answers will vary, but students should use specifics from the report and from their school to support the comparison.

4. What is your opinion of the suppression of using students' first language in classes?

Students should mention specifics from the text and their personal experience.

✪✪✪ B   LISTENING TWO: The Words Escape Me

📁 Go to www.mynorthstarlab.com to listen to *The Words Escape Me*.

Suggested Time: 20 minutes

In Listening Two, students listen to a song about someone who lives in a place where he can't understand or speak the language. The purpose of this listening is to further challenge students to think about the problems immigrants encounter when they don't speak the language of the place where they live.

1. Have students read the song title and ask them to say what they think it means. Then have them look at the questions in **Exercise 1** and the possible answers before listening.

2. Play the song once without pausing to give students an overall context for the exercise. After listening, ask students to circle the answers. Check the answers with the class or have students compare answers in pairs or groups.

3. Have students read the instructions for **Exercise 2** and the song lyrics. Play the song, pausing to give students time to fill in the blanks. Put students in pairs to compare their answers. Then play the song again to allow students to check their answers.

Expansion/Homework
You might want to reverse the order of Exercises 1 and 2. Have students fill in the song lyrics first, and then have them circle the meanings for particular lines.

 Link to *NorthStar: Reading and Writing 4*
If students are also using the companion text, have them compare the feelings expressed in the poem in Reading Two and the song they just heard.

✪✪✪ C INTEGRATE LISTENINGS ONE AND TWO

◖ SKILLS

Organize the information from the listenings in a chart; synthesize the information in a role play.

STEP 1: Organize   Suggested Time: 15 minutes

1. Have students look at the chart and read the list of topics. Put students in small groups to complete the chart with information from Listenings One and Two. Replay sections of the listenings, if requested.

2. Have groups compare charts with those of another group before going over the answers with the entire class.

 Link to *NorthStar: Reading and Writing 4*
If students are also using the companion text, you can ask them about how feelings of nostalgia and homesickness can be addressed in a school setting. Have students refer to Integrate Readings One and Two for a chart summarizing the themes addressed in both readings. Ask students: *Should teachers and school administrators do anything to help their immigrant students deal with the types of feelings expressed by the writers? If not, why not? If so, what should they do?*

STEP 2: Synthesize   **Suggested Time: 15 minutes**

1. Read the instructions with the class. Put students in pairs to decide what to say and to continue the example conversation. Remind students to cover the topics in the chart.

2. Have the pairs practice their conversations. Remind students to use the vocabulary from the unit where possible. Have a few pairs perform their conversations for the class.

   Go to www.mynorthstarlab.com for *Notetaking* and *Academic Skills Practice*.

FOCUS ON SPEAKING

Ⓐ VOCABULARY

◀ SKILLS

Review vocabulary from Listenings One and Two; expand students' understanding of vocabulary items by seeing them in additional contexts; use new vocabulary creatively in a speaking activity.

✪ REVIEW   **Suggested Time: 10 minutes**

 Go to www.mynorthstarlab.com for *Review*.

1. Have students take turns reading aloud the words and phrases in the box, helping them with their pronunciation. Then have them read the PowerPoint presentation all the way through before rereading it to complete the exercise.

2. Put students in pairs to compare and discuss their answers before going over the answers as a class.

✪✪ EXPAND   **Suggested Time: 10 minutes**

Have students read the background information. Explain the concept of a suggestion box for those unfamiliar with it. You might want to have students read the problems and suggestions first, attempting to understand the meaning of each boldfaced word or phrase from the context, before matching them to their meanings. Then go over the answers as a class.

VOCABULARY EXPANSION: Derivations
1. Exploring derivations of words can help students to make connections that will improve their understanding and retention of vocabulary. Learning that the word

(continued on next page)

flourish is derived from flowers, meaning "to bloom," can help them to visualize development or healthy growth. Provide these vocabulary words and have students work in small groups to locate derivations in a dictionary: *flourish, assimilate, suppress, relieve,* and *intimidate.*

2. Allow time for groups to discuss each of these derivations to come to an understanding of how that information can be helpful. Then have student groups write a simile for each word (for example, A family that is **uprooted** is <u>like</u> a plant that was pulled from the ground.).

Expansion/Homework
You could have students make a suggestion box for your classroom or your school. Have students decide on some questions that get placed in the box, and then have them write suggestions in pairs, groups, or individually.

✪ CREATE   Suggested Time: 20 minutes

1. Read the instructions and the boxed words and phrases, checking students' comprehension and pronunciation of each one. Then have students read through each statement and decide how strongly they agree or disagree with it.

2. Put students in pairs and have them explain their choices to their partners, using vocabulary from the list. Move around the room to make sure the boxed words and phrases are being used correctly.

Link to NorthStar: Reading and Writing 4
If students are also using the companion text, you can also include some of the vocabulary from Unit 9 of the *Reading and Writing* strand.

Go to www.mynorthstarlab.com for additional *Vocabulary* practice.

✪✪ B GRAMMAR: Present and Past—Contrasting Verb Tenses

Go to www.mynorthstarlab.com for *Grammar Chart* and *Exercise 2.*

◖ SKILLS

Practice the form and meaning of present and past verb tenses.

Suggested Time: 40 minutes

1. Have students work in pairs to read the three sentences in **Exercise 1** and answer the questions. Discover students' knowledge of the grammar by eliciting answers from the class.

2. Go over each section in the chart with the class providing more examples, or eliciting more examples from students. You might want to point out that there are three times being expressed, one in the past, one in the present or always, and one that is started in the past but has some relevancy to the present, as well.

3. Have students read the instructions for **Exercise 2** and choose the appropriate verb forms to complete the interview individually. Tell students to pay attention to the time words, the tense, and subject-verb agreement, when necessary. Move around the room to offer individual assistance. To check their answers, put students in pairs to read the interview aloud.

4. Have students read the instructions for **Exercise 3** and get into pairs. Have Student A ask the questions using the appropriate verb tense, and then have Student B answer. Encourage Student A to ask follow-up questions to get more information about Student B's answers, especially for the more open-ended questions. Have students switch roles after question 6. Monitor the pairs and correct their verb-tense errors as necessary. You may want to have a few pairs perform segments of their "interviews" for the class.

Expansion/Homework
(1) For more practice with the verb tenses, you can ask the pairs to discuss their response to the opinions expressed in the story, giving specific examples to illustrate their ideas while being careful to use the appropriate verb tenses. Then they can choose one opinion and write a short response to it. (2) For further practice, offer exercises from *Focus on Grammar 4, 3rd Edition,* and Azar's *Understanding and Using English Grammar, 3rd Edition.* See the Grammar Book References on page 226 of the student book for specific units and chapters.

 Go to www.mynorthstarlab.com for additional *Grammar* practice.

ⒸSPEAKING

◀SKILLS

Practice discriminating between the sounds *sh, z, ch,* and *j*; practice using language to express hesitation; integrate the concepts, vocabulary, grammar, pronunciation, and function from the unit to role-play a town meeting.

✪ PRONUNCIATION: *ship /ʃ/, measure /ʒ/, cheap /tʃ/, and jazz /dʒ/*

Suggested Time: 25 minutes

1. Put a few of the example words from the box on the board and pronounce them. Draw attention to the target sounds, introduce the corresponding phonetic symbols, and explain how to produce the sounds. Then play the example sentence for students and have them listen and repeat.

2. Read the boxed information with students giving them time to try out the voiced and voiceless pronunciations. Go over the example words again, and have students read about the common and uncommon spellings.

3. Read the instructions for **Exercise 1**. You might want to have students try to do the exercise first in pencil and then again while listening to the recording. Check their answers, and then replay the exercise as students repeat the words.

4. Read the instructions for **Exercise 2** with students and put them in pairs to read the questions or comments and construct answers. Have Student A read the statement or question, and then have Student B respond using the words provided in parentheses, switching roles after item 6. Remind students to pay attention to their pronunciation of the target sounds, and monitor the pairs as they work, making corrections as needed.

Expansion/Homework

To check students' pronunciation individually, you can have them record the list of words on pages 187–188 and the responses to the statements on pages 188–189. Listen to the recordings and record your feedback, modeling corrections for them on the tape.

✪✪ FUNCTION: Hesitating in Response to a Question

Suggested Time: 25 minutes

1. With books closed, ask students what they say when someone asks a question and they need time to think before answering. Write the phrases on the board. Then have students open their books and read the introductory statement and the phrases in the box. Have them write down phrases from the board that don't appear in the box.

2. Read the instructions for **Exercise 1** with students and have them read the short conversation together. Have them circle the hesitancy expressions and go over them together.

3. For **Exercise 2**, put students in pairs to take turns asking the questions and responding with the target phrases. Monitor the pairs and remind students to use the phrases as necessary.

Expansion/Homework

To get a better feel for how these phrases are used by native speakers, students can do some research by watching an English language program on television or listening to the radio. Help students choose a show that contains unscripted conversation (such as a panel news discussion or a talk show). Ask them to listen for ten minutes and write down the phrases of hesitation used in the conversation. Then have students report back to the class on what they heard.

✪✪✪ PRODUCTION: A Town Meeing

Suggested Time: 50 minutes

If you wish to assign a different speaking task than the one in this section, see page 192. The alternative topics relate to the theme of the unit, but may not target the same grammar, pronunciation, or function taught in the unit.

1. Go over the information in the box with the class. Then have all students read the five categories of immigrants in Step 1. Answer any questions. Then have students take notes on the questions individually.

2. Divide students into small groups to discuss the benefits and challenges they decided the immigrants and the town will face in Step 1. Tell them to rank the immigrant categories as specified in Step 2. Suggest that students make a note of the justification for their ranking.

3. Have the groups share their ideas and their rankings with the class. You might want to keep a tally of the different groups rankings on the board for further discussion. Encourage students to question other groups if they are unsure of or disagree with anything they said.

 Link to *NorthStar: Reading and Writing 4*
If students are also using the companion text, you can ask the groups to address how their town might address issues such as homesickness, nostalgia, and culture shock among the immigrants as discussed in the two readings.

✪ ALTERNATIVE SPEAKING TOPICS

These topics give students an alternative opportunity to explore and discuss issues related to the unit theme.

✪ RESEARCH TOPICS

Suggested Time: 30 minutes in class

1. Have students turn to page 223. Review the instructions for the activity with the class. Tell students that they will work in small groups and decide on which questions to ask the person they interview. Remind them that the questions should be the same for all interviewees.

2. Have students present the results of their interview to their groups. Compare the similarities and differences.

3. Have a representative of each group of students present the results to the class.

 Go to www.mynorthstarlab.com for *Student Speaking Models, Integrated Task, Video Activity, Internet Activity,* and *Unit 9 Achievement Test.*

UNIT 10

No Technology? No Way!

OVERVIEW

Theme: Technology

This unit focuses on the ways modern technological inventions that are supposed to make life simple can sometimes end up causing annoyance or frustration. Students think about their own experiences with modern technology, and the problems it can cause at times.

Listening One: *Noise in the City* is a news report about car-alarm vigilantes in New York City who go to extreme measures to silence annoying car alarms.

Listening Two: *Technology Talk* is an interview with the author of an article on cell phone etiquette.

Critical Thinking

Interpret cartoons	Make judgments
Draw conclusions from a graph	Hypothesize scenarios
Compare opinions about technology	Draw conclusions
Infer situational context	Define a problem and propose a solution

Listening

Make predictions	Take notes while listening
Listen for main ideas	Listen for specific information
Listen for supporting details	Listen for emphasis in speech
Interpret speakers' tone and word usage	Identify and name sounds

Speaking

Discuss opinions	Practice gambits to express frustration
Act out scripted dialogues	Role-play a conflict between neighbors
Discuss possible future outcomes	Develop and present a new technological gadget

Vocabulary

Find and use synonyms
Define words
Use context clues to find meaning
Use descriptive adjectives

Grammar

Future perfect and future progressive

Pronunciation

Adverbial particles

 MyNorthStarLab
Readiness Check, Background and Vocabulary, Listenings One and Two, Notetaking and Academic Skills Practice, Vocabulary and Grammar, Achievement Test

NorthStar: Reading and Writing 4
Unit 10 deals with contrasting views of technology in the home, from Bill Gates's computer-controlled house to Henry David Thoreau's simple cabin.

① FOCUS ON THE TOPIC

◖ SKILLS

Predict the content of the unit based on a cartoon and the title of the unit; activate prior knowledge; express opinions; infer the meaning of new vocabulary from context.

✪✪✪ Ⓐ PREDICT

Suggested Time: 5 minutes

1. Before opening the book, ask students to think about how many battery operated gadgets they have with them at the moment, for example, MP3s, cell phones, etc. Ask them whether there is ever anything that they find annoying when they are around other people using these gadgets. Have them discuss this in pairs or groups before sharing their thoughts with the class.

2. Have students open their books and look at the cartoon. Then have them look at the unit title. Check students' comprehension of the phrase, *No way.* Put students in pairs or small groups to discuss the questions.

✪✪ Ⓑ SHARE INFORMATION

Suggested Time: 20 minutes

1. Have students look at the graph. Ask them to make statements from the information in the graph. Then put students in groups to complete the first item.

2. Look at the list of boxed items, and have students underline the ones they either own, or use, and put a check beside the ones they would like to have or use. Have groups discuss questions 2 and 3.

3. Have a few groups share summaries of their discussions with the class.

 Link to *NorthStar: Reading and Writing 4*
If students are also using the companion text, you can have them refer to the chart in Share Information in Unit 10. Students can discuss the items in the chart that they feel can cause problems and/or those in the chart that have been the most beneficial to people or had the greatest impact.

Suggested Time: 20 minutes

 Go to www.mynorthstarlab.com for *Background and Vocabulary*.

1. Have students read and listen to the blog. Suggest that they focus first on the meaning of the text and not the boldfaced words. Then let them reread the blog focusing on the meaning of the boldfaced words.

2. Have students match the boldfaced words with their definitions individually. Put students in pairs to compare and discuss their answers. For disputed words, have students use the context to defend or explain their choice. Go over the answers as a class.

Expansion/Homework
You can assign this exercise as homework and use class time to check answers.

 Go to www.mynorthstarlab.com for additional *Background and Vocabulary* practice.

②FOCUS ON LISTENING

◖SKILLS

Make predictions about the content of the listening; differentiate between main ideas and details; make inferences about speakers' meaning from tone of voice and word choice; express opinions; listen to an interview.

°°°**A** LISTENING ONE: Noise in the City

Go to www.mynorthstarlab.com to listen to *Noise in the City*.

Suggested Time: 10 minutes

In Listening One, students listen to a radio program about the problem of car alarms going off unnecessarily in New York City, and what some New Yorkers have decided to do about it. The segment should get students thinking in more depth about the problems some very common technology can cause.

1. Have students read the title of the listening, and ask what kind of noise they think the title might refer to. After eliciting a few comments, ask them to keep in mind the topic of the unit when they make their predictions.

2. Ask students to read the background information and the questions. Play the audio and have students answer the questions. Remind students that these questions are going to be answered in the rest of the listening. Call on students to read their predictions. Affirm each prediction as a possibility.

Provide large chart paper and markers and have students in small groups do a process similar to a word splash or free-form web, where each student contributes random single words that come to mind from the report. Tell students to use the words to generate complete sentences that connect the word to the topic (car alarms). Then instruct each student to use the sentences to complete his or her own summary of the report.

✪✪✪ LISTEN FOR MAIN IDEAS   Suggested Time: 15 minutes

1. Have students read the instructions and the statements. You might suggest that, while they are reading them prior to listening, they think about whether the statement is true or false.

2. Play the entire report while students decide if the statements are true or false. If students seem to have trouble, play the audio one more time, having students raise their hands to indicate they've heard a relevant piece of information and then pausing the segment to allow students to discuss what they heard.

REACHING ALL STUDENTS: Listen for Main Ideas

• **Less Proficient:** Suggest that students read each statement with a partner and make a logical guess before listening to the report and marking the statements true or false.	• **More Proficient:** Have students elaborate on each statement by giving examples from the report or creating their own. Remind them that examples are specific (names, numbers, places, percentages, dates).

✪✪✪ LISTEN FOR DETAILS   Suggested Time: 20 minutes

1. First, have students read the questions. Then play the report again, and have students take notes on the answers to the questions. You may want to give them time to fill in their notes after listening.

2. Put students in pairs to discuss their answers with a partner. If needed, play the report again. Go over the answers as a class. If disagreements arise, replay the segments rather than simply giving the answers.

Link to NorthStar: Reading and Writing 4
If students are also using the companion text, you can ask them to extrapolate on the possible problems that could result if the technology in Bill Gates's "Smart Home" were to malfunction as often as many car alarms do. Have students work in pairs to pick one technological advance that Bill Gates has proposed. Have the pairs work together to think of how the technology could malfunction and what problems it could cause. Then have them create a call to the manufacturer of the

technology that malfunctioned, with one student being the manufacturer and the other being the caller who is complaining about his or her Smart Home. Have the pairs perform the role plays for the class.

✪✪✪ MAKE INFERENCES   Suggested Time: 10 minutes

1. Have students read the instructions and look at the chart. Check students' comprehension of the difference between *mostly serious* or *humorous* and *somewhat serious* or *humorous*. Emphasize that students should listen for what the person says as well as how he or she says it, and evaluate both aspects for their seriousness or humor. Emphasize that it's possible for students to have varying opinions as long as their reasoning is sound.

2. Play each excerpt, stopping the audio while students check off their choices. Replay the segment as needed. Then go over the answers as a class, eliciting from students what about the speakers' tone of voice or word choice indicated their sense of humor or seriousness for them.

Expansion/Homework
After the group discussions, you may want to lead a short discussion on why some speakers chose to use humor when discussing a serious subject, as this point may be difficult for students to discuss on their own. Replay Excerpts Two and Four for students. Explain the humorous references in the segments, if students haven't picked them out already, such as when Lucille DiMaggio calls her car "innocent" (as if it were human), and when the Egg Man uses the invented word "eggworthy" (like "praiseworthy" or "trustworthy") to refer to a car whose alarm is going off. Ask students if they think these people are upset about their experiences, and if so, why they are making a joke about it.

✪✪✪ EXPRESS OPINIONS   Suggested Time: 10 minutes

1. Have students read the questions and get into groups to discuss them. You might want to give students some time to gather their own thoughts before putting them into groups. Encourage them to give specific examples to support their opinions.

2. If time allows, have groups share their thoughts on one or both of the questions with the class.

CRITICAL THINKING

Give students the following questions for discussion in small groups before discussing as a whole class:

1. Do you think that car alarms are useful in stopping crime?

   Answers will vary, but students should give specific reasons and examples to support their opinions.

2. Are the people who punish car owners acting responsibly?

Answers will vary, but students should give specific reasons and examples to support their opinions.

3. Are owners who set their alarms to go off easily acting responsibly?

Answers will vary, but students should give specific reasons and examples to support their opinions.

4. How would you solve this problem?

Answers will vary, but students should give specific reasons and examples to support their opinions.

✱✱✱ B LISTENING TWO: The Ten Commandments of Cell Phone Etiquette

Go to www.mynorthstarlab.com to listen to *The Ten Commandments of Cell Phone Etiquette.*

Suggested Time: 20 minutes

In Listening Two, students listen to an interview with a man who has written about annoying use of cell phones. The purpose of this interview is to further challenge students to think about the negative aspects of the cell phone.

1. Have students read the title and ask them to say what "The Ten Commandments" might refer to. Then have them read the background information on the interview, checking their comprehension of *blogosphere* and *obnoxious.*

2. Have students look at the incomplete statements in **Exercise 1** and the possible completions before listening. Then play the interview while students choose their answers. Replay the interview as needed. Check the answers with the class, or have students compare and discuss answers in pairs or groups.

3. Have students read the instructions for **Exercise 2** and the discussion questions. Put students in small groups to discuss the questions. You may want to have the groups make lists of potentially bothersome technology to share with the class. Write each group's list on the board to see which gadgets people thought of in this context the most.

✱✱✱ C INTEGRATE LISTENINGS ONE AND TWO

◖ SKILLS

Organize the information from the listenings in a chart; synthesize the information in a role play.

STEP I: Organize

Suggested Time: 15 minutes

Have students read the instructions and look at the chart. Put students in small groups to complete the "problem" column of the chart with information from Listenings One and Two. Replay excerpts from both listenings as requested to help students fill in the chart. Have groups compare charts with another group's before going over the answers with the entire class.

STEP 2: Synthesize

Suggested Time: 15 minutes

Read the instructions and put students in pairs to discuss the responses in the chart. Remind students to use the vocabulary from the unit where possible. Move around the room and make a note of errors or language issues that come up to present to the class later.

Expansion/Homework

You might also have students talk about what the response to each problem might be in their own countries. After completing the chart, you might like to ask the students to reflect on their own cell phone use in view of the problems mentioned in Listening Two and discuss their own cell phone etiquette in groups.

 Link to *NorthStar: Reading and Writing 4*

If students are also using the companion text, you can ask them to think about what Henry David Thoreau from Reading Two might say about cell phones, and why.

 Go to www.mynorthstarlab.com for *Notetaking* and *Academic Skills Practice*.

③ FOCUS ON SPEAKING

Ⓑ VOCABULARY

◀ SKILLS

Review vocabulary from Listenings One and Two; expand students' understanding of vocabulary items by seeing them in additional contexts; use new vocabulary creatively in a speaking activity.

✪ REVIEW

Suggested Time: 15 minutes

 Go to www.mynorthstarlab.com for *Review*.

1. Divide the class into two groups; group A and B. Have each group read their own instructions and complete their part of the conversation while you move around the room to offer help as needed. Have students take turns reading aloud the words and phrases in the box, helping them with pronunciation.

2. Pair A students with B students and have them read and respond to each other's statements using the word in parentheses.

Expansion/Homework
Before the pairs read the conversations, you can have A students pair up and B students pair up to compare their answers for the fill-in sections. For more oral practice, you can have students improvise additional conversations using the target vocabulary. Have each student think of a type of technology they find annoying and start a conversation complaining about it.

✪✪ EXPAND   Suggested Time: 15 minutes

1. Have students look at the list of noises in the left-hand column of the chart in **Exercise 1**. They may not be familiar with most of the words, but explain that they will hear sounds on the audio that will illustrate the words for them. Play the sounds as students write in the left-hand column what the source of the noise probably is. Then elicit the descriptions from students, recreating the chart on the board.

2. Have students look at the list of adjectives in **Exercise 2**, clarifying any that they don't know. Students can use dictionaries if they wish. Play the sounds again as students write down the adjectives they think best describe the sounds. Then have students share their answers with the class.

Expansion/Homework
To find definitions of the adjectives, you can assign one word to each student (preferably as homework the day before). Have students look up the word in a dictionary, and tell them to read the definitions carefully so that they note down the relevant definitions only. In class, have each student present the definition of his or her word to the class.

VOCABULARY EXPANSION: Words in Context

Remind students that context clues are often the best ways to determine the meaning of words in a text. Provide the following sentences and have students work with their partner to underline the clues that help them to understand the meaning and identify the kind of clue (definition, example, synonym, antonym, general clues).

- Modern life is full of nasty noises in the cities . . . Sirens . . . loud music . . . there's one form of **sonic** pollution at the top of the list.

- Each night, hundreds of people like Judy Evans are jolted out of their sleep by the nagging **wail** of a car alarm.

- After that police can break into a car or even **tow away** a wailing vehicle.

✪ CREATE   Suggested Time: 20 minutes

1. Read the instructions and have students look at the chart. Give them a little time to think about each device or service before pairing them up to create their own "commandments" about each one.

2. Put students in pairs to discuss the items and complete the chart. Move around the room to help with any individual questions. Encourage students to use the vocabulary from the unit. Have each pair present one or two of their "commandments" to the class.

 Link to *NorthStar: Reading and Writing 4*
If students are also using the companion text, you can include some of the vocabulary from Unit 10 and encourage students to use it in their discussions.

 Go to www.mynorthstarlab.com for additional *Vocabulary* practice.

✪✪B GRAMMAR: Future Perfect and Future Progressive

Go to www.mynorthstarlab.com for *Grammar Chart* and *Exercise 2*.

◖ SKILLS

Practice the form and meaning of the future perfect and future progressive tenses.

Suggested Time: 40 minutes

1. Have students work in pairs to read the three examples in **Exercise 1** and answer the questions. Discover students' knowledge of the grammar by eliciting answers from the class.

2. Go over each section in the chart with the class providing more examples, or eliciting more examples from students. You might want to illustrate the points made by placing the events in the example sentences on a timeline.

3. Explain to students that in **Exercise 2**, they will be playing a partner game to guess from clues what the mystery item is. Read through the instructions with the class.

4. Divide the class into two groups; group A and group B. Have group A students look at page 206, while Student B looks at page 216. Have students look at the clues and fill in the blanks with the future perfect. Circulate to check students' answers.

5. Put A and B students in pairs and have them take turns reading the clues one at a time while their partners guess which item is being described. Monitor the pairs to correct any errors.

6. Have the class read the instructions for **Exercise 3** and the list of types of new technology. Ask them to think about technology in the near future and to use the future progressive to describe what people will be doing then.

7. Put students in pairs to practice the future progressive while discussing their predictions. They can discuss the items suggested in the box and also make predictions of their own. Encourage them to explain their ideas with more than one sentence. After students finish, ask the pairs to share some of their predictions with the class. Monitor the pair work and class discussion, correcting any errors.

Expansion/Homework
For further practice, offer exercises from *Focus on Grammar 4, 3rd Edition,* and Azar's *Understanding and Using English Grammar, 3rd Edition.* See the Grammar Book References on page 226 of the student book for specific units and chapters.

 Go to www.mynorthstarlab.com for additional *Grammar* practice.

C SPEAKING

SKILLS

Practice the pronunciation of adverbial particles; use language to express frustration; integrate the concepts, vocabulary, grammar, pronunciation, and function from the unit in a role play of a technology fair.

◑◐ PRONUNCIATION: Adverbial Particles

Suggested Time: 20 minutes

1. Have students listen to the example sentences and repeat to practice the stress pattern. Then read through the boxed explanation with the class.

2. Have students listen to the sentences in **Exercise 1** and circle the stressed particles. Check answers as a class. You may want to play the audio again, pausing to let students repeat after each one.

3. Go over instructions for **Exercise 2**. For Part A, have students listen to the complaint and circle the stressed particles. Check by having students take turns reading sentences from the excerpt. For Part B, have students read the instructions and mark the blended consonant-vowel. Then put students in pairs to take turns reading the complaint to each other with the correct stress and joined words. Move around the room to listen and correct individuals as needed.

4. Have students work in pairs for **Exercise 3** to match the comments and responses and create a short dialogue. Have them practice the dialogue as you listen for stress and pronunciation problems. If time allows, have a few pairs role-play their dialogues for the class.

◑◐ FUNCTION: Expressing Frustration

Suggested Time: 30 minutes

1. With books closed, ask students to think back to the listenings and try to remember any phrases the speakers used to express their frustration with modern technology. Write the phrases students remember on the board. Have students open their books and read the introductory statement and the phrases in the box. Have them write down phrases from the board that don't appear in the box.

2. Divide the class into pairs to do the exercise. Have students read the situations one at a time and make up a role play, using the phrases on page 209 to express frustration as much as they can. Ask students to choose one role play to perform for the class. To encourage students to use the target phrases in the role plays, ask the other students to write down the phrases expressing frustration that they hear during the role play. To give feedback to the pair that is performing, students can give their notes to the pair.

Expansion/Homework

To get a better feel for how these phrases are used by native speakers, students can do some research by watching an English language program on television or listening to the radio. Situation comedies on television would probably be good for this. Ask them to listen for ten to twenty minutes and write down the phrases of frustration used in the conversation. Then have students report back to the class on what they heard.

✪✪✪ PRODUCTION: A Technology Fair

Suggested Time: 45 minutes

If you wish to assign a different speaking task than the one in this section, see pages 212–213. The alternative topics relate to the theme of the unit, but may not target the same grammar, pronunciation, or function taught in the unit.

1. Go over the information in the task box with the class. If possible, bring in some magazines or catalogs that advertise strange or interesting gadgets. Have students discuss how these gadgets solve problems. Then, as a class or in pairs, have students brainstorm other frustrating problems.

2. Then put students in small groups and have them look at the chart in the exercise to decide if they want to present an idea to solve a problem from the chart, or another one. Then have them complete the chart with their notes.

3. Once they are ready, have students circulate telling each other about their solutions.

4. For Step 3, have the students vote on the solution they thought was the best after you list them all on the board. You might want to assign a number for each solution and then have the students put the number of the solution they preferred on a small slip of paper so that the voting can by secret. Discuss with the students why these were chosen, or have the students discuss it in groups.

⊙ ALTERNATIVE SPEAKING TOPICS

These topics give students an alternative opportunity to explore and discuss issues related to the unit theme.

⊙ RESEARCH TOPICS

Suggested Time: 30 minutes in class

1. Have students turn to page 224. Review the instructions for the activity with the class. Tell students that they will choose one of the items from the list to research, and that they should include not only recent developments, but also the history of the particular technology.

2. Have students prepare their reports. Remind students that they need to include how the technology affects them personally.

3. Have students present the summaries of their research to the class. As the students listen, they should think of questions to ask the presenter.

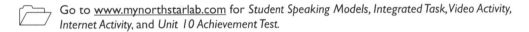 Go to www.mynorthstarlab.com for *Student Speaking Models, Integrated Task, Video Activity, Internet Activity,* and *Unit 10 Achievement Test.*

Student Book Answer Key

UNIT 1

1C BACKGROUND AND VOCABULARY

3, page 4

1. e	3. f	5. h	7. a	9. b	11. k
2. l	4. g	6. j	8. c	10. i	12. d

2A LISTENING ONE, page 5

1. Dr. Weil recommends reducing our news intake slowly until we manage to live with no news for one week.

LISTEN FOR MAIN IDEAS, page 5

1. c   2. a   3. e   4. b   5. d

LISTEN FOR DETAILS, page 6

1. c	3. a	5. b	7. b
2. a	4. b	6. b	8. b

MAKE INFERENCES, page 7

1. b   2. a   3. b   4. a

2B LISTENING TWO, page 8

1. a	3. a	5. a	7. b
2. b	4. b	6. b	

STEP 1: Organize, page 9

Answers will vary. Suggested answers:

	News Resisters	Is Media Overwhelming?
Effects on individuals' behavior	• we become addicted • not enough time in life for everything • media prevents us from being comfortable alone • people don't know how to be alone with themselves and just think	• we're experiencing a national attention deficit disorder
Effects on individuals' feelings	• creates antagonism between immediate (news) and eternal (religion) • media creates sense of despair	• we're evading who we are
Effects on children	• children don't have a lot of time to be by themselves	• kids are developing attention deficit disorder • kids don't do well in school
Effects on society as a whole	• prevents us from contributing to the benefit of society and others	• we focus on people like ourselves, which hurts our sense of community

REVIEW

1, pages 10–11

1.	repetitive	7.	comes in second
2.	bias	8.	regardless of
3.	inconsequential	9.	perspective
4.	newsworthy	10.	barrage
5.	lethal	11.	evading
6.	makes a connection	12.	remedy

2, page 11

Positive connotation	Negative connotation
make a connection newsworthy remedy	barrage bias evade inconsequential lethal repetitive

EXPAND, page 11

1. addicted to; catch
2. take a break from; coverage; get the scoop on; daily
3. remedy; humor; underlying
4. recommends; track down; distract; attention deficit disorder

3B GRAMMAR

2, page 14

2. were provided
3. were flooded
4. have been treated
5. is being reported
6. is predicted
7. is considered
8. was released
9. have been received
10. is being planned
11. will be followed
12. was rescued
13. had been warned
14. was interviewed
15. will be given

3, page 15

1. was attracted
2. are being filled
3. is stimulated
4. have been depressed
5. are being overloaded
6. is weakened
7. have been plunked
8. was inspired

PRONUNCIATION

2, page 16

1. are
2. is
3. has
4. are
5. have
6. is
7. are
8. have

UNIT 2

1C BACKGROUND AND VOCABULARY

1, pages 22–23

a. crutches
b. scars
c. in store for
d. landscape
e. soared
f. collapsed
g. limitations
h. overcome
i. revelation
j. proof
k. crushed

LISTEN FOR MAIN IDEAS, page 24

1. Richard dreamed of flying over different landscapes.
2. When Richard was a young boy, an accident with a runaway truck mangled his left leg.
3. Richard realized that everyone is born with gifts, but we all run into obstacles.
4. Richard believes that if we recognize our talents and make the most of them, we can succeed in life.

LISTEN FOR DETAILS, page 25

F 1. As a child, Richard used to dream he was ~~in an airplane~~. (flying)
F 2. Richard always dreamed about ~~the same~~ landscape. (different)
F 3. Richard had an accident when he was ~~six~~. (four)
F 4. He was forced to get around ~~in a wheelchair~~. (on crutches)
F 5. Richard was ~~standing on the ground~~ when he had a revelation. (sitting on the rooftop of a cathedral)
F 6. He heard a song called "~~Drive~~ Away with Me." (Fly)
F 7. Richard ~~can now~~ walk. (cannot)
F 8. He dreamed he ~~was a boy again~~. (could fly)

MAKE INFERENCES, page 25

1. b
2. b
3. a
4. b

2B LISTENING TWO

1, pages 26–27

1. 7
2. blindness, deafness, cancer survivor, amputee
4. The largest group of disabled climbers to scale Mt. Kilimanjaro
5. They inspired each other

STEP 1: Organize, page 28

Answers will vary. Suggested answers:

Richard
Challenges — Physical problems (cannot stand, can hardly walk) and psychological challenges (stopped dreaming, as a young boy)
Goals and hopes — To go to college
Personal qualities — Perseverance and imagination

Achilles
Challenges — Variety of physical challenges: blind, deaf, asthmatic, cancer survivor, amputee: tough physical challenge
Goals and hopes — To climb Mt. Kilimanjaro; to take message of hope up the mountain for others
Personal qualities — Perseverance and endurance

Ways the stories overlap
Everyone shows great perseverance and determination.
Everyone is facing great odds.

REVIEW, page 29

1. challenging
2. determined
3. inspiration
4. landscape
5. scattered
6. eagles
7. collapsed
8. recognize
9. inspirational
10. recognition
11. perseverance
12. judging
13. limitations
14. courageous
15. empowerment
16. peak
17. proof
18. tough
19. in store for
20. altitude
21. soaring

EXPAND, pages 31–32

1. L, F	**3.** F, L	**5.** L, F
2. L, F	**4.** L, F	**6.** F, L

PRONUNCIATION

1, page 36

1 When Richard was little // he dreamed he was flying.
2 He looked at his scar // and imagined it was an eagle.
3 When he visited Venice // he realized that he had great gifts.
4 He suddenly realized // that he could overcome his obstacles.
5 The essay he wrote about his experience // was chosen for broadcast.

UNIT 3

1C BACKGROUND AND VOCABULARY, pages 42–43

a. 11	**c.** 5	**e.** 1	**g.** 7	**i.** 2	**k.** 4
b. 9	**d.** 8	**f.** 6	**h.** 10	**j.** 3	

2A LISTENING ONE, page 44

1. 9½ hours
2.–3. *Answers will vary.*

LISTEN FOR MAIN IDEAS, page 44

1. It's a hormone that affects sleep.
2. Teens are out of synch because melatonin is not secreted in their body until 11 hours later than it is in childhood.
3. They fall asleep whenever they can.
4. They face dangers driving.
5. They feel frustrated, irritable, and sad.

LISTEN FOR DETAILS, page 45

1. b	**3.** c	**5.** b	**7.** c	**9.** c
2. a	**4.** b	**6.** b	**8.** b	

MAKE INFERENCES, page 46

Excerpt One

1. playful, amused
2. F

Excerpt Two

1. respectful, enthusiastic
2. T

Excerpt Three

1. confused
2. F

Excerpt Four

1. shocked
2. F

2B LISTENING TWO

1, pages 47–48

1. b	**3.** b	**5.** b	**7.** b
2. a	**4.** b	**6.** a	

STEP 1: Organize, page 48

Answers will vary. Suggested answers:

	Teenagers	Parents of young children
Symptoms of sleep deprivation	—eyelids droop —get drowsy in class —fall asleep after a few minutes in a quiet environment	—crankiness —lack of concentration —no time for others —drink lots of coffee
Dangers of sleep deprivation	—risk of accidents —slower reaction time, less concentration —emotional impact	—makes us perform badly in all situations —make bad decisions —can be dangerous on the job
Recommendations from professionals	—understand and be sensitive to these issues —raise awareness —find ways to deal with the problem	—make sleep a priority —realize that sleep debt accumulates

REVIEW, pages 49–50

a. 1	**d.** 4	**g.** 5	**j.** 11	**m.** 14
b. 10	**e.** 2	**h.** 12	**k.** 13	**n.** 15
c. 3	**f.** 7	**i.** 8	**l.** 9	**o.** 6

EXPAND, pages 51–52

1. run by	**5.** nodded off
2. naps	**6.** burning the midnight oil
3. irritable	**7.** shut-eye
4. power nap	**8.** caught 40 winks

3B GRAMMAR

2, pages 54–56

2. wouldn't get	**12.** fell
3. would you do	**13.** took
4. slept	**14.** would be
5. showed up	**15.** didn't get
6. worked	**16.** would be
7. would be	**17.** would happen
8. worked	**18.** didn't sleep
9. weren't allowed	**19.** would increase
10. would be	**20.** didn't enforce
11. would happen	

PRONUNCIATION

1, page 57

1. I <u>need</u> to go to bed, but I'm <u>feeling</u> energetic.
2. <u>Adolescents</u> wake up late, but <u>children</u> wake up early.
3. <u>Lian</u> is fast asleep, but <u>her children</u> are awake.
4. <u>My husband</u> has insomnia, but <u>I</u> need to sleep.
5. I'm <u>sleepy</u> in the morning, but I'm <u>wide awake</u> at night.

UNIT 4

IC BACKGROUND AND VOCABULARY, pages 64–65

1. f	**3.** c	**5.** g	**7.** h	**9.** e
2. b	**4.** a	**6.** i	**8.** d	

2A LISTENING ONE, page 66

1. bird   2. chimp   3. dolphin

LISTEN FOR MAIN IDEAS, page 66

1. a   2. c   3. c

LISTEN FOR DETAILS, page 67

1. F; Sara, the older chimp, helped the new, injured chimp by ~~giving her food.~~ (taking her to a door)
2. T
3. F; Alex the parrot ~~uses~~ a computer to communicate. (does not use)
4. F; Alex can answer questions about ~~what he wants to eat and do.~~ (similarities and differences)
5. T
6. T
7. T
8. F; When Alex answers questions, he ~~doesn't seem to understand the questions; instead, he is answering in a rote manner.~~ (seems to understand the questions)

MAKE INFERENCES, pages 67–68

Excerpt One

1. c   2. a

Excerpt Two

1. a   2. b

Excerpt Three

1. a   2. b

Excerpt Four

1. b   2. a

2B LISTENING TWO, pages 68–69

1. Y	3. N	5. Y	7. Y	9. Y
2. Y	4. N	6. N	8. Y	10. Y

STEP I: Organize, page 69

Animal	The Infinite Mind	What Motivates Animals?
I. Chimps	One chimp understood that another chimp was disabled and helped the disabled chimp.	Sneaks around a barrier to get food when a human is watching and may take the food.
2. Birds	Parrot: • can answer questions he has not heard before about objects. • can tell difference in objects' shapes, colors, sizes. • can vocalize the differences. • can ask for specific food, ask to be taken places, ask to go on the trainer's shoulder.	Scrub jays and crows: • try to hide where they bury food from other birds. • can also come back later and change the location if they think another bird saw them bury the food.
3. Killer whales	• can solve problems by using air lift object it can't normally pick up. • can use bait to attract and catch seagulls.	

REVIEW, page 70

1.	gorilla	chimpanzee
2.	mindful	conscious
3.	protected	restricted
4.	understanding	perception
5.	fascinating	mysterious
6.	handle	use
7.	current	established
8.	experiment	study
9.	tame	friendly
10.	instant	unplanned

EXPAND

2, page 72

1. a	4. e	7. l	10. h	12. f
2. i	5. g	8. j	11. b	13. d
3. c	6. m	9. k		

UNIT 5

1B SHARE INFORMATION

2, page 84

Answers will vary. Suggested answers:

Graph 1

1. males
2. females
3. ten
4. Japan
5. 85.52
6. 78.56
7. live longer than men

Graph 2

8. 65 years and up
9. seven
10. 1950
11. 2030
12. Italy
13. Japan
14. will probably have the highest percentage of elderly people

1C BACKGROUND AND VOCABULARY, pages 86–87

1. j
2. h
3. f
4. i
5. d
6. e
7. a
8. c
9. g
10. b
11. l
12. k

2A LISTENING ONE, page 87

1. an organization for women over fifty
2. for solidarity

LISTEN FOR MAIN IDEAS, pages 87–88

Answers will vary. Suggested answers:

1. A Californian, Sue Ellen Cooper, founded the organization after reading a poem called "Warning." It's a supportive organization for women over 50 who have spent their lives up until this time nurturing their families.
2. They instantly understand the message of the organization.
3. A kind of détente, an agreement to stop competing with each other, and a refusal to be invisible

LISTEN FOR DETAILS, pages 88–89

1. a
2. b
3. b
4. c
5. c
6. c
7. a
8. c

MAKE INFERENCES, page 89

Excerpt One

1. humorous, playful
2. D

Excerpt Two

1. informative, serious
2. D

Excerpt Three

1. serious, emphatic
2. D

Excerpt Four

1. thoughtful
2. A

2B LISTENING TWO, page 91

1. a
2. b
3. a
4. b
5. a
6. a
7. b

STEP 1: Organize, page 92

Answers will vary. Suggested answers:

	Red Hatters	**Susie Potts Gibson**
Age	50 years old and older	lived to be 115
In the eyes of other people	unusual, exciting, flamboyant	independent, unusual, stubborn
In their own eyes	proud, friendly, supportive	self-directed, healthy, believed in her own advice
Examples of their behavior	join clubs and celebrate age together in same color clothing	bathed her feet in vinegar, took own decision about living facilities

REVIEW, pages 92–93

2. mourning
3. generation
4. go in for
5. life expectancy
6. elderly
7. facility
8. bitter
9. generation
10. attendant
11. take care of

EXPAND, page 94

1. physician
2. sit on the sidelines
3. face
4. pass away
5. bunch of
6. widow
7. the ripe old age of
8. it's a different story
9. keep an eye on

GRAMMAR

2, page 97

2. isn't it
3. do they
4. haven't you
5. isn't it
6. do they
7. didn't you

3, page 98

1. don't wear
2. hasn't operated
3. can't
4. don't feel
5. has
6. didn't die
7. wasn't
8. didn't believe
9. didn't say
10. was

PRONUNCIATION

2, page 99

2. i	4. g	6. f	8. d
3. e	5. a	7. b	9. h

FUNCTION

2, page 100

The following sentences are incorrect:

1. b   2. a   3. a   4. a

UNIT 6

IC BACKGROUND AND VOCABULARY

2, pages 105–106

1. h	3. d	5. a	7. b	9. g	11. k
2. c	4. f	6. l	8. e	10. i	12. j

2A LISTENING ONE, page 107

People who raise money for charities

LISTEN FOR MAIN IDEAS, page 107

2   tax benefits
7   required by school
4   prevent something bad from happening
1   passion for the cause
6   family tradition
3   desire to repay someone for something
5   see the direct effects of what they're doing

LISTEN FOR DETAILS, pages 107–108

1. b	3. b	5. a	7. a	9. a
2. a	4. a	6. b	8. c	

MAKE INFERENCES, page 108

1. T   2. T   3. T   4. T

2B LISTENING TWO, page 110

1. a   2. b   3. c   4. b   5. c   6. b

STEP 1: Organize, page 111

Answers will vary. Suggested answers:

	Why We Give	The Mystery Donor
1. Who volunteers or donates money?	• ½ of all Americans volunteer • 75% of people give money	A woman called the "Mystery Donor" from Seattle
2. Why do people give?	• Passion for a cause • To prevent negative things from happening • Because they are forced to	She sympathizes with others like her
3. What background factors cause people to give?	They see a need	She sees a need
4. Who receives the money or time?	Many different people	The people she chooses
5. How does the giver feel?	Very satisfied	Very satisfied
6. Does the donor prefer to be public or anonymous?	Public	Anonymous

REVIEW, page 113

Noun	Verb	Adjective
1. anonymity	—	anonymous
2. catastrophe	—	catastrophic
3. charity	—	charitable
4. contribution	contribute	contributed
5. donation, donor	donate	donated
6. generosity	—	generous
7. inheritance	inherit	inheritable
8. motivation	motivate	motivated, motivating
9. moral, morality	moralize	moral
10. passion	—	passionate
11. philanthropy, philanthropist	—	philanthropic
12. wealth	—	wealthy

EXPAND

1, pages 114–115

1. catastrophic
2. moralize
3. wealth
4. inherited
5. motivated
6. passion
7. charity
8. contribution
9. generous
10. anonymously

2, page 115

1. appeal
2. fundraiser
3. benefactors
4. cause
5. rewarding
6. freelance
7. under the radar

3B GRAMMAR

1, page 117

1. Sting; The Rainforest Foundation; Brazil; A frog
2. who, whose, where, that

2, pages 118–119

1. that
2. who
3. where
4. which
5. that
6. whose
7. who
8. which
9. that
10. which
11. who
12. who
13. who
14. who
15. which
16. when
17. who
18. who
19. whose
20. whose
21. that

3, pages 119–120

1. that
2. when
3. where
4. whose
5. that
6. that

PRONUNCIATION

1, page 121

2. F
3. U
4. F
5. F
6. U

UNIT 7

IC BACKGROUND AND VOCABULARY

1, pages 129–130

1. b
2. b
3. a
4. a
5. a
6. b
7. a
8. a
9. a
10. b
11. b
12. b

2A LISTENING ONE, page 130

1. They are spending time as a family doing the child's homework.
2. *Answers will vary.*

LISTEN FOR MAIN IDEAS, page 131

1. c   2. f   3. e   4. b   5. d   6. a

LISTEN FOR DETAILS, pages 131–132

1. c   3. b   5. a   7. a
2. a   4. b   6. b   8. a

MAKE INFERENCES, pages 132–133

Excerpt One

1. a   2. b

Excerpt Two

1. b   2. a

Excerpt Three

1. b   2. a

Excerpt Four

1. b   2. a

2B LISTENING TWO

1, page 134

2. She would consider a grade less than ~~65~~ to be a failure. (85)
3. Ying Ying's considers duty a combination of pride, ~~fear~~, and self-esteem. (love)
4. Ying Ying wanted to do well for her family, her country, and her ~~classmates~~. (heritage)
5. She used to want to be a ~~teacher~~. (gardener)
6. Her parents want her to become a ~~doctor~~. (lawyer)
7. She doesn't want any more ~~pressure~~. (dreams)
8. She believes it ~~isn't~~ too late to change her future. (is)

STEP 1: Organize, page 135

Effects of Homework on:	Why Homework Is Harmful (A Parent's View)	Why Homework Is Important (A Student's View)
1. Children's physical health	Staying up late to do homework has bad impact on children's health (they don't get enough sleep)	Good grades lead to satisfaction and happiness
2. Children's mental health	Kids are exhausted: they need mental health days	Achievements are tied up with pride and self-esteem
3. Parents	Homework involves entire family: not feasible for parents with more than one child	Good grades lead to parental approval
4. The relationship between parents and children	• In practice, homework falls on family, not just children • Leads to family problems	Children must follow their parents' lead
5. Other	Homework is longstanding historical battle in the U.S. despite some research showing benefits	Only hard work brings results

REVIEW, pages 135–136

1. a; parent / student
2. a; parent
3. a; parent
4. a; teacher or professor
5. a; teacher or professor
6. b; parent
7. a; parent / student
8. b; teacher or professor
9. a; teacher or professor
10. b; parent / student

EXPAND, pages 136–139

1. c   3. g   5. h   7. j   9. f
2. d   4. a   6. b   8. e   10. i

3B GRAMMAR

2, pages 140–141

2. make him sit down
3. let him watch
4. have him stop
5. help him understand
6. have him take
7. make him give up
8. get him to do

PRONUNCIATION

1, page 143

2. ōptional
3. distraūght
4. promōtions
5. sōcial
6. abōlish
7. hēritage
8. tāngible
9. decīsion
10. respōnsible

2, page 144

2. accountable
3. achievement
4. excellent
5. complete
6. assignments
7. monitor
8. demanding
9. agree
10. ridiculous
11. opinion
12. abolished

UNIT 8

1C BACKGROUND AND VOCABULARY, page 151

1. a   3. a   5. a   7. b   9. a
2. b   4. a   6. c   8. b   10. c

2A LISTENING ONE, page 152

1. lunch
2. *Answers will vary.*

LISTEN FOR MAIN IDEAS, page 152

1.
Women's lifestyles have changed.
Men's lifestyles have changed.
People are adjusting their working hours.

2.
It is open longer hours.
It has expanded its staff.
It offers take-out food.

LISTEN FOR DETAILS, page 153

1. b   3. b   5. a   7. c   9. b
2. c   4. a   6. b   8. c

MAKE INFERENCES, page 154

1. a   2. b   3. b   4. b   5. b

2B LISTENING TWO

1, page 155

1. a   3. b   5. a   7. a
2. a   4. b   6. b

STEP 1: Organize, page 156

Answers will vary. Suggested answers:

Categories	Goodbye, Sit-down Meal	Food in a Bowl
1. Examples of changes in our diet	• French bakeries are serving sandwiches now • French people are eating more take-out food • Sandwiches have more traditional French ingredients	Food is often now served in bowls, including lasagna, Mexican food, etc.
2. Reasons why our eating habits are changing	• More women are working • Men are working at desks, and are eating less • People are in a hurry • Parents want to spend less time at lunch, and then leave work early so they can pick up their children	• We're in a hurry • We are eating more • We don't emphasize good manners
3. Speakers' attitudes toward these changes	Accepting: Thinks these changes reflect a deeper change in French society as a whole	• We're eating too much food, too quickly • Worried about children not appreciating food and not having good manners
4. Speakers' tone	Intellectual, informative, analytical, educated	Humorous, informal

REVIEW, page 157

1. a   3. b   5. b   7. b   9. b
2. a   4. b   6. b   8. a   10. a

EXPAND, page 158

a. 7   c. 2   e. 3   g. 5   i. 4   k. 11
b. 6   d. 12   f. 8   h. 9   j. 1   l. 10

3B GRAMMAR

2, pages 160–162

1. call you up
2. caught on
3. check it out
4. ask you over
5. turn him down
6. put him off
7. calling it off
8. letting you down
9. thinking it over
10. hand it in
11. work it out
12. call me back
13. turned it in
14. try it out
15. run into them

3, pages 162–163

2. e   5. k   8. l   11. h   14. j
3. b   6. m   9. o   12. f   15. n
4. c   7. a   10. g   13. i

PRONUNCIATION

1, page 164

1. one   4. boot
2. shoot   5. boost
3. body   6. cook

2, page 164

/uw/ **too:** food, boom, cool, noodles, noon, too, tool
/ʊ/ **good:** book, cook, look
/ə/ **cut:** blood, flood

3, page 164

/ɑ/ **not:** popular, done, job, money, oven, possible, products, shock
/ow/ **no:** explode, frozen, go, grocery, home, whole
/ə/ **Monday:** come

UNIT 9

1C BACKGROUND AND VOCABULARY, pages 170–171

1. a   3. g   5. l   7. d   9. h   11. b
2. k   4. c   6. i   8. j   10. e   12. f

LISTEN FOR MAIN IDEAS, page 172

1, 3, 5

LISTEN FOR DETAILS, page 173

Person Being Interviewed	Student	Teacher	What This Person Likes About The School
Jennifer Shenke		✓	Students have a successful learning experience; they enjoy themselves
Priscilla Billarrel	✓		Students feel supported
Aaron Listhaus		✓	Students feel at home: they feel valued
Evelyna Namovich	✓		Students are not punished for speaking their own language
Kathy Rucker		✓	School is providing practical skills that are needed for economic success

MAKE INFERENCES, page 173

Excerpt One: A

Excerpt Two: D

Excerpt Three: A

Excerpt Four: A

Excerpt Five: A

2B LISTENING TWO

1, pages 174–175

1. a	3. b	5. c	7. b
2. c	4. a	6. a	8. a

2, pages 175–176

1. foreign
2. fast
3. breath
4. words
5. miss
6. studying
7. stupid
8. escape
9. tongue
10. cold

STEP 1: Organize, page 177

Answers will vary. Suggested answers:

Topics	New Student at the International High School	Singer of "Words Escape Me"
Specific problems these people face	Inability to speak English	Inability to speak English
Feelings about their new life in the United States	Feel uprooted, intimidated, isolated	Feels uprooted, intimidated, isolated
Things that would help them to adapt better and find a niche in this country	Being supported by others: being able to speak their own language while they learn English	Being able to speak English more fluently

REVIEW, pages 178–179

1. tight-knit
2. unique
3. assimilate
4. support
5. intimidated
6. niche
7. interpret
8. set him apart
9. boned up on
10. mainstream

EXPAND, page 180

1. e	3. a	5. b	7. c	9. i
2. f	4. g	6. d	8. h	

3B GRAMMAR

2, pages 183–185

1. came
2. was
3. didn't speak
4. went
5. weren't
6. had
7. was
8. didn't understand
9. was talking
10. asked
11. became
12. told
13. wanted
14. felt
15. thought
16. felt
17. doesn't speak
18. has changed
19. isn't
20. are
21. have changed
22. is
23. look
24. have spoken
25. attend
26. are learning
27. love
28. have become
29. teach
30. help
31. teach
32. hasn't spoken
33. doesn't remember
34. wishes
35. has been taking

3, pages 185–186

1. How long has she been in the United States?
2. How did she feel about speaking Chinese when she was in school in the U.S.?
3. How does she feel about it now?
4. Why have her feelings changed?
5. What new technology has changed the way people learn other languages?
6. How do you feel when people speak a language you don't understand?
7. What is Dr. Chin's native language?
8. What are the benefits of a bilingual school?
9. How has the bilingual school helped Dr. Chin's children?
10. What types of jobs require a bilingual person?
11. How do Dr. Chin's views about language differ from her grandparents' views?
12. In your opinion, what kind of school is best for immigrant children?

PRONUNCIATION

1, pages 187–188

	/ʃ/ she	/ʒ/ pleasure	/tʃ/ child	/dʒ/ just
3. enjoy				✓
4. adjust				✓
5. measure		✓		
6. lecture			✓	
7. traditional	✓			
8. culture			✓	
9. usual		✓		
10. punishment	✓			
11. special	✓			
12. subject				✓
13. Chile		✓		
14. television		✓		
15. educators				✓
16. occasion		✓		
17. communication	✓			
18. encourage				✓
19. treasure		✓		
20a. niche	✓			
20b. niche			✓	
21. flourish	✓			

UNIT 10

1C BACKGROUND AND VOCABULARY, pages 194–196

1. a   3. a   5. c   7. a   9. c   11. b
2. c   4. b   6. c   8. a   10. a   12. b

LISTEN FOR MAIN IDEAS, page 196

1. T   2. T   3. F   4. T   5. F   6. T

LISTEN FOR DETAILS, page 197

1. a. They wake people up.
   b. They get arrested.
2. a. They put a note on the car.
   b. They smear Vaseline on the windshield or break it.
3. a. It was kicked.
   b. No one bothered to get up.
4. a. The police arrived 40 minutes after the alarm went off.
   b. They should be banned.
5. a. It affects their ability to sleep and work.
   b. It could cause hearing loss.
6. a. Police can break into people's cars.
   b. They would be less sensitive to trucks.

2B LISTENING TWO

1, page 199

1. a   3. c   5. b   7. b
2. b   4. a   6. a

STEP 1: Organize, page 200

Answers will vary. Suggested answers:

	Problem	Response	Is Response Appropriate?
Noise in the City	1. Car alarms going off in the middle of the night.	Leave note on car saying, "Fix your car alarm. It disturbed hundreds of people last night."	Yes
		Break an egg on windshield.	No
		Put grease on windshield.	No
		Break windshield.	No
Ten Command-ments	1. annoying ring tone	Select music that won't offend anyone.	Yes
		Set ring tone to vibrate.	Yes
	2. phone ringing during a performance	Make announcements that remind people to turn off phones.	Yes
	3. phone ringing in a quiet place/ talking loudly in front of others	Go to a vestibule.	Yes

REVIEW, pages 201–202

Conversation One

1. getting under my skin
2. jolts
3. frustrated

Conversation Two

4. irritated
5. drive you crazy
6. offense
7. pay a fine
8. vigilantes

3B GRAMMAR

2, page 206

Mystery Item 1

1. will have replaced
2. will have produced

Mystery Item 2

1. will have used
2. will have used

Mystery Item 3

1. will have turned on
2. will not have become

PRONUNCIATION

3, page 208

1. e   2. a   3. c   4. b   5. d

Unit Word List

The **Unit Word List** is a summary of key vocabulary from the student book. The words are presented by unit, in alphabetical order.

UNIT 1

addict (verb)
addicted to
addiction
attention deficit disorder (ADD)
barrage
bias
catch
catch the news
come in second
coverage
daily
despair
disengage from
distract
evading
fantasy
focus
get the scoop on
have a focus on
humor

immobilized
inconsequential
intake
lethal
make connection to
make a connection
newsworthy
perspective
plug into
put an emphasis on
raise
reason
recommend
regardless of
remedy
repetitive
sense of humor
take a break from
take on
track down
underlying

UNIT 2

altitude
challenging
collapse
courageous
crush (verb)
crutch
determined
eagle
empowerment
in store for
inspiration
inspirational
judging
landscape
limitations

overcome
peak
perseverance
proof
reach a high point
reach deep down
recognition
recognize
revelation
scars
scatter
soar
soaring
tough
turn around

UNIT 3

accumulate
alert
alertness
blink
burn the midnight oil
captivating
catch 40 winks
catnap
chronic
chronically
cranky
dim
do without
droop
fatigue
hormones

irritable
miserable
nap
nod off
out of sync
power nap
priority
run by
shut-eye
snore
spontaneous
subtle
surge
suspect
waves of sleepiness

UNIT 4

ape
aware
categorize
chimp (chimpanzee)
cognition
compassion
context
deceive
disease
dolphin
endangered
figure out
get it
give someone the floor
gorilla
hazard
humane
in captivity
intriguing
killer whale

manipulate
nuisance
off the top of (someone's) head
parrot
pest
prevailing
push the envelope
remarkable
research
rote memorization
seagull
socialize
spontaneous
spontaneously
squirrel
superior
unethical
vocalize

UNIT 5

anxious
assisted living facility
attendant
bitter
bitterness
bold
brag (about)
bunch of
chapter
citizen
elderly
emphatic
ensemble
face (verb)
facility
flamboyant
generation
get together with
go in for
gorgeous
hotspot
it's a different story
jealous
keep an eye on
life expectancy
mourning
nurturing
pass away
physician
population
self-improvement
senior
serious
sit on the sidelines
solidarity
take care of
the ripe old age of
widow

UNIT 6

anonymity
anonymous
anonymously
appeal (noun)
benefactor
catastrophe
catastrophic
cause
charity
contribute
donation
donor
freelance
fundraiser
generosity
inherit
inheritance
mandatory
moral
morality
moralize
motivated
motivation
passion
passionate
philanthropist
philanthropy
rewarding
under the radar
wealth
wealthy

UNIT 7

a cinch
accountable
advocate
buckle down
come to mind
conked out
count on
demanding
distraught
duty
fluctuate
foundation
have (one's) nose to the
    grindstone
hold accountable for
hopping mad
monitor
obedient
outlawed
over the top
pay off
pull (one's) weight
ritual
sacrifice
self-esteem
tangible

UNIT 8

ask over
be (something) city
be a hit
bean (someone) with
    something
bread and butter
breadwinner
bring home the bacon
core
delicacy
dough
exploding
food for thought
get cooking
hard to swallow
intimate
leave a bad taste in one's
    mouth
make (one's) tastes
    known
overrun
phenomenon
put bread on the table
put (something) on the
    back burner
salt of the earth
shift
shovel (food) in
sit-down
stack
stir up
take it with a grain of
    salt
there's trouble brewing
tough
witness (verb)
workforce

UNIT 9

assimilate
blend in
bone up on
deal with
dialect
do (your) part
encouragement
flourishing
have a hard time
in the process
interpret
intimidated
intimidating

learn by doing
mainstream
native tongue
niche
punishment
relieved
set apart
support (noun)
suppress
tight-knit
unique
uprooted

UNIT 10

annoying
awful
bang
banned
beep
buzz
clang
comforting
constant
defective
drive you crazy
faint (adjective)
frustrated
getting under my skin
honk
hum
irritated
irritating
jolted
jolting
loud
low
offense

pay a fine
piercing
prompt
rattle
ring
retaliatory
rhythmic
screech
sending me over the
    edge
shatter
shrill
siren
soft
sonic
startling
tick
tow
vibration
vigilante
wail
whistle

Achievement Tests
Unit 1

Name: _____

Date: _____

PART 1: LISTENING

1.1 🔊 *Listen to the beginning of a talk show. Check (✔) the best prediction of what the listening is about. There is only one right answer.*

_____ **A.** a debate about dieting

_____ **B.** the sociology of television

_____ **C.** opinions about daily news

_____ **D.** issues concerning mental health

1.2 🔊 *Now listen to the entire talk show. Use the information to choose the correct answers. Check (✔) the answers.*

1. The two men who are speaking on the show _____.

_____ **A.** want better coverage of complex problems

_____ **B.** believe it is hard to connect the events in a story

_____ **C.** have different opinions about the news on TV

_____ **D.** think it is important to show what is currently newsworthy

2. According to Lauren Hall, how often does a person watch the news?

_____ **A.** at least once a day

_____ **B.** twice a day

_____ **C.** every other day

_____ **D.** twice a week

3. What will Mr. Tucker probably think about Professor Gibson's book?

_____ **A.** He won't want to read the book.

_____ **B.** He won't agree with the ideas in the book.

_____ **C.** He will think it doesn't put events into perspective.

_____ **D.** He will think it doesn't show the negative side of TV news.

4. Mr. Tucker believes that _____.

_____ **A.** addiction is not a good thing

_____ **B.** issues in the world are not complicated

_____ **C.** viewers are getting too much information

_____ **D.** people need to decide what stories are important

(continued on next page)

5. About how long is the coverage of a story on the news?

_____ **A.** two and a half minutes

_____ **B.** three and a half minutes

_____ **C.** twenty minutes

_____ **D.** thirty minutes

6. 🔘 _Listen again to a part of the talk show. Then answer the question._

Why does Professor Gibson say, "But are viewers getting the information they need from the news on television?"

_____ **A.** He is asking Mr. Tucker what he means.

_____ **B.** He is emphasizing what he will say next.

_____ **C.** He wants the viewers to answer his question.

_____ **D.** He wants to know the answer to his question.

1.3 🔘 _Listen to the excerpt from "News Registers" from_ NorthStar: Listening and Speaking 4, _Unit 1. Use the information from this listening and the listening from Part 1.2 to complete the activity. Write the letter of the statement under the name of the person/people who would agree with it. Not all the statements will be used._

~~**A.** Paying attention to the daily news is addicting.~~

B. People should watch the news every morning and night.

C. People should decide what is important in the media.

D. The news presents problems but does not give solutions.

E. The daily news makes it hard to make logical connections.

F. It is hard to get a perspective when all stories are a standard size.

People on the News Program	Mr. Tucker
A	

PART 2: VOCABULARY

2.1 *Read the paragraph. Use the words and phrases from the box to fill in the blanks. Not all the words will be used.*

addicted to	catch the news	make a connection	plugged in
bias	evade	newsworthy	

Every night I used to turn on the TV to _____. I suddenly realized
                                                 1.

that I was _____ it. Even though I knew some of the stories weren't
                  2.

_____, I felt I had to be _____ or I wouldn't know
       3.   **4.**

what was happening in the world. Some stories would continue for several days,

and I worried that I wouldn't be able to _____ between the events if
                                               5.

I missed a day of the news.

2.2 *Match the words and phrases in Column A with their definitions in Column B. Write the letter of the definition on the line. Not all the definitions will be used.*

Column A	Column B
_____ 1. daily	**A.** make something not real or believable
_____ 2. coverage	**B.** point of view
_____ 3. distract	**C.** opinion based on only one side of an issue
_____ 4. perspective	**D.** every day
_____ 5. regardless of	**E.** no matter how / what
	F. reporting of events on the news
	G. take someone's attention away from something

PART 3: SKILLS FOR SPEAKING

3.1   *Complete the news report. Fill in the blanks with the passive voice of the verb in parentheses. Use the tense that is indicated.*

People say the only news that _____*is reported*_____ is bad news. Well, tonight we
                                   (report / present)

have a story about a baby girl who _____ by her pet cat Ginger. The
                                    1. (save / past)

10-month-old girl was sleeping in a crib that _____ thirty years ago.
                                               2. (make / past perfect)

The wood was so old that the legs broke and the girl _____ under
                                                      3. (trap / past)

the crib. Ginger ran to get the girl's mother, who was sleeping in the next room.

She meowed until the mother woke up and picked up the crying baby. Ginger

_____ with a bowl of milk. She is now sleeping contentedly.
   4. (reward / past)

3.2   ᶜ ᴰ ¹ *Listen. Fill in the blanks with the reduced form of the auxiliary verb that you hear.*
          ⑥   *Write the reduced sounds as follows:*

   have = əv   has = əz   are = ər

John ___*əz*___ been trying to stop watching the news. This week _____ been
                                                                   1.

easy. He's watched the news six days instead of seven. Luckily, his friends _____
                                                                             2.

going to help him continue with this plan. Next week he'll only watch the news five

days of the week. His friends _____ promised to distract him, so he won't be
                               3.

tempted to turn on the TV.

3.3 *Read the conversation. The underlined phrases are expressions of giving or responding to an opinion. Decide whether each phrase is used to state an opinion, agree with someone else's opinion, politely disagree, or avoid giving an opinion. Check (✔) the correct answer.*

STAN: John, are you watching the news again? It really doesn't give you any important information.

JOHN: <u>Well, as far as I know,</u> there's no other way to find out what's happening in the world today.

    ✓ **A.** opinion   ____ **C.** disagreement

    ____ **B.** agreement   ____ **D.** not an opinion

STAN: (1)<u>You have a good point, but</u> I think you get a much broader coverage of what's going on by reading the newspaper.

    ____ **A.** opinion   ____ **C.** disagreement

    ____ **B.** agreement   ____ **D.** not an opinion

JOHN: (2) <u>Yes, but on the other hand,</u> some of the newspapers are so biased you can't believe what you read.

    ____ **A.** opinion   ____ **C.** disagreement

    ____ **B.** agreement   ____ **D.** not an opinion

STAN: I haven't been keeping up on the news lately so (3) <u>I'm not really sure about that</u>.

    ____ **A.** opinion   ____ **C.** disagreement

    ____ **B.** agreement   ____ **D.** not an opinion

PART 4: SPEAKING

4.1 *Say one reason that was given in Part 1.2 for not watching the daily news. You may listen again to Part 1.2.*

4.2 *Say whether you agree or disagree with the reason you gave in 4.1.*

4.3　*Expressing an Opinion*

Speak for 1–2 minutes. Give your opinion about the daily news.

Here are several points you may want to include:
- how often you watch the news on TV or read the newspaper
- the positive and negative points of the daily news
- why you think people should or should not watch the daily news on TV

- Take notes.
- Use the passive voice.
- Use expressions for stating an opinion.
- Use the vocabulary and grammar from Unit 1.

<table>
<tr><td colspan="5" align="center">Unit 1 Vocabulary Words</td></tr>
<tr>
<td>addicted to
bias
catch the news</td>
<td>coverage
daily
focus</td>
<td>inconsequential
make a connection
newsworthy</td>
<td>perspective
plugged in
recommend</td>
<td>regardless of
repetitive
take a break from</td>
</tr>
<tr><td colspan="5" align="center">Unit 1 Grammar: Passive Voice</td></tr>
<tr><td colspan="5">• Some people are addicted to the news
• John has been addicted to the news for a long time.
• Before he watched the news on TV, he had been addicted to reading the daily news.</td></tr>
</table>

Achievement Tests
Unit 2

Name: _____

Date: _____

PART 1: LISTENING

1.1 CD 7 ⑦ *Listen to the beginning of an interview. Check (✔) the best prediction of what the listening is about. There is only one right answer.*

_____ **A.** John will talk about the students he met.

_____ **B.** Professor Kim will talk to John about his classes.

_____ **C.** Professor Kim will ask John about his background.

_____ **D.** John will tell Professor Kim his impression of the campus.

1.2 CD 7 ⑧ *Now listen to the entire interview. Use the information to choose the correct answers. Check (✔) the answers.*

1. What do John and Professor Kim mainly discuss?

_____ **A.** John's family problems

_____ **B.** a dream John used to have

_____ **C.** a job that John found challenging

_____ **D.** obstacles that John has had to overcome

2. What limitations did John face?

_____ **A.** discrimination and poverty

_____ **B.** family problems and poverty

_____ **C.** learning disabilities and discrimination

_____ **D.** unemployment and lack of self-confidence

3. Why don't many people in John's neighborhood have jobs?

_____ **A.** They don't want to work.

_____ **B.** There are no jobs they want.

_____ **C.** There is high unemployment.

_____ **D.** They are not trained for any jobs.

4. How does John most likely feel about the kids in his neighborhood?

_____ **A.** superior to them

_____ **B.** impressed by them

_____ **C.** sympathetic towards them

_____ **D.** discriminatory to them

(continued on next page)

5. John's dream is to _____.

_____ **A.** get an education

_____ **B.** overcome obstacles

_____ **C.** fight against discrimination

_____ **D.** teach kids from his neighborhood

6. Professor Kim most likely thinks that John _____.

_____ **A.** has a tough job

_____ **B.** will be a serious student

_____ **C.** has too many limitations

_____ **D.** will be a challenging person

1.3 CD 1 *Listen to the excerpt from "Dreams of Flying and Overcoming Obstacles" from*
 9 *NorthStar: Listening and Speaking 4, Unit 2. Use the information from this*
listening and the listening from Part 1.2 to complete the activity. Put the letter of
the obstacle and the letter of the dream under the correct name.

A. imagination

B. fly

~~**C.** physical disability~~

D. go to college

E. teach

F. poverty

	Richard	John
Obstacle	C	2.
Dream	1.	3.

PART 2: VOCABULARY

2.1 *Read the paragraph. Use the words from the box to fill in the blanks. Not all the words will be used.*

determined	in store for	learning disability	tough
discrimination	inspiration	overcome	

Teresa had never done well in school. Figuring out math problems was easy for her, but reading had always been a problem. Finally the school counselors discovered that she had a / an _____. She received tutoring to help her
_____
1.

_____ this problem. The extra hours with the tutor helped her
2.

improve her reading, but she had not realized how _____ it would
3.

be to catch up with her classmates. Every subject required that she could read well.

As soon as she knew what she was _____, she became even more
4.

_____ to succeed.
5.

2.2 *Check (✔) the correct definition of each word.*

1. proof

   _____ **A.** something that is provable

   _____ **B.** something that is evidence

   _____ **C.** something that has value

2. perseverance

   _____ **A.** persistent effort to achieve something

   _____ **B.** great ability to endure something

   _____ **C.** easily able to succeed at something

3. limitation

   _____ **A.** something that makes you wonder

   _____ **B.** something that you don't realize

   _____ **C.** something that keeps you from doing well

(continued on next page)

4. revelation

_____ **A.** a feeling of wonder

_____ **B.** a feeling that anything is possible

_____ **C.** feeling of surprise and inspiration

5. recognize

_____ **A.** recall

_____ **B.** understand

_____ **C.** locate

PART 3: SKILLS FOR SPEAKING

3.1 *Complete each sentence by writing either the gerund or infinitive form of the verb in parentheses.*

During the interview at Simpson College, Professor Kim wanted

_____to get to know_____ more about John. John hoped _____ Professor
(get to know)   1. (impress)

Kim. He thought that _____ about his dream for the future would
                                   2. (talk)

show Professor Kim that he would be a serious student. Professor Kim was

interested in _____ more about the obstacles John had had to
                     3. (hear)

overcome. For John, _____ high school was the first obstacle to
                              4. (finish)

overcome before he could accomplish his dream.

3.2 (CD 7, track 10) *Listen to the sentences. Write the number of thought groups in each sentence.*

___2___   Both John and Richard were applying to college.

_____ **1.** Richard's essay was about overcoming a physical disability.

_____ **2.** John had an interview with Professor Kim.

_____ **3.** John told Professor Kim about his dream to become a teacher.

3.3 *Match the facts about John with the elements of personal achievement. Write the letter of the fact on the line.*

Elements of Personal Achievement	Facts about John
__D__ Background	**A.** John knows what he wants to study when he goes to college.
_____ I. Challenge	**B.** John grew up in a neighborhood of poverty.
_____ 2. Accomplishment	**C.** John has talked to some students at Simpson College, and he thinks he will get along well at the college.
_____ 3. Life Lesson	~~**D.** John is at an interview at the college he hopes to attend~~.
	E. John stayed in high school and will go to college.
	F. By overcoming his situation and going to college, John can show children they have options.

PART 4: SPEAKING

4.1 *Say one of the obstacles that John from Part 1.2 faced. You may listen again to Part 1.2.*

4.2 *Say one other thing about John's personal story. It can be about his background, challenge, accomplishment, or life lesson.*

4.3 *Overcoming Obstacles*

Speak for 1–2 minutes. Talk about how an obstacle or limitation can become something positive in a person's life. You can talk about a real person, including yourself, or you can talk about this topic in a general way.

- Take notes.
- Use gerunds and infinitives.
- Provide details about background information, obstacles, accomplishments, and life lessons.
- Use the vocabulary and grammar from Unit 2.

Unit 2 Vocabulary Words					
determined discrimination illness in store for	injury inspiration lack of money	lack of self- 　confidence learning disability limitation	overcome physical or mental 　disability	proof recognize revelation	shyness tough
Unit 2 Grammar: Gerunds and Infinitives					
[gerund] • ***Achieving*** a goal is a rewarding experience. [infinitive] • It is difficult **to overcome** shyness.					

Achievement Tests
Unit 3

Name: _____

Date: _____

PART I: LISTENING

1.1 CD 1 (11) *Listen to the beginning of a conversation. Check (✔) the best prediction of what the listening is about. There is only one right answer.*

_____ **A.** what REM sleep is

_____ **B.** what melatonin is

_____ **C.** how REM affects melatonin

_____ **D.** why melatonin is called the sleep hormone

1.2 CD 1 (12) *Now listen to the entire conversation. Use the information to choose the correct answers. Check (✔) the answers.*

1. The purpose of this conversation is to _____.

_____ **A.** explain what melatonin is

_____ **B.** review last week's lecture

_____ **C.** discuss Donald's sleep problems

_____ **D.** tell Donald what he missed in class

2. How many stages of sleep do humans have?

_____ **A.** two

_____ **B.** three

_____ **C.** four

_____ **D.** five

3. What happens during REM sleep?

_____ **A.** You begin to dream.

_____ **B.** A sleep hormone is released.

_____ **C.** Your muscles don't move.

_____ **D.** You have problems with memory.

4. During non-REM sleep _____.

_____ **A.** you don't dream

_____ **B.** you are not fully asleep

_____ **C.** your eyes move rapidly

_____ **D.** your breathing is regular

(continued on next page)

5. If you are deprived of REM sleep, you might have trouble _____ .

_____ **A.** moving your eyes

_____ **B.** learning new things

_____ **C.** falling back to sleep

_____ **D.** releasing sleep hormones

🔊 CD 7
13 *Listen again to a part of the conversation. Then answer the question.*

6. Why does Donald say, "What"?

_____ **A.** He wants Sonia to repeat what she said.

_____ **B.** He wants Sonia to speak more loudly.

_____ **C.** He wants Sonia to give an explanation.

_____ **D.** He wants Sonia to continue what she was saying.

1.3 🔊 CD 7
14 *Listen to the excerpt from "Teen Sleep Needs" from* NorthStar: Listening and Speaking 4, *Unit 3. Use the information from this listening and the listening from Part 1.2 to complete the activity. Use the phrases to complete the outline.*

A. occur after 10 minutes

B. affect alertness

C. a stage of sleep

D. affect memory

E. ~~a hormone released to make you sleepy~~

F. occurs when you first fall asleep

I. Sleep

   A. Melatonin

      1. is _____E_____

   (1) a. lack of sleep can _____

   B. REM sleep

   (2) 1. is _____

   (3) a. lack of REM sleep can _____

PART 2: VOCABULARY

2.1 *Read the letters. Use the words and phrases from the box to fill in the blanks. Not all the words and phrases will be used.*

alertness	dim	hormone	melatonin	snoring
blinking	do without	insomnia	priority	surge
chronically	fatigue	irritable	sleep-deprived	

Dear Dr. Sleep:

I suffer from terrible _____. It doesn't matter how tired
                                    1.

I am during the day. As soon as I lie down to go to sleep, I feel a

_____ of energy. Then I don't fall asleep until it's almost time
         2.

to get up, so I am _____ _____. I can't stand
                            3.   **4.**

this much longer.

Sleepless in Boston

Dear Sleepless:

What you have is not only a problem for you; it can also be a danger to

others. Lack of sleep leads to _____ and this can affect your
                                        5.

_____. Here are some suggestions: After 1 P.M., you must
        6.

_____ coffee, tea, or any other beverage that contains caffeine.
        7.

Do not exercise after 4 P.M. Try relaxation therapy. If none of these remedies

helps, then you must see your physician. Sometimes sleep medication is

necessary.

Dr. Sleep

(continued on next page)

Dear Dr. Sleep:

My problem is my husband. He sleeps like a baby, but his

_____ keeps me up all night. Then he can't understand
      8.

why I am so _____ the next day.
          9.

Cranky in Minneapolis

Dear Cranky:

Of course I understand why you're cranky. But don't get rid of your

husband yet. He may have a sleep disorder called apnea. Your first

_____ is to get your husband to see a doctor. Sleep apnea can
     10.

be treated very easily. Once his apnea is under control, then you'll be sleeping

like a baby, too.

Dr. Sleep

PART 3: SKILLS FOR SPEAKING

3.1 *Read the paragraph. Circle the errors, and write the correct form of the verbs on the lines.*

If I (don't) have a cup of coffee after dinner, I would sleep better. If I sleep better, I could get up earlier. If I got up earlier, I can get to work on time. At work, I won't be yawning and falling asleep at my desk. I would get much more accomplished if I stop drinking coffee after dinner.

     didn't
    ————————

1. ————————

2. ————————

3. ————————

4. ————————

3.2 CD 7 (15) *Listen to the sentences with contrastive stress. The second half of each sentence is below. The boldfaced words are stressed. Check (✔) the phrase you hear.*

_____ ✓ **A.** but my **sister** likes to stay up **late**

_____ **B.** but my **sister** likes to **stay up** late

1.

_____ **A.** but I **sleep** well on the **weekend**

_____ **B.** but I sleep **well** on the **weekend**

2.

_____ **A.** whereas **nightmares** occur when you're **asleep**

_____ **B.** whereas **nightmares** occur **when** you're asleep

3.

_____ **A.** **sleep** a **little** and wake **up** a **lot**

_____ **B.** **sleep** a little and **wake up** a lot

3.3 *Read the conversations. Check (✔) the sentence that best completes the conversation.*

TOM: What'd I miss in class today?
CHRIS: The lecture was about melatonin.
TOM: _____
CHRIS: It was about melatonin.

_____ **A.** What is melatonin?

_____ **B.** Could you say that another way?

_____ ✓ **C.** I'm sorry. I didn't catch that. Could you repeat it?

_____ **D.** No, I don't know what you said.

(continued on next page)

1. **CHRIS:** I wasn't in class yesterday. What did I miss?
   TOM: We learned about melatonin.
   CHRIS: _____.
   TOM: Yeah, that's what it's called.

   _____ **A.** Oh, the sleep hormone.

   _____ **B.** Could you say that another way?

   _____ **C.** I'm sorry. I didn't catch that. Could you repeat it?

   _____ **D.** No, I don't know what you said.

2. **CHRIS:** I wasn't in class yesterday. What did I miss?
   TOM: The professor talked about REM sleep.
   CHRIS: _____
   TOM: Rapid Eye Movement.

   _____ **A.** I know. Rapid Eye Movement.

   _____ **B.** Could you say that another way?

   _____ **C.** I'm sorry. I didn't catch that. Could you repeat it?

   _____ **D.** No, I don't know what you said.

3. **TOM:**   My wife was snoring so loudly I couldn't sleep last night.
   CHRIS: Maybe she has sleep apnea.
   TOM: _____.
   CHRIS: She might have sleep apnea.

   _____ **A.** Sleep apnea.

   _____ **B.** Could you say that another way?

   _____ **C.** I'm sorry. I didn't catch that. Could you repeat it?

   _____ **D.** No, I don't know what you said.

PART 4: SPEAKING

4.1 *Say one fact about REM sleep. You may listen again to Part 1.2.*

4.2 *Tell Sonia that you didn't understand something that she said. Ask for clarification.*

4.3 *Giving an Explanation*

Speak for 1–2 minutes. Imagine that your friend had trouble sleeping last night. Tell your friend about the effects of not getting enough sleep. Say why he or she had trouble sleeping and suggest what he or she could do to sleep better.

- Take notes.
- Use present unreal conditionals.
- Use contrastive stress to emphasize certain information.
- Use the vocabulary and grammar from Unit 3.

Unit 3 Vocabulary Words				
alert	chronically	hormone	melatonin	snoring
alertness	do without	insomnia	priority	surge
blinking	fatigue	irritable	sleep-deprived	yawn
Unit 3 Grammar: Present Unreal Conditional				
• If you went to bed earlier, you wouldn't be so tired. • You could sleep better if you didn't drink coffee after dinner.				

Achievement Tests
Unit 4

Name: _____

Date: _____

PART I: LISTENING

1.1 CD7 ⑯ *Listen to the beginning of a lecture. Check (✔) the best prediction of what the listening is about. There is only one right answer.*

_____ **A.** what intelligence is

_____ **B.** whether animals are smarter than humans

_____ **C.** whether animals have language

_____ **D.** which animals can speak

1.2 CD7 ⑰ *Now listen to the entire lecture. Use the information to choose the correct answers. Check (✔) the answers.*

1. What is this lecture mainly about?

    _____ **A.** proof that animals possess language skills

    _____ **B.** an animal that was taught to communicate with humans

    _____ **C.** evidence that gorillas are almost as intelligent as humans

    _____ **D.** an experiment done by linguists about animal communication

2. Why did many linguists believe that only humans were able to use language?

    _____ **A.** Animals had no system of communication.

    _____ **B.** Language could not be used to express what animals feel.

    _____ **C.** Humans were the only beings socialized to learn language.

    _____ **D.** Only the human brain had a specific function for language.

3. Based on the lecture you can conclude that _____.

    _____ **A.** linguists worked with psychologists to study language

    _____ **B.** linguists didn't do experiments on animals

    _____ **C.** psychologists didn't study theories about language

    _____ **D.** psychologists believed linguists' theories about language

4. Where did Koko live?

    _____ **A.** in a zoo

    _____ **B.** with a linguist

    _____ **C.** at a nature park

    _____ **D.** with psychologists

5. Why did Koko learn American Sign Language?

_____ **A.** She couldn't vocalize words.

_____ **B.** Patterson wanted her to memorize words.

_____ **C.** She wanted to communicate with humans.

_____ **D.** Her caretakers could only understand American Sign Language.

6. One necessary quality of language is that _____.

_____ **A.** humans can be taught to use it

_____ **B.** it can be used to make up new words

_____ **C.** animals cannot use it to communicate

_____ **D.** it has a vocabulary of at least 1,000 words

1.3 ^{CD 1} 18 *Listen to the excerpt from "The Infinite Mind: Animal Intelligence" from* NorthStar: *Listening and Speaking 4, Unit 4. Use the information from this listening and the listening in Part 1.2 to complete the activity. Choose the examples of Koko's behavior that support the argument that some animals have language.*

Argument: Some animals have language.	
Examples that Support This Argument	**Examples of Koko's Behavior**
F	**A.** had an argument
1.	**B.** had a vocabulary of over 1,000 words
2.	**C.** created a word for *mask*
3.	**D.** asked for food
	E. told a dentist about her level of pain
	F. ~~used the words *finger* and *bracelet* for the word *ring*~~
	G. not able to vocalize

PART 2: VOCABULARY

2.1   *Read the paragraphs. Use the words and phrases from the box to fill in the blanks. Not all the words and phrases will be used.*

endangered	intriguing	socialized	unethical
hazard	rote memorization	superior	vocalize

Many people know the _____ story of Koko, the gorilla who was
  1.

_____ among humans. Koko was said to have gone beyond
  2.

_____ of words and phrases to actually possess language. Since apes
  3.

cannot _____ as humans do, she communicated through American
  4.

Sign Language.

  In many ways, Koko's environment in human conditions can be seen as

_____ to the life she might have had in a zoo. However, some people
  5.

believe that it is _____ to take a gorilla away from its life among
  6.

animals of its own species.

2.2   *Match the words and phrases in Column A with their definitions in Column B. Write the letter of the definition on the line. Not all the definitions will be used.*

Column A	Column B
_____ 1. context	**A.** do a problem
_____ 2. figure out	**B.** compassionate
_____ 3. deceive	**C.** like a person
_____ 4. humane	**D.** solve
	E. do deliberately to trick someone
	F. information that helps determine the meaning of a word

PART 3: SKILLS FOR SPEAKING

3.1 *Read the statements. Check (✔) the sentence that is a correct form of reported speech.*

Dr. Pepperberg: You can talk to the birds the way you talk to a very young human.

_____✓___ **A.** Dr. Pepperberg said that you could talk to the birds the way you talk to a very young human.

_____ **B.** Dr. Pepperberg said that you can talk to the birds the way you talk to a very young child.

_____ **C.** Dr. Pepperberg said that you can have talked to the birds the way you talk to a very young child.

1. Goodwin: An elephant secretly learned how to open his cage.

    _____ **A.** Goodwin reported that an elephant secretly learned how to open his cage.

    _____ **B.** Goodwin reported that an elephant has secretly learned how to open his cage.

    _____ **C.** Goodwin reported that an elephant had secretly learned how to open his cage.

2. Liz: The chimp understands that a human is watching them.

    _____ **A.** Liz said the chimp understood that a human was watching them.

    _____ **B.** Liz said the chimp understood that a human is watching them.

    _____ **C.** Liz said that the chimp understands a human was watching them.

3. Researcher: I must continue my research on animal intelligence.

    _____ **A.** The researcher said I had to continue my research on animal intelligence.

    _____ **B.** The researcher said he had to continue his research on animal intelligence.

    _____ **C.** The researcher said he must continue his research on animal intelligence.

4. Koko's caretaker: Koko could understand more than a thousand words.

    _____ **A.** Koko's caretaker reported that Koko could have understood more than a thousand words.

    _____ **B.** Koko's caretaker reported that Koko could understand more than a thousand words.

    _____ **C.** Koko's caretaker reported that Koko could understood more than a thousand words.

3.2 ᵈ⁷ ⒚ *Listen to the questions. Check (✔) A if the question is a Yes/No question and B if it is a choice question.*

Does Alex understand colors or numbers?

_____ **A.** Yes/No

___✓___ **B.** Choice

1. Can animals show sadness or distress?

_____ **A.** Yes/No

_____ **B.** Choice

2. Do parrots communicate with each other or with humans?

_____ **A.** Yes/No

_____ **B.** Choice

3. Does Koko speak or sign?

_____ **A.** Yes/No

_____ **B.** Choice

3.3 *Read the conversation. Circle the three phrases that show the speaker is either giving an example or asking for an example.*

BETH: Here's an animal you'd never think of as intelligent. The octopus!

SAM: You've got to be kidding.

BETH: Apparently they have long- and short-term memory.

SAM: (What do you mean?)

BETH: Well, for instance, they've been given problem-solving tests and done well on them.

SAM: Problem-solving tests? Such as?

BETH: Like going through a maze. You know what a maze is, right? A place you enter and you have to go through all kinds of passages to find your way out. And there's one kind of octopus that can trick other sea animals so it can catch them.

SAM: Could you give me some more details?

BETH: I'm not an expert, but its brain is not only in its head. Some of it is in its arms, so the arms can tell what kind of animal is near and then copy the other animal's behavior.

SAM: Wow. I'll have to use that as an example on the test we're going to have.

PART 4: SPEAKING

4.1 *Say one thing you learned about Koko. You may listen again to Part 1.2.*

4.2 *Say the same thing as reported speech. Begin with the phrase "The professor ..."*

4.3 *Talking About a Class*

Speak for 1–2 minutes. Your friend missed a class on animal language. Tell your friend what the professor said about this.
- Take notes.
- Use reported speech.
- Give examples.
- Use the vocabulary and grammar from Unit 4.

Unit 4 Vocabulary Words					
ape	deceive	experiment	humane	manipulate	socialize
aware	emotion	figure out	in captivity	research	superior
context	establish	gorilla	intriguing	rote memorization	vocalize

Unit 4 Grammar: Reported Speech
• My friend said that gorillas could learn language. • He said that they had to be taught to use sign language.

Achievement Tests
Unit 5

Name: _____

Date: _____

PART 1: LISTENING

1.1 CD 7 [20] *Listen to the beginning of an interview. Check (✔) the best prediction of what the listening is about. There is only one right answer.*

_____ **A.** the oldest living person

_____ **B.** the life of a very old woman

_____ **C.** life in the Andes Mountains

_____ **D.** travel to a village in the Andes Mountains

1.2 CD 7 [21] *Now listen to the entire interview. Use the information to choose the correct answers. Check (✔) the answers.*

1. What is the main idea of this interview?

_____ **A.** to discuss the longevity of Sra. Cantez

_____ **B.** to learn how people should change their diet

_____ **C.** the discovery of the world's oldest living person

_____ **D.** finding out how life in the Andes promotes longevity

2. Sra. Cantez will celebrate her birthday with _____.

_____ **A.** her neighbors

_____ **B.** her closest friends

_____ **C.** her husband and family

_____ **D.** her son and his children

3. What does Sra. Cantez most likely think about assisted living facilities?

_____ **A.** She thinks they are a good way to take care of the elderly.

_____ **B.** She thinks they are not a good way to take care of the elderly.

_____ **C.** She thinks there should be more of them in the village.

_____ **D.** She thinks there should be more of them in the cities.

4. According to Sra. Cantez, what contributes to her longevity?

_____ **A.** fresh fish

_____ **B.** fresh fruits

_____ **C.** no red meat

_____ **D.** no alcohol

CD 7 (22) *Listen again to a part of the interview. Then answer the question.*

5. Why does Sra. Cantez say, "Those are places where families put their parents when they get old, aren't they?"

_____ **A.** to show that she's not completely sure and she wants confirmation

_____ **B.** to express that she wants an explanation from Jaime

_____ **C.** to say that this is her opinion and she believes that Jaime agrees with her

_____ **D.** to express that she does not approve of assisted living facilities

CD 7 (23) *Listen again to a part of the interview. Then answer the question.*

6. Why doesn't Sra. Cantez want to admit that she takes an aspirin every day?

_____ **A.** She thinks that aspirin is unhealthy.

_____ **B.** She believes that aspirin will hurt her heart.

_____ **C.** She doesn't want to think there is anything wrong with her heart.

_____ **D.** She doesn't want to accept assistance from modern life in the city.

1.3 **CD 7 (24)** *Listen to "On Vinegar and Living to the Ripe Old Age of 115" from NorthStar: Listening and Speaking 4, Unit 5. Use the information from this listening and the listening from Part 1.2 to complete the activity. Write the letter of the behavior under the correct name.*

	Susie Potts Gibson	Asención Cantez
A. uses vinegar	A	
B. doesn't drink alcohol		
C. takes aspirin		
D. doesn't worry		
E. never goes to the doctor		
F. eats pickles		

PART 2: VOCABULARY

2.1 *Read the paragraph. Use the words and phrases from the box to fill in the blanks. Not all the words and phrases will be used.*

assisted living facilities	get together	life expectancy
bitter	it's a different story	seniors
generations	keep an eye on	

It used to be common for families to _____ for celebrations. Several
                                          1.

_____ would be represented, and grandparents, aunts and uncles,
        2.

cousins, and grandchildren could all learn what was happening in each other's

lives. Today, _____. Families don't keep in touch. The notion of the
                3.

extended family hardly exists. Often, _____ don't want to be
                                        4.

completely on their own, so they move into _____.
                                            5.

2.2 *Match the words and phrases in Column A with their definitions in Column B. Write the letter of the definition on the line. Not all the definitions will be used.*

Column A	Column B
_____ 1. ripe old age	A. a man whose wife has died
_____ 2. go in for	B. old people
_____ 3. the elderly	C. like to participate in
_____ 4. widow	D. very advanced in years
_____ 5. pass away	E. die
	F. a woman whose husband has died

PART 3: SKILLS FOR SPEAKING

3.1 *Read the conversations. Fill in the blanks with the correct tag question.*

ANA: You heard about the man who lived to be 115, _____*didn't you*_____?

PETER: Yeah, but he isn't the oldest person on record. Officially, a French woman named Jeanne Clament lived to be 122 years old! That's amazing,

_____?
       1.

ANA: It sure is. She must have had an incredible life.

PETER: Yeah. She experienced so many changes in the world, _____?
                                                                    2.

TONY: I went with my parents to look at an assisted living facility over the weekend.

CARMEN: Oh, that can be pretty depressing, _____?
                                                3.

TONY: Well, I thought it would be, but I was surprised. It's like a small community. There are apartments for people who can still take care of themselves, and then there are other facilities for people who need a doctor or nurse to come every day.

CARMEN: Well, that doesn't sound so bad, _____?
                                               4.

3.2 CD 7 (25) *Listen to the sentences. Check (✔) the line in front of the phrase you hear.*

_____ hear the interview about the 115-year-old woman who just died?

_____ **A.** Do you   ✔ **B.** Did you

1. _____ mean Susie Potts Gibson?

_____ **A.** Do you   _____ **B.** Did you

2. Yeah. That's her name. _____ ask?

_____ **A.** Why do you   _____ **B.** Why did you

3. I thought it was so interesting. _____ think?

_____ **A.** What do you   _____ **B.** What did you

3.3 *Complete the conversation. Use the suggestion phrases from the box to fill in the blanks.*

~~could~~	could have	why didn't you
could consider	how about	why don't you

JOHN: I'm trying to eat a healthy diet so I can live to be 100.

CAROL: I read about a woman who lived to be 115 and she only ate green vegetables

and yogurt. You _____*could*_____ try to follow her diet.

Or _____ going on the new high protein diet? You eat
          1.

nothing but steak and French fries for a month.

JOHN: I think I'd like that. A steak every day. That sounds perfect.

CAROL: Well, actually, that sounds like a fad diet to me. _____ just
                                                                        2.

eat healthy food and stay away from junk foods?

JOHN: I suppose you're right.

CAROL: And you _____ exercising three times a week.
                        3.

JOHN: True. There's no real secret to longevity.

PART 4: SPEAKING

4.1 *Say one thing that Asención from Part 1.2 does to live a long life. You may listen again to Part 1.2.*

4.2 *Suggest to a friend that he or she do something Asención does to live a long life.*

4.3 *Making Suggestions*

Speak for 1–2 minutes. A friend has asked you how she can live a long life. Suggest what she can do to live a long life.

- Take notes.
- Use tag questions.
- Make suggestions.
- Use the vocabulary and grammar from Unit 5.

<table>
<tr><td colspan="5" align="center">**Unit 5 Vocabulary Words**</td></tr>
<tr>
<td>assisted living facilities
bitter
elderly</td>
<td>generations
get together
go in for</td>
<td>it's a different story
keep an eye on
life expectancy</td>
<td>longevity
pass away
ripe old age</td>
<td>seniors
widow</td>
</tr>
<tr><td colspan="5" align="center">**Unit 5 Grammar: Tag Questions**</td></tr>
<tr>
<td colspan="5">• You want to live a long life, **don't you**?
• It wouldn't be too hard to stop eating junk food, **would it**?</td>
</tr>
</table>

Achievement Tests
Unit 6

Name: _____

Date: _____

PART 1: LISTENING

1.1 CD7 26 *Listen to the beginning of a talk show. Check (✔) the best prediction of what the listening is about.*

_____ **A.** the life of an anonymous donor

_____ **B.** a person who received a contribution

_____ **C.** reasons people make anonymous contributions

_____ **D.** the number of Americans who donate to charities

1.2 CD7 27 *Now listen to the entire show. Use the information to choose the correct answers. Check (✔) the answers.*

1. This main idea of this listening is to tell _____.

_____ **A.** how important it is to prioritize choices

_____ **B.** the challenges that a single mothers faces

_____ **C.** the benefit of making anonymous contributions

_____ **D.** how an anonymous donation helped a young woman

2. What percentage of Americans is said to have made charitable contributions?

_____ **A.** less than 25%

_____ **B.** 30–40%

_____ **C.** 45–50%

_____ **D.** greater than 50%

3. Why did people write letters to the *Afternoon Update*?

_____ **A.** They wanted to receive contributions.

_____ **B.** They wanted to thank their benefactors.

_____ **C.** The donors were trying to find people in need.

_____ **D.** Their benefactors wanted to know they were grateful.

4. Most Americans make contributions to _____.

_____ **A.** causes they feel are important

_____ **B.** ideas they think are interesting

_____ **C.** organizations that are prosperous

_____ **D.** individuals who need financial help

T-32

5. How old were the woman's children when she received the donation?

_____ **A.** One child was one year old and the other was about five years old.

_____ **B.** One child was one month old and the other was about five years old.

_____ **C.** One child was one year old and the other was about ten years old.

_____ **D.** One child was five years old and the other child was fifteen years old.

6. How would the anonymous donor most likely feel if she heard the letter read on the radio?

_____ **A.** lucky

_____ **B.** curious

_____ **C.** pleased

_____ **D.** amazed

1.3 CD 1 / 28 *Listen to the excerpt from "The Mystery Donor" from* NorthStar: Listening and Speaking 4, *Unit 6. Use the information from this listening and the listening in Part 1.2 to complete the activity. Write the letter of the most and least important item each woman decided to buy in the correct column.*

Necessities

A. gas bill	~~**C.** diapers~~	**E.** tuna fish
B. light bill	**D.** canned goods	**F.** milk

	Donor	Recipient
Top Priority	C	
Last Priority		

PART 2: VOCABULARY

2.1   *Read the paragraph. Use the words from the box to fill in the blanks. Not all the words will be used.*

anonymous	charitable	donors	morality
cause	contributions	freelance	passion

More people than ever are making _____ to organizations they feel

                            1.

are important. Interestingly, an increasing number of _____ do not

                                               2.

want their identities known. Some prefer to remain _____ in order

                                                3.

to avoid being bothered by relatives or fundraisers asking for money. Others believe

that giving to a _____ _____ without asking for

                    4.   **5.**

recognition is a more sincere form of giving. Politics can also be a factor. Giving a

large donation to a political campaign can be seen as a way of gaining influence.

2.2   *Complete the chart with the different forms of the words.*

	Noun	Verb	Adjective	Adverb
1.	catastrophe	X		X
2.		X	generous	generously
3.	inheritance		X	X
4.	reward	X		X
5.		X	wealthy	X

PART 3: SKILLS FOR SPEAKING

3.1 *Read the paragraph. Use the relative pronouns from the box to fill in the blanks.*

that	when	where	which	~~who~~	whom	whose

The American Red Cross was founded in 1881 by Clara Barton, a nurse ____who____

had served on the battlefield during the Civil War. It is a charitable organization

_____ mission is to respond to national disasters _____ threaten thousands
     1.   **2.**

of lives. Many times _____ the government has needed assistance, the
                          3.

American Red Cross has come to its aid. For example, in 1993 the Red Cross

provided food and shelter to thousands of people in the Midwest, an area

_____ floods had destroyed thousands of homes.
     4.

3.2 CD 🔊 *Listen to the lists in the sentences. Check (✔) U if the list is unfinished and F if the*
   29 *list is finished.*

      ___✓___ U   _____ F

1. _____ U   _____ F

2. _____ U   _____ F

3. _____ U   _____ F

3.3   *Read the paragraph. Fill in the blanks with phrases from the box.*

above all	~~is also important~~	of least concern
aside from that	not a priority	the top priority

A: It's the first time I've bought a house. I have no idea what to look for.

B: Well, you can start by thinking about where you want to live, what the house looks like, and, of course, how much it costs.

A: I want to live in a neighborhood that has good transportation because I hate to drive.

B: So that's a good start.

A: But I'm going to be living in this house for at least ten years so what it looks like ___is also important___.

B: You have to make a lot of decisions when you're buying a house. What about cost? Usually that's everyone's first concern.

A: Believe it or not, money is _____ since I just got that huge
     1.
inheritance.

B: That's the first time I've heard that!

A: So I have to decide between the neighborhood and what the house looks like.

Now that I think about it, _____ is the neighborhood. It has to
     2.

have a good transportation system, but _____, it has to be safe.
     3.

PART 4: SPEAKING

4.1 *Say one of the things that the woman from Part 1.2 had to make a decision about. Say whether it is a high or low priority. You may listen again to Part 1.2.*

4.2 *Say what your priorities would be if you had to make the decisions that the woman had to make.*

4.3 *Retelling a Story*

Speak for 1–2 minutes. Tell the story of the woman who received an anonymous donation. Here are some things you could include:

- the situation she was in before she received the money from the anonymous donor
- the decisions she had to make
- the reasons for her decisions
- how her life changed

- Take notes.
- Use the correct relative pronouns in adjective clauses.
- Use proper intonation in lists.
- Use vocabulary for prioritizing and ranking ideas.
- Use the vocabulary and grammar from Unit 6.

Unit 6 Vocabulary Words				
anonymous	cause	contributions	generous	passion
benefactor	charitable	donate	inherit	rewarding
catastrophe	charity	donors	inheritance	wealth
catastrophic	contribute	generosity	motivate	wealthy

Unit 6 Grammar: Adjective Clauses
• Some people make only donations **which** are tax deductible. • A donor **whose** identity was anonymous helped a young single mother. • The government called on the Red Cross at a time **when** there was a flood in the Midwest. • The Red Cross helps in places **where** disasters have struck.

Achievement Tests
Unit 7

Name: _____

Date: _____

PART I: LISTENING

1.1 CD 7 ⟨30⟩ *Listen to the beginning of a news report. Check (✔) the best prediction of what the listening is about. There is only one right answer.*

_____ **A.** how to make parents satisfied

_____ **B.** whether homework is too hard or too easy

_____ **C.** what good and bad effects of homework are

_____ **D.** why students complain about doing homework

1.2 CD 7 ⟨31⟩ *Now listen to the entire news report. Use the information to choose the correct answers. Check (✔) the answers.*

1. This report is mainly about _____.

_____ **A.** studies about homework

_____ **B.** parent-teacher conferences

_____ **C.** students' worries about tests

_____ **D.** concerns about tired students

2. Who is the reporter talking to?

_____ **A.** students

_____ **B.** teachers

_____ **C.** parents

_____ **D.** researchers

3. Ms. Kim believes that _____.

_____ **A.** students should have homework

_____ **B.** homework is not good for children

_____ **C.** teachers give students difficult homework

_____ **D.** parents should discuss homework with teachers

4. Why can't Camilla pay attention in school?

_____ **A.** Her parents make her stay up late.

_____ **B.** She has problems focusing on things.

_____ **C.** She is too tired from doing homework.

_____ **D.** Her father and mother don't get along.

5. The survey done by the University of Michigan indicates that
   _____.

   _____ **A.** family meals have a bad effect on children's homework

   _____ **B.** homework should be done after the family finishes dinner

   _____ **C.** homework is not more important than family meals

   _____ **D.** too much homework makes it difficult for families to eat together

6. With which of the following statements would the National Association of Educational Progress most likely agree?

   _____ **A.** Homework is the foundation for students' success in the future.

   _____ **B.** Elementary school children should not be given very much homework.

   _____ **C.** Only high school students should be given a large amount of homework.

   _____ **D.** Standardized tests are the only way to measure student performance.

1.3 🔘 *Listen to the excerpt from "Effects of Homework on Family Life" from* NorthStar: Listening and Speaking 4, *Unit 7. Use the information from this listening and the listening from Part 1.2 to complete the activity. Check (✔) the survey that each person would be pleased with. If you do not have enough evidence, do not check either column.*

	National Association of Educational Progress	University of Michigan
Margot Adler		
Cecilia Bluer		✓
Joyce Epstein		
Robert Martino		
Chris Roberts		
Steven Russo		

PART 2: VOCABULARY

2.1 *Read the conversation. Use the words and phrases from the box to fill in the blanks.*
Not all the words and phrases will be used.

accountable	distraught	monitor	sacrifice
demanding	duty	pays off	way over the top

A: I'm worried about students these days. I think the amount of homework they

get is way too _____.
   1.

B: I agree. My daughter will stay up until 11 doing homework, and she gets so

_____ if she hasn't finished everything. I don't see how it
   2.

_____ in the end if she's too tired to concentrate in class the
   3.

next day.

A: And the demands on the parents are _____. How am I supposed
   4.

to have time to help with her art projects, math homework, language classes?

I don't even understand half of her homework. In the end, all I can do is

_____ her to see that she completes the assignments. I really can't
   5.

be expected to do them with her.

2.2 *Match the words and phrases in Column A with their definitions in Column B. Write the letter of the definition on the line. Not all the definitions will be used.*

Column A	Column B
_____ **1.** tangible	**A.** the basis on which beliefs develop
_____ **2.** fluctuate	**B.** a rite of passage
_____ **3.** advocates	**C.** something concrete; something measurable
_____ **4.** ritual	**D.** fluid; unformed
_____ **5.** foundation	**E.** someone who speaks against something
	F. change from one level to another
	G. people who publicly support something
	H. an action that is done regularly

PART 3: SKILLS FOR SPEAKING

3.1 *Read the sentences. Use the causative verbs from the box and the words in parentheses to fill in the blanks. Use each verb only once.*

get	have	help	let	~~make~~

I hate to do my homework, but my mom ___*makes me do*___ it before I can
                                           (me, do)
go out and play.

1. I don't understand my math homework, but my dad doesn't understand it

either, so he can't _____ it.
                                   (me, do)

2. This study says that parents should not tell their children when to do their

homework. They should _____ on their own.
                             (their children, decide)

3. My son never wants to do his homework. I don't know what I can do to

_____ it without complaining.
                      (him, do)

4. When you see Helga, would you _____ to my office?
                                       (her, come)

3.2 (CD7 33) *Listen to the sentences. Circle the **unstressed** vowel in the underlined words.*

What is the (e)ffect of too much homework on students?

1. Completing homework assignments is said to improve a student's <u>self-esteem</u>.

2. I just had to give her <u>mental</u> health days.

3. I think the <u>amount</u> of homework that elementary students get is ridiculous.

3.3 *Read the pairs of sentences. If the sentences are connected with a phrase that restates what is said, circle the phrase that is used. If the sentences are not connected with a phrase that restates what is said, do not circle anything.*

Well don't get me wrong. I *absolutely* feel that homework is necessary. (What I mean is) that the amount of homework is way too demanding.

1. Is there any tangible evidence that schools are giving too much homework? To put it another way, can we really believe what the research says?

2. I agree. In fact, I think this might have the opposite effect.

3. When my wife and I get home after work, one of us cooks dinner and the other monitors Camilla to make sure she finishes her assignments. What this means is that we have no time to be a family anymore.

PART 4: SPEAKING

4.1 *Say one thing that the reporter from Part 1.2 says about research done on the effects of homework on students. You may listen again to Part 1.2.*

4.2 *Restate what you said to make it clearer.*

4.3 *Discussing Homework*

Speak for 1–2 minutes. Talk about whether students are given too much homework either in your country or in the United States. What are some of the positive or negative effects of this?

- Take notes.
- Use expressions for restating for clarity.
- Use the vocabulary and grammar from Unit 7.

Unit 7 Vocabulary Words				
accountable	demanding	fluctuate	pay off	self-esteem
advocate	distraught	foundation	ritual	tangible
come to mind	duty	monitor	sacrifice	way over the top

Unit 7 Grammar: Causative Verbs

- Some teachers **make students do** too much homework.
- If I don't understand my English assignment, my friend **helps me (to) do** it.
- Will you **let me look** at your notes after class?
- How can we **get the schools to assign** less homework?

Achievement Tests
Unit 8

Name: _____

Date: _____

PART 1: LISTENING

1.1 🎵 CD7 34 *Listen to the beginning of a report on an American phenomenon. Check (✔) the best prediction of what the listening is about. There is only one right answer.*

_____ **A.** Americans' love of Starbucks coffee

_____ **B.** Starbucks' gain in the American market

_____ **C.** The effects of Starbucks on American cities

_____ **D.** Reasons for Starbucks' success in America

1.2 🎵 CD7 35 *Now listen to the entire interview. Use the information to choose the correct answers. Check (✔) the answers.*

1. The reporter is explaining _____.

_____ **A.** who supports Starbucks' business

_____ **B.** why businesses are more casual

_____ **C.** what social changes have occurred

_____ **D.** which social groups prefer Starbucks

2. According to the listening, what is one reason Americans like Starbucks?

_____ **A.** The drinks are not fattening.

_____ **B.** The coffee is not expensive.

_____ **C.** No one makes them leave.

_____ **D.** People often feel pressured.

3. What is one reason why there is such a demand for places like Starbucks?

_____ **A.** The coffee is relatively inexpensive.

_____ **B.** The work environment has changed.

_____ **C.** Businesses give people longer coffee breaks.

_____ **D.** Peoples tastes have become more sophisticated.

4. What was the customer's reason for coming to Starbucks?

_____ **A.** He felt his office was too rigid.

_____ **B.** He wanted to go someplace to cool off.

_____ **C.** He needed to get away from the office.

_____ **D.** He could stay and work while he was there.

5. How did the customer most likely feel before he came to Starbucks?

_____ **A.** hungry

_____ **B.** surprised

_____ **C.** unappreciated

_____ **D.** overwhelmed

6. What changes will probably occur in the way people will work?

_____ **A.** Most employees will work from home.

_____ **B.** More people will do their work at Starbucks.

_____ **C.** The number of unemployed people will increase.

_____ **D.** A larger number of people will work for Starbucks.

1.3 ᴄᴅ 7 *Listen to the excerpt from "French Sandwiches" from* NorthStar: Listening and
       36 Speaking 4, *Unit 8. Use the information from this listening and the listening from
       Part 1.2 to complete the activity. If a change was not mentioned in either of the
       listenings, do not put a check in the table.*

Changes	French lifestyle	American lifestyle
workforce is almost 50% women	✓	
more time for lunch breaks		
more men have white collar jobs		
more workers who don't work directly for a company		
not enough space in office buildings		
a greater variety of take-out food available		
offices are more casual		

PART 2: VOCABULARY

2.1 *Read the sentences. Use the words and phrases from the box to fill in the blanks. Not all the words and phrases will be used.*

breadwinners	phenomenon	take with a grain of salt
core	put it on the back burner	the salt of the earth
delicacy	shift	witnessed
intimate	sit-down	workforce
overrun	stacked	

1. The latest _____ is the coffee house that offers wireless Internet.

2. He exaggerates a lot. Whatever he tells you, you have to _____.

3. You see these coffee houses on every corner; the city is _____ with them.

4., 5. As companies hire fewer full-time employees, you see a _____ in the _____ toward freelance workers.

6. You're very busy at work. You can go on vacation later. You should _____.

7. Recently we have _____ a change in the atmosphere of the workplace.

8. At the very _____ of a business are its employees.

9. Paul's refrigerator was _____ with bags of coffee beans. He had bought every variety of coffee that Starbucks sold.

10. Every week the chef prepared a new _____ to please the restaurant's customers.

PART 3: SKILLS FOR SPEAKING

3.1 *Read the sentences. Check (✔) A if the phrasal verb is used correctly and B if it is used incorrectly.*

People were lined up outside the new Starbucks.

___✓___ **A.** correct   _____ **B.** incorrect

1. Could you pick a double grande cappuccino with whipped cream and cinnamon up since you're going to Starbucks?

_____ **A.** correct   _____ **B.** incorrect

2. People used to think that fast food would never catch it on in France.

_____ **A.** correct   _____ **B.** incorrect

3. It's such a sunny day, so I don't want to eat lunch inside. Let's take it out to the park, OK?

_____ **A.** correct   _____ **B.** incorrect

4. Watch how I make this latte. Now you try out it.

_____ **A.** correct   _____ **B.** incorrect

3.2 CD 1 ③⑦ *Listen to the sentences as you read them. The underlined words contain one of the following sounds: /uw/ /ʊ/ /ə/ /a/ /ow/. Check (✔) the sound you hear.*

I am <u>done</u> with my homework.

_____ **A.** /uw/   ___✓___ **C.** /ə/   _____ **E.** /ow/

_____ **B.** /ʊ/   _____ **D.** /a/

1. She had a <u>job</u> at a coffee house.

_____ **A.** /uw/   _____ **C.** /ə/   _____ **E.** /ow/

_____ **B.** /ʊ/   _____ **D.** /a/

2. The French now eat fast <u>food</u>.

_____ **A.** /uw/   _____ **C.** /ə/   _____ **E.** /ow/

_____ **B.** /ʊ/   _____ **D.** /a/

3. The fast food tastes very <u>good</u>.

_____ **A.** /uw/   _____ **C.** /ə/   _____ **E.** /ow/

_____ **B.** /ʊ/   _____ **D.** /a/

T-47

3.3 *The instructions are missing phrases used to focus the listener's attention. Use the phrases from the box to fill in the blanks.*

Look at what I'm holding

Notice what I'm doing

See this

This ingredient is very special

Watch how I

~~Watch me carefully~~

Instructions:

I'm going to show you how to make a garden-fresh salad. First you'll need lettuce

tomatoes, mushrooms, carrots, and anything else you'd like to add. Now

___watch me carefully___. I need to clean the vegetables. _____? This is a

1.

special brush used to clean mushrooms. _____ very carefully brush

2.

any dirt off the mushrooms because they can be delicate. _____ next.

3.

I'm using a sharp knife to slice the tomatoes, but I hold the tomato like this so I

don't cut myself. When everything is cleaned and cut, put it all in a big bowl. Mix all

the ingredients with your fingers or another utensil, add dressing, and voilà! You

have a delicious and healthy salad.

PART 4: SPEAKING

4.1 *Name one reason why places like Starbucks have become so popular. You may listen again to Part 1.2.*

4.2 *Say one thing that people order at Starbucks.*

4.3 *Discussing an American Phenomenon*

Speak for 1–2 minutes. Explain why your city or town does or does not have places like Starbucks. If it does, tell whether these places are popular or not and why this is so.

- Take notes.
- Make a list of other places like Starbucks.
- When presenting, try to use phrasal verbs.
- Use the vocabulary and grammar from Unit 8.

Unit 8 Vocabulary Words			
breadwinners	intimate	phenomenon	stacked
core	make up	shift	witnessed
delicacy	overrun	sit-down (meal)	workforce
Unit 8 Grammar: Phrasal Verbs			
• Fast food **caught on** in France. • You should **try this out**. • I'm here to **pick up** the sandwich I ordered.			

Achievement Tests
Unit 9

Name: _____

Date: _____

PART 1: LISTENING

1.1 CD7 38 *Listen to the beginning of a debate. Check (✔) the best prediction of what the listening is about. There is only one right answer.*

_____ **A.** how many immigrants need to learn English

_____ **B.** how immigrants should be taught in school

_____ **C.** why immigrant children should be allowed in our schools

_____ **D.** why immigrants should learn English

1.2 CD7 39 *Now listen to the entire debate. Use the information to choose the correct answers. Check (✔) the answers.*

1. This is a debate between _____.

   _____ **A.** someone who thinks immigrants should be assimilated as quickly as possible and someone who thinks immigrants should be in mainstream classes

   _____ **B.** someone in favor of multilingual classes and someone who thinks immigrants should be in mainstream classes

   _____ **C.** a student who is in a multilingual class and a student who is in a mainstream class

   _____ **D.** a teacher from a multilingual class and a teacher from a mainstream class

2. What happens in a multilingual classroom?

   _____ **A.** Students learn to assimilate to American classes.

   _____ **B.** Students go to a mainstream class for their English lesson.

   _____ **C.** Students from many countries learn in a cooperative way.

   _____ **D.** Students learn to speak the languages that other immigrants speak.

3. Students in multicultural classrooms most likely _____.

   _____ **A.** want to learn English

   _____ **B.** have only had classes taught in English

   _____ **C.** speak only their native language in class

   _____ **D.** learn best outside of school

4. The teachers in multicultural classrooms _____.

_____ **A.** take students out of mainstream classes

_____ **B.** do not want their students to assimilate

_____ **C.** do not teach classes in English

_____ **D.** let students speak their native languages

5. After the debate, Mr. Green and Ms. Anopolis will most likely

_____.

_____ **A.** agree that immigrant students should be in mainstream classes

_____ **B.** disagree about how immigrant students should be taught

_____ **C.** agree that immigrant students should be in multicultural classes

_____ **D.** be unsure about how immigrant students should be taught

🎧 CD 1 **40** *Listen again to a part of the debate. Then answer the question.*

6. Why does Mr. Green say, "Hang on a minute, are you saying that they're allowed to speak in their native tongues?"?

_____ **A.** He wants Ms. Anopolis to stop speaking.

_____ **B.** He is disagreeing with what Ms. Anopolis said.

_____ **C.** He is asking Mr. Haas, the moderator, to stop the debate.

_____ **D.** He is thinking about what Ms. Anopolis said before he responds.

1.3 🎧 CD 1 **41** *Listen to the excerpt from "A World within a School" from* NorthStar: Listening and Speaking 4, *Unit 9. Use the information from this listening and the listening from Part 1.2 to complete the activity. Check (✔) the lines next to the statements that teachers from International High School and Mr. Green do not agree on.*

Immigrants should:

___✓___ **A.** assimilate as fast as possible

_____ **B.** learn to speak English

_____ **C.** feel like other students in mainstream schools

_____ **D.** interpret lessons to new classmates

_____ **E.** keep their native language

_____ **F.** learn from each other

PART 2: VOCABULARY

2.1 *Read the paragraph. Use the words and phrases from the box to fill in the blanks.*

assimilate	mainstream	relieved	tight-knit
bone up on	native tongues	support	unique

Some people believe that immigrants who want to _____ into a new
                                                    1.

culture should not use their _____. They also think that immigrant
                                        2.

students should be put directly into _____ classes. However, many
                                              3.

people who have come to the U.S. from _____ communities do not
                                                4.

want to give up their native identities. They rely on other members of their culture

to _____ them while they are coping with problems they encounter
        5.

in the new environment.

2.2 *Check (✔) A if the word or phrase has a positive meaning, B if the word has a negative meaning, and C if the meaning is neutral (neither positive or negative).*

1. flourish   _____ **A.** positive   _____ **B.** negative   _____ **C.** neutral

2. uprooted   _____ **A.** positive   _____ **B.** negative   _____ **C.** neutral

3. suppressed   _____ **A.** positive   _____ **B.** negative   _____ **C.** neutral

4. niche   _____ **A.** positive   _____ **B.** negative   _____ **C.** neutral

5. intimidated   _____ **A.** positive   _____ **B.** negative   _____ **C.** neutral

PART 3: SKILLS FOR SPEAKING

3.1 *Complete the sentences with the correct form of the verb in parentheses.*

A: How long <u>have you been attending</u> an international school?
        (you, attend)

B: Only one year. I came to this school last June. While I _____ to
                                                                                                    1. (go)

regular school, I really felt uncomfortable because I _____.
                                                                                           2. (not fit in)

Since I've been at this school, my attitude _____ so much. I
                                                                                   3. (change)

like my classmates and the teachers. This semester I _____
                                                                                              4. (take)

three classes and I like all of them.

3.2 (CD 7 / 42) *Listen to the sentences. Check (✔) the sound you hear.*

You've really <u>adjusted</u> well to <u>international</u> school.

adjusted

_____ **A.** /ʃ/   _____ **B.** /ʒ/   _____ **C.** /tʃ/   ✓ **D.** /dʒ/

1. international

_____ **A.** /ʃ/   _____ **B.** /ʒ/   _____ **C.** /tʃ/   _____ **D.** /dʒ/

2. I <u>generally</u> don't watch TV before I've finished my homework, but today is a special <u>occasion</u>.

generally

_____ **A.** /ʃ/   _____ **B.** /ʒ/   _____ **C.** /tʃ/   _____ **D.** /dʒ/

3. occasion

_____ **A.** /ʃ/   _____ **B.** /ʒ/   _____ **C.** /tʃ/   _____ **D.** /dʒ/

3.3 *Check (✔) the lines that begin with phrases used to hesitate before answering a question.*

✓ **A.** Let me think for a minute before I give you an answer.

_____ **B.** I think so, but I don't know for sure.

_____ **C.** Maybe you're right, but I still don't agree with you.

_____ **D.** Well, let's see. The report says that there were three studies.

_____ **E.** I'm not sure. I'll have to think about that.

_____ **F.** OK. I'll let you know.

_____ **G.** Hang on a minute. I think that he's right.

PART 4: SPEAKING

4.1 *State one advantage of mainstream classes for immigrants, according to Part 1.2. You may listen again to Part 1.2.*

4.2 *State one advantage of multicultural classes for immigrants.*

4.3 *Giving an Opinion*

Speak for 1–2 minutes. Say whether you think that mainstream classes or multicultural classes are better for immigrants. Explain why.

- Take notes.
- Discuss the pros and cons of mainstream classes.
- Discuss the pros and cons of multicultural classes.
- State your opinion and support it with information from Part 1.2.
- Use the vocabulary and grammar from Unit 9.

Unit 9 Vocabulary Words			
assimilate	intimidating	relieved	tight-knit
bone up on	mainstream	set apart	unique
flourish	native tongue	suppressed	uprooted

Unit 9 Grammar: Contrasting Verb Tenses
• Last year Lim **went** to the International High School, but now **he's going** to a mainstream high school. • Dmitri **was learning** English, but he **didn't forget** his native language. • Marian **has been teaching** English for five years, but **she's thinking** about doing something else next year.

Achievement Tests
Unit 10

Name: _____

Date: _____

PART 1: LISTENING

1.1 *CD7* *Listen to the beginning of a news report. Check (✔) the best prediction of what the* **43** *listening is about. There is only one right answer.*

_____ **A.** the dangers of car alarms

_____ **B.** the effectiveness of car alarms

_____ **C.** laws passed against car alarms

_____ **D.** people's concerns about their car alarms

1.2 *CD7* *Now listen to the entire report. Use the information to choose the correct answers.* **44** *Check (✔) the answers.*

1. This report is mainly about _____.

_____ **A.** how citizens can ban car alarms

_____ **B.** what level of noise is safe for humans

_____ **C.** why parents are worried about car alarms

_____ **D.** what lawmakers are doing about car alarms

2. A study found that children living in areas with high levels of noise _____.

_____ **A.** had lower reading skills

_____ **B.** showed low attention levels

_____ **C.** reported elevated blood pressure

_____ **D.** suffered from increased heart rate

3. Ms. Carera is worried about the noise level of _____.

_____ **A.** sirens

_____ **B.** planes

_____ **C.** city traffic

_____ **D.** car alarms

(continued on next page)

4. One can assume that a safe level of noise is _____.

    _____ **A.** less than 85 decibels

    _____ **B.** 90 decibels or less

    _____ **C.** around 120 decibels

    _____ **D.** approximately 60 decibels

5. The group Parents to Silence Car Alarms wants to _____.

    _____ **A.** ban car alarms

    _____ **B.** study the effects of car alarms

    _____ **C.** punish people who have car alarms

    _____ **D.** make owners of car alarms pay a fine

6. Members of Parents to Silence Car Alarms will most likely _____.

    _____ **A.** talk to the makers of car alarms

    _____ **B.** send letters to government officials

    _____ **C.** have their children's hearing tested

    _____ **D.** measure the noise level in their neighborhood

1.3 CD 1 / 45 *Listen to the excerpt from "Noise in the City" from* NorthStar: Listening and Speaking 4, *Unit 10. Use the information from this listening and the listening from Part 1.2 to complete the activity. Write the letter of the effect of car alarms under the name of the person who discussed it. Not all effects will be used.*

Senator Catherine Abate	Jonathan Dworsky
B	

A. poor reading skills

B. ~~loss of hearing~~

C. difficulty paying attention

D. decrease in heart rate

E. increase in stress hormones

F. loss in ability to work

PART 2: VOCABULARY

2.1   *Read the paragraph. Use the words and phrases from the box to fill in the blanks. Not all words will be used.*

banned	jolted	shrill	towed
drive you crazy	pay a fine	sick and tired	vibrations
fed up with	prompted	sirens	wail
irritated	retaliatory		

Are you _____ the noisy city? _____ of being
           1.   **2.**

_____ awake by the screech of a car alarm at 2 A.M.? And just
        3.

when you fall back to sleep, you are awakened by the _____ of
                                        4.

ten _____ all heading to a fire two blocks away. Then don't just feel
        5.

_____ and helpless. Join the Citizens for Peace and Quiet. We
        6.

are meeting to write a letter to our senator proposing that the first time

someone's car alarm goes on for more than 3 minutes, the owner of the car will

have to _____ of fifty dollars. If we continue to be awakened by the
          7.

_____ noise of alarms going off in the middle of the night, we
        8.

propose that all car alarms be _____. Don't let our noisy streets
                    9.

_____. Join us Wednesday at 7:00 P.M. and make your voice be heard.
    10.

PART 3: SKILLS FOR SPEAKING

3.1   *Fill in the blanks with the form of the verb that best completes the sentence.*

SUE: I can't wait to get away from all of this noise. Tonight I'm leaving for Hawaii.

Tomorrow I ____will be lying____ on the beach.
(lie)

TOM: You went there last year, didn't you?

SUE: I go every year. After this trip I _____ there 8 times.
1. (be)

JOHN: Can you come to the meeting at 8 P.M. tomorrow?

GORDON: Sorry, but I have a test the next day. I _____ all night.
2. (study)

SARAH: Did you see my new phone? I can watch movies on it while I'm talking.

ANNE: They come up with something new every month. By next year, they

_____ a phone that cleans your house.
3. (invent)

SARAH: You're probably right, but I _____ this one for a long time.
4. (still use)

3.2   🔘 *Listen to the sentences. Check (✔) the line in front of the word that is stressed.*
CD 7
46

I handed the paper <u>in</u> <u>on</u> Wednesday <u>at</u> 4:00.

___✔___ **A.** in   _____ **B.** on   _____ **C.** at

1. The thunder set all the car alarms <u>off</u> <u>at</u> the same time <u>on</u> Sunday.

_____ **A.** off   _____ **B.** at   _____ **C.** on

2. Everyone <u>on</u> the block is fed <u>up</u> <u>with</u> the noise.

_____ **A.** on   _____ **B.** up   _____ **C.** with

3. Do you know where to get my laundry?

Go to the cleaner's <u>on</u> the corner and pick it <u>up</u> <u>for</u> me, please.

_____ **A.** on   _____ **B.** up   _____ **C.** for

3.3 *Check (✔) the sentences that express frustration.*

  ✓   **A.** I'm so fed up with the noise I could scream.

_____ **B.** I'm not crazy about the noise, but you expect it in the city.

_____ **C.** You're driving me crazy! Could you please turn the TV down?

_____ **D.** I'm so annoyed when people let their cell phones ring at work.

_____ **E.** Some people get annoyed with this music, but I just can't get enough of it.

_____ **F.** That music really gets under my skin.

PART 4: SPEAKING

4.1 *Say one thing that bothers people about living in the city, according to Part 1.2. You may listen again to Part 1.2.*

4.2 *Say that what you said in 4.1 bothers you. Include an expression of frustration when you say it.*

4.3 *Solving a Problem*

Speak for 1–2 minutes. Imagine that you live in a neighborhood where car alarms frequently go off, and you and your neighbors have been woken up several times by their irritating noise. Talk about what you would say to your neighbors about this problem and what you might do about it.

- Take notes.
- Make a list of problems and possible solutions.
- Use the future perfect and the future progressive.
- Use expressions of frustration.
- Use the vocabulary and grammar from Unit 10.

Unit 10 Vocabulary Words				
banned	irritated	pay a fine	shrill	towed
drive you crazy	jolted	prompted	sick and tired	vibrations
fed up with	offense	retaliatory	sirens	wail

Unit 10 Grammar: Future Perfect and Future Progressive
[future perfect] • By the time you call 911, the car alarm **will have stopped.** • The mother worries that as the neighborhood gets more   [future progressive] crowded, they **will be living** in an even noisier environment.

Achievement Tests Audioscript

UNIT 1

1.1

Ms. Hall: Good evening. This is Lauren Hall on *Face-to-Face*. Tonight we'll hear from Professor John Gibson, a sociologist who specializes in media and society, and Mr. Daniel Tucker, the producer of CND's *Evening News*. Tonight's topic: television news.

So, you're probably asking, what's the issue? We all check the headlines before heading to work or race home to catch the news before dinner. TV news has become a part of our daily diet. Now some experts are suggesting that a daily diet of the nightly news can actually be bad for your mental health.

1.2

Ms. Hall: Good evening. This is Lauren Hall on *Face-to-Face*. Tonight we'll hear from Professor John Gibson, a sociologist who specializes in media and society, and Mr. Daniel Tucker, the producer of CND's *Evening News*. Tonight's topic: television news.

So, you're probably asking, what's the issue? We all check the headlines before heading to work or race home to catch the news before dinner. TV news has become a part of our daily diet. Now some experts are suggesting that a daily diet of the nightly news can actually be bad for your mental health.

Gentlemen, thank you for being with us tonight. We'll begin with Professor Gibson.

Prof. Gibson: Well, I've actually just finished writing a book about this topic called *No News Can Be Good News*.

Mr. Tucker: Sounds interesting.

Prof. Gibson: Well, I'll send you a copy. Anyway, I think it's essential to be informed about what's happening in the world, but like Ms. Hall said, we turn on the TV every morning or evening to get our information. We're *addicted* to television news.

Mr. Tucker: Perhaps, but is that such a bad thing? In my opinion, you have to be plugged in or you won't know what's going on in the world today.

Prof. Gibson: But are viewers getting the information they need from the news on television? The problems of today are very complex, but the coverage of the problems is very superficial. In a thirty-minute program, each story is covered in about three and a half minutes. It's impossible to put things into perspective. The same amount of time is devoted to the healthcare crisis in this country as it is to the latest Hollywood divorce.

Mr. Tucker: Well, it's really the responsibility of the viewer to decide what's important. We just show what seems to be newsworthy on that day.

Prof. Gibson: Exactly. That's another problem. How can a viewer make a connection between the developments of a story? Each day a different story is presented, regardless of its importance.

Ms. Hall: I'm afraid that's all the time we have. Thank you, gentlemen, for sharing your thoughts with us tonight.

1.2, Question 6

Mr. Tucker: Perhaps, but is that such a bad thing? In my opinion, you have to be plugged in or you won't know what's going on in the world today.

Prof. Gibson: But are viewers getting the information they need from the news on television? The problems of today are very complex, but the coverage of the problems is very superficial.

1.3

Margot Adler: When I was a kid, I loved a baseball novel called *The Southpaw*. It was the first volume of a baseball quartet written by Mark Harris. One of the books, *Bang the Drum Slowly*, became a famous movie. What I only learned recently was that Harris wrote a long essay in the *New York Times* back in the early '70s in which he said reading a daily newspaper was a useless addiction. Thirty years later, Harris still believes that.

Mark Harris: Somebody gets up in the morning and the first thing he or she has to do is get that newspaper, and then they have to have it with the coffee and it's kind of two addictions go together.

Margot Adler: John Sommerville is a professor of history at the University of Florida and the author of works on the history of religion in England. He has written a book called *How the News Makes Us Dumb: The Death of Wisdom in an Information Society,* and he argues that bias is fixable, but the real problem isn't. His main argument against daily news is the daily part. He argues that dailiness, as he puts it, chops everything down to a standard size, making it harder to get perspective, to know the appropriate size and scale of any problem.

John Sommerville: That one feature by itself, regardless of the competence and the professionalism of the journalist, it's lethal. If dumbness is the inability to make connections, logical connections and historical connections, then you can see how taking in everything on a daily basis is going to hurt our ability to make the connections.

3.2

John has been trying to stop watching the news. This week has been easy. He's watched the news six days instead of seven. Luckily, his friends are going to help him continue with this plan. Next week he'll only watch the news five days of the week. His friends have promised to distract him, so he won't be tempted to turn on the TV.

UNIT 2

1.1

Administrative Assistant: OK, John. You can see Professor Kim now.

Professor Kim: Please, sit down. So have you had a chance to look around the campus?

John: Yes. I got to talk to some of the students, and I think I would really get along well here.

Prof. Kim: Good. Well, we're very impressed with your essay. But we like to get to know prospective students a little better before we make our final decision.

1.2

Administrative Assistant: OK, John. You can see Professor Kim now.

Professor Kim: Please, sit down. So have you had a chance to look around the campus?

John: Yes. I got to talk to some of the students, and I think I would really get along well here.

Prof. Kim: Good. Well, we're very impressed with your essay. But we like to get to know prospective students a little better before we make our final decision.

It looks like you've had to overcome quite a few obstacles to get this far. I used to live near your neighborhood and it . . .

John: Yes, it's still in a poverty zone. That's actually one reason I've always wanted to go to college. You see, most of my friends dropped out of high school either to get a job or because they just didn't see the point.

Prof. Kim: By that you mean . . . ?

John: Well, not many people have jobs in my neighborhood. Most haven't had any training, and, then, there's still a lot of discrimination.

Prof. Kim: I see you haven't let those limitations get in the way.

John: No, in fact I recognized that getting an education was really the only way out. For a while I thought going to college was just a dream. But I found out about a scholarship, so lack of money is not really a problem anymore.

Prof. Kim: Do you know what you'd like to study?

John: Education. It's kind of a dream of mine to go back and teach kids that they have options. They don't have to stay in the same situation they're in now.

Prof. Kim: Seems like that's going to be a tough job.

John: Yeah, but I really know what these kids are faced with. A lot of them miss school because of family problems. And I don't know the numbers, but I bet over half have some kind of learning disability.

Prof. Kim: You've chosen a very challenging career. Now do you have any questions you'd like to ask about Simpson College?

1.3

Richard Van Ornum: When I was little, I dreamed I was flying. Each night, I was up in the air, though never over the same landscape. Sometimes in the confusion of early morning, I would wake up thinking it was true and I'd leap off my bed, expecting to soar out of the window. Of course, I always hit the ground, but not before remembering that I'd been dreaming. I would realize that no real person could fly and I'd collapse on the floor, crushed by the weight of my own limitations. Eventually, my dreams of flying stopped. I think I stopped dreaming completely.

After that, my earliest memory is of learning to count to 100. After baths, my mother would perch me on the sink and dry me, as I tried to make it to 100 without a mistake. I had to be lifted onto the sink. An accident with a runaway truck when I was four had mangled my left leg, leaving scars that stood out, puckered white against my skin. Looking at the largest of my scars in the mirror, I imagined that it was an eagle. It wasn't fair, I thought, I had an eagle on my leg, but I couldn't fly. I could hardly walk, and the crutches hurt my arms.

Bob Edwards: The college essay of Richard Van Ornum, who attends the Seven Hills School in Cincinnati.

UNIT 3

1.1

Donald: Hey Sonia, I went to the lecture hall, but there was no one there.

Sonia: Well, if you ever went to class, you'd know that we were meeting in Jones Hall today.

Donald: No wonder. Anyway, what'd I miss?

Sonia: We finished the unit on melatonin and . . .

Donald: What?

Sonia: Melatonin, the sleep hormone. I'll give you my notes from last week so you can catch up. Now we're starting the unit on REM sleep.

1.2

Donald: Hey Sonia, I went to the lecture hall, but there was no one there.

Sonia: Well, if you ever went to class, you'd know that we were meeting in Jones Hall today.

Donald: No wonder. Anyway, what'd I miss?

Sonia: We finished the unit on melatonin and . . .

Donald: What?

Sonia: Melatonin, the sleep hormone. I'll give you my notes from last week so you can catch up. Now we're starting the unit on REM sleep.

Donald: Boy, I'm really behind. I've missed class because I keep oversleeping.

Sonia: Sounds like you need a new alarm clock.

Donald: What I need is a good night's sleep. I've had insomnia lately and I'm so sleep-deprived. When I'm awake, I'm so cranky and irritable even I can't stand to be around myself.

Sonia: I can imagine. Your body just can't do without sleep.

Donald: Yeah, I *know*. Anyway, you said you were learning about *what*?

Sonia: REM sleep. It means, Rapid Eye Movement. R for rapid, E for eye . . .

Donald: I got it. M for movement. REM. So is it like blinking?

Sonia: No, blinking occurs when you're awake. And during REM it's your *eyes* not your *eyelids* that move.

Donald: Oh, so what *is* REM then?

Sonia: It's part of the sleep cycle. You see, you go through five stages of sleep. The fifth stage is REM sleep. During REM sleep your breathing becomes quicker and irregular, your muscles are paralyzed, and your eyes move rapidly. This is when you have the most dreams.

Donald: Since I'm not getting *any* sleep these days, I guess I'm missing out on REM sleep, then.

Sonia: Well, REM sleep is really important. If you didn't have REM sleep, you might have memory problems. Also researchers have found that if you were deprived of REM sleep, you might have trouble learning new things.

Donald: This is really interesting. I wish I hadn't missed the last two classes.

Sonia: Here. You can read over my notes.

Donald: Thanks a lot. I'll see you tomorrow.

1.2, Question 6

Donald: Hey Sonia, I went to the lecture hall, but there was no one there.

Sonia: Well, if you ever went to class, you'd know that we were meeting in Jones Hall today.

Donald: No wonder. Anyway, what'd I miss?

Sonia: We finished the unit on melatonin and . . .

Donald: What?

Sonia: Melatonin, the sleep hormone.

1.3

Michelle Trudeau: But there's also a big push from biology that makes teenagers such night owls. It comes from that mighty sleep hormone, melatonin.

Mary Carskadon: Melatonin is a wonderfully simple signal that turns on in the evening.

Michelle Trudeau: You're getting sleepy. . . .

Mary Carskadon: And it turns off in the morning.

Michelle Trudeau: And you awaken. During adolescence, melatonin isn't secreted until around 11:00 P.M., several hours later than it is in childhood. So the typical teenager

doesn't even get sleepy until that melatonin surge signals the brain that it's night, no matter how early the teen goes to bed. And the melatonin doesn't shut off until nine hours later, around 8:00 A.M. But of course most high schools start around 7:30. The result is all too evident. A teenager's body may be in the classroom, but his brain is still asleep on the pillow.

Michelle Trudeau: Reaction time, alertness, concentration, all slowed down by insufficient sleep. The Federal Department of Transportation estimates teenage drivers cause more than half of all fall-asleep crashes.

Ronald Dahl: But in addition to those straightforward effects on attention and the ability to stay awake and alert, there are more subtle effects on emotion.

Michelle Trudeau: Dahl is studying how adolescents balance their cognitive thoughts and their emotions. When tired, he says, teens are more easily frustrated, more irritable, more prone to sadness. And their performance on intellectual tasks drops.

3.2

I like to go to bed early, but my **sister** likes to stay up **late**.

1. I have insomnia during the week, but I sleep **well** on the **weekend**.
2. Daydreams occur when you're awake, whereas **nightmares** occur when you're **asleep**.
3. I have two children who **sleep** a **little** and wake **up** a **lot**.

UNIT 4

1.1

Professor: OK, so last week we were discussing whether animals possess what we consider intelligence. Let's take language as an example.

1.2

Professor: OK, so last week we were discussing whether animals possess what we consider intelligence. Let's take language as an example. Before studies had been done with animals, linguists had a theory about why only humans have language. They believed that a specific part of the brain was used for one purpose: to acquire and use language. They also thought that only the human brain was specialized for this. However, experiments from the field of psychology produced intriguing results that suggest that humans are not the only animal to possess language.

Early studies had failed to show that animals could do anything more than repeat things that they had heard a person say in a kind of rote memorization. However, in the 1960s researchers studied apes because of their superior intelligence. One well-known case is that of Koko, who is perhaps the most famous gorilla in the 20th century. That is, excluding King Kong.

Koko was socialized in a human environment. A researcher named Francine Patterson raised Koko and taught her how to communicate. But because gorillas are not physically able to vocalize words, Patterson taught Koko to use American Sign Language. When Koko was very young, she used language to ask for food or other rather basic things. Now that can be seen as simply putting words together to get a desired result. Hardly as developed as human language.

I see you have a question?

Student: So what exactly do you mean by language?

Professor: Well, for one thing, language is used in novel ways and in new contexts. For example, Patterson said that Koko invented her own term for ring, a word she had never been taught. She put together the signs for *finger* and *bracelet* to come up with her way of saying *ring*. In many other situations, Koko figured out how to communicate rather complex ideas. For example, Patterson reported that when Koko had a toothache, she told the dentist the level of her pain on a scale from 1 to 10. According to Patterson, Koko's language was so developed that she could have an argument with her human caretaker.

Koko is said to have a vocabulary of over 1,000 words. However, some scientists caution that one shouldn't be deceived into believing that vocabulary by itself is language.

1.3

Good morning. Today we'll consider whether animals are "intelligent" in the same way that humans are. Why do we say humans are intelligent? Is it because we create and use language, create art, and use tools? Because we have emotions? Because we are socialized to a particular cultural environment? Because we lie and deceive others? Do other animals do these things as well? Let's look at some recent research.

First, humans are conscious beings. When we look into a mirror, for example, we know we are seeing our own image. Can animals do the same? Well, when some apes look into a mirror for the first time, they spontaneously examine their teeth. In fact, some researchers put paint on chimps' faces when they were asleep. After waking, the chimps looked into a mirror and tried to get the paint off. Scientists say this shows self-awareness.

Second, we've also learned some intriguing things about the ability of animals to communicate, both with each other and with humans. Of course, most animals don't have the ability to vocalize words. However, some animals raised in captivity have learned to communicate with humans through computers or gestures. Actually, some apes learn hundreds of words. While some people claim that this is just rote memorization, and not true communication, studies have shown that they can ask and answer questions they have never heard before and even create new "words." For example, a gorilla named Koko saw a picture of a mask for the first time and called it an "eye hat."

UNIT 5

1.1

Host: This is *Living Today* with Pauline Falcon. Today we'll celebrate the birthday of Asención Cantez and find out how she has lived to the ripe old age of 107. Jaime Martín has traveled to the Andes Mountains, where Señora Cantez has spent her entire life in a small village.

1.2

Host: This is *Living Today* with Pauline Falcon. Today we'll celebrate the birthday of Asención Cantez and find out how she has lived to the ripe old age of 107. Jaime Martín has traveled to the Andes Mountains, where Señora Cantez has spent her entire life in a small village.

Jaime Martín: Happy birthday, Señora Cantez. How will you be celebrating today?

Sra. Cantez: I don't go in for anything special. I'll just sit outside and enjoy the fresh air.

Jaime: Will you be celebrating alone?

Sra. Cantez: I've been a widow now for 20 years, and all of my closest friends have passed away. But I live with my son's family. And tonight we'll have three generations together. It's not unusual, though. We often get together whether it's a birthday or not.

Jaime: I know this probably seems like a silly question, but what about the seniors who don't have family? Do you have any assisted living facilities?

Sra. Cantez: Those are places where families put their parents when they get old, aren't they?

Jaime: Yes, that's right.

Sra. Cantez: I believe there are some in the cities. But here the elderly are the most respected members of the community. Such a thing would never exist in this village.

Jaime: Our listeners are curious. What's your secret to longevity?

Sra. Cantez: I live a very simple life. One of the most important things for us is that we don't worry.

Jaime: I can't *imagine*. What about diet? Do you have any suggestions for the rest of us?

Sra. Cantez: It's very simple. A lot of fresh fruits and vegetables.

Jaime: So how are you feeling at the age of 107?

Sra. Cantez: I can't say I have anything to worry about. Just the normal aches and pains that anyone would expect at my age, wouldn't they?

Jaime: Amazing. 107 and nothing but a few aches and pains.

Sra. Cantez: Well, there was a little problem with my heart a few years ago. My son took me to a doctor in the city. He said it was just a small heart attack.

Jaime: Well, you certainly seem to have recovered well.

Sra. Cantez: I don't like to admit it, but I take an aspirin every day. The doctor said it would help my heart.

Jaime: So an aspirin a day, and the rest is simple—fresh air, simple food, and no worrying.

1.2, Question 5

Jaime: I know this probably seems like a silly question, but what about the seniors who don't have family. Do you have any assisted living facilities?

Sra. Cantez: Those are places where families put their parents when they get old, aren't they?

1.2, Question 6

Jaime: Amazing. 107 and nothing but a few aches and pains.

Sra. Cantez: Well, there was a little problem with my heart a few years ago. My son took me to a doctor in the city. He said it was just a small heart attack.

Jaime: Well, you certainly seem to have recovered well.

Sra. Cantez: I don't like to admit it, but I take an aspirin every day. The doctor said it would help my heart.

1.3

Madeleine Brand, host: This is *Day to Day,* from NPR News. I'm Madeleine Brand.

Alex Chadwick, host: I'm Alex Chadwick. We're a little late with this next item, an obituary for a woman who died over the weekend. Susie Potts Gibson is someone to know about anyway, because she had achieved a couple of distinctions. First, she lived to the age of 115, one of the oldest people in the world, and second, she apparently lived not just a long life, but a remarkably happy one as well. Her granddaughter, Nancy Paetz, is on the phone from her office in Huntsville, Alabama. Ms. Paetz, welcome to *Day to Day.*

Ms. Nancy Paetz: Thank you.

Chadwick: Your grandmother, Susie Potts Gibson, she was born in Mississippi. She lived in Sheffield, Alabama, in the same house for 80 years, I read, in an obituary in the *L.A. Times.* What did she think about being 115 years old?

Ms. Paetz: You know, she was very proud of it. She often referred to herself as one of the oldest people in the world, and she would constantly say, okay, so am I still one of the oldest people in the world? So that was kind of exciting for her, I think.

Chadwick: She had a secret of longevity?

Ms. Paetz: If you asked her what her secret was, she would tell you that it was probably three things. One, she lived for her pickles. She ate lots and lots of pickles.

Chadwick: Okay, pickles is one.

Ms. Paetz: And vinegar.

Chadwick: Vinegar.

Ms. Paetz: We kept, every time we visited, we had to go and buy big jars of vinegar, and big jars of pickles.

Chadwick: How did she take her vinegar?

Ms. Paetz: Well, she put it on everything. I don't think she ever just drank it, but she certainly drank the pickle juice.

Chadwick: She did?

Ms. Paetz: Oh, yes. Yes, she soaked her feet in it. She put it on any parts of her body that hurt, that was her end all, be all.

Chadwick: All right, pickles, vinegar, and number three . . .

Ms. Paetz: And number three was she didn't take medicines unless she absolutely had to, until the last few years when she really was getting old in her mind, they made her take some of the medicines that she needed in the nursing home, but she was the kind that would never take an aspirin for a headache. She figured it'd go away, and it couldn't be good for you.

Chadwick: She lived alone to the age of 106, and then moved into some sort of assisted living facility there, I read. Weren't you all a little anxious about having your grandmother living on her own, independently, at an age over 100?

Ms. Paetz: Yes, especially since she was so far away, but she's always been a very strong woman and a very stubborn woman, and she would not even allow the conversation to be held, and in fact, when it came time for her to move, she called us on the phone, and she says, okay, the time has come. I've sold my house. I've got me a room. Come move me.

Chadwick: She took care of all the arrangements herself?

Ms. Paetz: Oh, yes. Oh, yes. There was never anything wrong with her mind or her physical abilities.

Chadwick: Nancy Paetz, mourning, but mainly remembering her grandmother, Susie Potts Gibson who died over this last weekend in Alabama at the age of 115. Nancy Paetz, thank you and our sympathies to you.

Ms. Paetz: Thank you very much.

3.2

Did you hear the interview about the 115-year-old woman who just died?
1. Do you mean Susie Potts Gibson?
2. Yeah. That's her name. Why do you ask?
3. I thought it was so interesting. What do you think?

UNIT 6

1.1

Host: This is Pat Miles on the *Afternoon Update.* Last week we heard from two people whose generosity has touched the lives of thousands. While over 50% of Americans donate to charitable causes, these two donors, who wish to remain anonymous, have chosen to make direct contributions to individuals in need. I hope they are tuned in this afternoon because they will hear how their acts of goodwill have changed one person's life.

1.2

Host: This is Pat Miles on the *Afternoon Update.* Last week we heard from two people whose generosity has touched the lives of thousands. While over 50% of Americans donate to charitable causes, these two donors, who wish to remain anonymous, have chosen to make direct contributions to individuals in need. I hope they are tuned in this afternoon because they will hear how their acts of goodwill have changed one person's life. After last week's show, we received hundreds of letters from people wishing to express their gratitude to their unidentified benefactor. Today I'll read a thank you note from one woman who is so grateful for the help she received that she now donates one third of her wealth to charity. She writes:

Dear Anonymous Donor:

I don't know where I would be today without your generosity. I am a single mother and the challenges that I faced when I was raising my two sons were sometimes overwhelming. I had one son in kindergarten and another still in diapers. It was a particularly cold winter and I had missed several payments to the gas company so we were without heat. One night, with the one-year-old in my lap and my older son warming his hands near the stove, I had to make a decision. Should I use the last of my money to send a check to the gas company, buy milk for the baby, pay for more diapers, or get enough canned goods to last until the next pay check? In the end, the top priority was milk. Above all, the baby's nutrition was what mattered. My older son and I could continue to survive on tuna fish. The temperature was supposed to rise, so the gas company was the last on the list. Of course diapers were crucial, but with a little creativity one could make do for a short time.

That afternoon, expecting to get another threatening letter from the gas company, I received the check that turned my life around. It got me through that catastrophic winter, and fifteen years later, I am a business woman with money to spare. For me, there is nothing more rewarding than contributing what I can to those in need.

Sincerely,

Grateful Recipient

1.3

Amy Radil: I had just done a story about a welfare mother who was having trouble feeding her children, when I got a phone message. The woman in the message, let's call her the Mystery Donor, said she would like to do something, anonymously, to help the woman in my story. She ended up paying off a $1,200 light bill to keep the woman's power from being shut off. Her career as a benefactor really began after she lost her husband.

Donor: My husband died about three years ago and I had access to more money than I needed for expenses. So it was an opportunity to start giving money away.

Amy Radil: At age 58, the Mystery Donor lives in a pretty but not extravagant Seattle home. When her husband was alive they gave money but tended to focus on established charities. Now she acts on her own. Altogether she donates a quarter of her income each year, and she says that amount will increase over time. She says she often gives secretly because she's learned that money can change relationships. Her first secret donation was to a massage therapist she knew.

Donor: She was a single mother and so this was really important work. And she broke her leg. And anybody who's been a single mother as I have knows what a catastrophe looks like on its way. And that looked awful to me. So what I did was to give her some money anonymously through having a cashier's check from the bank sent to her from another town.

Amy Radil: These small, personal gifts often go to helping single mothers. Their experience echoes her own years ago.

Donor: I know what that feels like to feel desperate and need to care for a child. I was poor as a single mother for a period, looking for a job and had a one-year-old. I do recall one night where I had to decide whether to buy tuna fish or diapers. And it was down to that before I got my next paycheck. Of course we got the diapers.

Amy Radil: She describes the past three years as a learning curve in the art of philanthropy. She contributes hundreds of thousands of dollars each year to her cause of choice: sustainable farming. She belongs to a group, the Women Donors Network that put her in touch with a University of Montana professor named Neva Hassanein. Hassanein had created a program to help local farmers supply the school's cafeteria food. The Mystery Donor wanted to help expand the program to other institutions. Hassanein says she then proposed having Americorp volunteers work with other colleges to replicate it.

3.2

Many donations can be declared as tax deductions: cars, clothes, furniture . . .
1. Every year, I contribute to several organizations: the Red Cross, the Children's Fund, my church . . .
2. We need your time, money, anything you can give.
3. You have to decide which of these gets top priority: studying, helping out at home, or volunteering your time.

UNIT 7

1.1

Anchor: Tonight our weekly report card on education looks at the issue of homework. Usually it's the students who do the complaining, but there is growing concern among parents about the effect of homework on their children.

1.2

Anchor: Tonight our weekly report card on education looks at the issue of homework. Usually it's the students who do the complaining, but there is growing concern among parents about the effect of homework on their children.

Chris Roberts reports.

Chris (reporter): I've spoken with several parents as they are leaving their parent-teacher conferences, and what I'm hearing is that they are dissatisfied with the amount of work their children take home. Ms. Kim, what exactly are you unhappy about?

Ms. June Kim: Well don't get me wrong. I *absolutely* feel that homework is necessary. What I mean is that the amount of homework is way too demanding. My son is in the third grade and sometimes he is up until 9 o'clock finishing his assignments. I just can't believe this makes him a better student.

Mr. Robert Martino: I agree. In fact, I think this might have the opposite effect. Sometimes my daughter is so tired the next morning that she can hardly keep her eyes open, much less pay attention in class. The amount of homework kids are given is way over the top. And this also means that when my wife and I get home after work, one of us cooks dinner and the other monitors Camilla to make sure she finishes her assignments. It's become a ritual. We have no time to be a family anymore.

Chris: So what does the research say? Is there any tangible evidence that schools are giving too much homework? Advocates of the push towards more homework, such as the National Association of Educational Progress, have evidence that supports their view as it relates to junior high and high school students. Research conducted in 2001 shows that both junior high and high school students who did more homework performed better than those who did less homework.

While the results did not show this correlation for elementary school children, NAEP believes that homework in elementary school still pays off because it "may lay the foundation for future success." (http://www.hoover.org/publications/digest).

Parents of elementary school children, like Ms. Kim and Mr. Martino, may be pleased with the result of a recent survey conducted by the University of Michigan. It indicates that having family meals together is one of the most important factors in performance on standardized tests.

Anchor: Thank you Chris. We'll have a look at teachers' performance next on the weekly report card on education.

1.3

Margot Adler: Thousands of families have had the experience of homework assignments that become family events: that wooden replica of the Mayflower that Dad and Mom finished after eight-year-old Johnny got bored, the science fair project that went over the top, the Internet search that took the whole weekend. These days, kids and families are doing lots of homework, and many of those parents are finding that the amount of hands-on help required is totally alien to their own experience growing up, where homework was pretty minimal until high school, and parents stayed way out of the picture. Steven Oloya, a professor of special education, lives outside of Los Angeles. He has five children who have been in public schools and Catholic schools. One of his daughters, Kaitlyn, attends Chaparral High School, and wants to be a teacher.

Kaitlyn: I usually get home around 5:00, and I'm usually doing homework until about 11 or 12 at night.

Professor Steven Oloya: We've had many nights, one and two in the morning.

Kaitlyn: I'll find myself just getting really, really tired doing my homework. I have to get up and move around to stay awake.

Prof. Oloya: That's a nightly ritual, because around 11:30 she starts to conk out in the chair, and I go, "Kate, Kate, you've got to wake up." We go outside, sprint down the street, sprint back up the street, just to get her to wake up so she can do one more hour of solid, intense reading and studying.

Adler: Oloya isn't the only parent who talks about sleep and homework. Cecilia Bluer thinks back to her daughter's previous year in the New York City public schools.

Ms. Cecilia Bluer: Last year, when she was in third grade, she got four hours of homework a night. She was up until 11 at night in tears. There were days that I did not take her to school the next day because she was so distraught over not doing homework, and we had gotten up at 5 to complete her assignment. I just had to give her mental health days. I wasn't the only mother in that class keeping their children out of school so they could just get a full night's sleep.

Adler: Advocates believe homework teaches responsibility, keeps kids off the streets, helps refine study skills and gets parents involved in their kids' schooling. Joyce Epstein, a sociologist at Johns Hopkins University's Center on Schools, Families and Communities, says her research over 20 years gives support for homework.

Ms. Joyce Epstein: It is helpful for showing that youngsters at any grade level who do their work and complete it do do better in school than kids just like them, similar youngsters, who don't complete their work.

Adler: It is the impact of homework on family life that has many parents hopping mad, particularly in a culture where two parents often work and home-life hours are already truncated by many social forces. Steven Russo, an administrator at a medical school, has two children in the New York City public schools, a daughter in sixth grade and a son in ninth grade.

Mr. Steven Russo: When you add it all up, you know, your child's in school for 30 hours a week, they're going to have another 10 hours of homework, then they're expected to read between a half an hour to an hour a night, and then there are projects and there's art, you're talking about a 45 to a 50-hour work week for a 10-year-old.

Adler: Margot Adler, NPR News, New York.

UNIT 8

1.1

Barista: May I help the following guest, please?

Customer A: Double tall no whip skinny latte, please.

Barista: That'll be $3.57. May I help the following guest, please?

Reporter: Sound familiar? Places like this are a fairly recent phenomenon—a kind of coffee shop/cafe where you can pick up your own specialized cup of coffee and hang out for as long as you want. No waiter will pressure you to leave because there are no waiters. Why are American cities overrun by Starbucks and a half a dozen other stores like it?

1.2

Barista: May I help the following guest, please?

Customer A: Double tall no whip skinny latte, please.

Barista: That'll be $3.57. May I help the following guest, please?

Reporter: Sound familiar? Places like this are a fairly recent phenomenon—a kind of coffee shop/cafe where you can pick up your own specialized cup of coffee and hang out for as long as you want. No waiter will pressure you to leave because there are no waiters.

Why are American cities overrun by Starbucks and a half a dozen other stores like it? Like many social phenomena, Starbucks is responding to a demand in the market. And in this case, the demand originates in part from a change in the atmosphere of the business world and the make up of the workforce. Nowadays offices are much more casual. Employees are not locked into such rigid schedules and can take a break when they want to. Here's a customer who looks like he just came from the office.

Excuse me, sir. May I ask you why you came to Starbucks?

Customer B: I just had to get out of the office and clear my head. I was looking at my desk stacked with papers, and I thought, boy, it's time for a coffee break.

Reporter: Any reason you came here?

Customer: Yeah, well it's just around the corner and I can pick up a latte and chill out before I have to face those stacks of papers.

Barista: Grande double latte.

Customer B: Oh, that's mine.

Barista: Enjoy it.

Reporter: We're also witnessing a shift in the structure of the business world. Where once the core of a business was the employees who worked there, today there is an increasing number of freelance workers. These are workers who are not employed directly by a company but contract to work for one or more companies. They usually don't have office space, other than the ten square feet that serves as an office in their own home. Rather than working in complete isolation, some freelancers use Starbucks as their office away from home. You've probably seen them working away at their computers, oblivious to the noise around them.

Well, I think I'll have a cup of coffee myself.

This is Judy Framer, and thank you for listening to the Afternoon Show.

1.3

Bob Edwards, Host: France, home of the two-hour, sit-down mid-day meal, is witnessing a boom in take-out sandwiches. At noon, customers line up outside Paris bakeries, waiting to buy long, thin versions of a shrimp salad and avocado sandwich, or other iconoclastic delicacies. The variation in eating habits is reflecting a deeper change in French society. NPR's Sarah Chayes reports.

Sarah Chayes: As with any major shift in something as intimate as eating, the story is complicated. Sociologist Claude Fishlere makes a living studying food habits here.

Claude Fishlere: It starts with a change in the workforce. So it's a feminization, white-collarization, if I can say so . . . services rather than industry. . . .

Sarah Chayes: The result has been a revolution in one of France's core industries—the bakery. Formerly, bakeries here offered a limited range of albeit excellent products—about four kinds of bread, breakfast and dessert pastries. Now, that's just the start.

Audile Gazier: (speaks French)

Sarah Chayes: She says, nowadays people want to eat faster at noon, and leave early at the end of the day. Life is changing, she says; we have to keep up. The changes include women making up almost half the labor force now, and making their tastes known, and men, more likely to be working behind a computer than behind a jackhammer, not needing to eat so much. Sociologist Fishlere:

Claude Fishlere: They also have to pick up the children as early as possible, from the *crèche*.

Sarah Chayes: . . . daycare center.

Claude Fishlere: Daycare center. So basically, they look for something that's very close to what is called fast food. And, eh, the interesting point is that the um, supply that has developed goes well beyond your, uh, basic McDonald's hamburgers.

UNIT 9

1.1

Moderator: This is Bill Haas on *Face-to-Face*. Tonight two experts discuss the issue of teaching immigrant children. Mr. Green represents Only English, a group whose mission is to make English the official language of the United States. Ms. Anopolis represents the Multicultural Society. So, let's start with Ms. Anopolis. Exactly what is your stand on this issue?

1.2

Moderator: This is Bill Haas on *Face-to-Face*. Tonight two experts discuss the issue of teaching immigrant children. Mr. Green represents Only English, a group whose mission is to make English the official language of the United States. Ms. Anopolis represents the Multicultural Society. So, let's start with Ms. Anopolis. Exactly what is your stand on this issue?

Ms. Anopolis: Certainly we feel that immigrant children need to learn English, but we also feel that putting them directly into mainstream classes is not the ideal way for them to succeed in school. What we've seen is that students who have been uprooted from their culture need time to assimilate. In a multilingual classroom, students whose native language isn't English learn together in cooperative settings where they support each other.

Moderator: Mr. Green, could you tell us how Only English feels about this issue?

Mr. Green: Pretty much the opposite of what Ms. Anopolis just described. First, cooperative learning is just a way for the teacher to be lazy. And taking the students out of the mainstream classes is a big mistake. When children are set apart from the other kids in their peer group we feel that A) they won't learn English very quickly and B) they will feel intimidated by their peers. Kids, especially teenagers, want to belong to the mainstream.

Ms. Anopolis: Well, uh for newly arrived immigrants who aren't familiar with either the culture or the language, it's too much for them to be thrown in with the American kids. They're actually relieved to be around kids in the same situation that they're in.

Moderator: So how does the teacher talk to students from so many different countries?

Ms. Anopolis: It's not easy. The students all support each other. And sometimes one student will interpret for a new student.

Mr. Green: Hang on a minute, are you saying that they're allowed to speak in their native tongues?

Ms. Anopolis: It's sometimes the best way for them to learn. And although we know that learning English is the only way they'll get ahead, we also think it's important that they don't forget their language.

Mr. Green: Well you know that's one of our beliefs also. We've fallen behind because we rely on everyone else to speak English. It puts us in a weaker position internationally.

Moderator: Well we'll have to end on that note. This Is Bill Haas with *Face-to-Face*.

1.2, Question 6

Ms. Anopolis: It's not easy. The students all support each other. And sometimes one student will interpret for a new student.

Moderator: Hang on a minute; are you saying that they're allowed to speak in their native tongues?

1.3

Mary Ambrose: Students in cities like New York are used to hearing wide variations of English. In a town where immigrant communities flourish, many dialects and languages mix with standard English. In fact, there's an international high school that encourages immigrant students to use and develop their native tongues while learning English. It's a new approach, and as Richard Schiffman reports, it seems to work.

Richard Schiffman: The philosophy of this school is that you learn by doing, and not by hearing the teacher lecture. In this math class, for example, six teams of young people are gathered around lab tables, building their own miniature temple out of cardboard. But to find out what really sets this school apart, you need to get up close.

The four teenage boys at this table are planning their temple in Polish. At the other tables, they're speaking Spanish, English, and Mandarin Chinese. This is not just a bilingual classroom; it's a multilingual one, and the pupils here are all recent immigrants to the United States. Their teacher, Jennifer Shenke, walks around the room, quietly helping out.

Jennifer Shenke: They love building things. This has been really successful, and they've learned a lot of math that they didn't have before, umm, just doing scale and proportion. And, and I feel pretty good about that because they, they didn't know that they were learning it until they had learned it.

Richard Schiffman: Shenke is happy that her pupils are learning math and enjoying themselves in the process, and she's especially pleased that they're teaching one another. She knows that many in her classroom wouldn't be able to follow her if she lectured. So she depends on the pupils who know more English and more math to help teach those who know less. That's what's happening now at the lab tables. They're helping each other out in their own languages. . . .

Priscilla Billarrel: . . . I think what we share the most is a feeling of not fitting in.

Richard Schiffman: Priscilla Billarrel left Chile when she was 14 years old. She says that although they come from all over the world, the students at the International High School understand each other very well.

Priscilla Billarrel: Since we all are immigrants in here, we all know what['s] to be different feels like, so we support one another. Whenever we have problems with pronunciation[s], or we're missing words or something, whatever we're saying, we correct one another kindly. We don't make fun of each other. That's what I really like about this school. . . .

Richard Schiffman: . . . New York City can be an intimidating place, even for those who have spent their whole lives here. But for young people who have just been uprooted from tight-knit, extended families and traditional communities abroad, the city can seem positively unfriendly. Teacher Aaron Listhaus says that young immigrants don't just need a place to learn English and other subjects. They need, above all else, a place that feels completely safe and welcoming.

Aaron Listhaus: It's particularly important for these students to have a comfort level in a place called school and for that school to feel like home . . . to feel like their needs are going to get met, um, they're going to be listened to, they're going to be valued for who they are and the diverse backgrounds that they come from, and that those things are viewed as what makes them special rather than what makes them a problem.

Richard Schiffman: The fact that immigrant youngsters speak a language other than English, Listhaus says, is seen by most educators as a problem that needs to be corrected. The usual approach is to teach students exclusively in English, and to suppress the use of their native language. Evelyna Namovich, who came to the U.S. three years ago from Poland, remembers what it was like to find herself in a typical New York City school.

Evelyna Namovich: Sometimes it was so difficult because I didn't know what was the subject all about, what was she speaking about, and I would need somebody to translate, even a little bit for me, you know. And we couldn't, because we would have to write something like . . . an essay, er, like punishment, if we spoke Polish.

Richard Schiffman: Evelyna says she was relieved when she transferred to the International High School, where she not only wasn't punished for speaking Polish, she was encouraged to bone up on her native language at the same time as she was learning English. Instructor Aaron Listhaus says that it's important that young immigrants don't lose their languages, as his own immigrant parents from eastern Europe did.

Richard Schiffman: . . . Today, as also in the past, immigrants to the U.S. often feel the need to assimilate as quickly as possible into mainstream American culture. But there is one place, at least, where new immigrants are being encouraged to keep what is unique to them. From the International High School in New York, I'm Richard Schiffman, for *The World*.

UNIT 10

1.1

Anchor: Almost anyone who has lived in a big city can tell you how irritating it is to be awakened in the middle of the night by the wail of a car alarm. The loss of sleep can drive you crazy, but this is just one in a long list of problems that such high decibel noises can cause.

1.2

Anchor: Almost anyone who has lived in a big city can tell you how irritating it is to be awakened in the middle of the night by the wail of a car alarm. The loss of sleep can drive you crazy, but this is just one in a long list of problems that such high decibel noises can cause. Jonathan Dworsky reports from New York City.

Jonathan: People in this noisy neighborhood in upper Manhattan are fed up with car alarms. They're angry enough at being jolted awake several times a week, but more than that they worry about what effect these alarms will have on their children. Already studies have shown that continuous exposure to high-decibel noise can cause an increase in heart rate and blood pressure. And studies on children who were surrounded by elevated noise levels found that these children had lower reading levels than children in less noisy areas. These studies were repeated after the noise from a nearby train had been lowered, and the children's reading scores improved.

Andrea Carera, mother of a two-year-old boy, says,

Andrea: By the time my child can read, he will already have been exposed to the constant roar of the traffic, but the intense siren of a car alarm is way above the level of safety.

Jonathan: Ms. Carera has a valid concern. According to The National Institute of Occupational Safety and Health, exposure to noise above 85 decibels for 8 hours or more is a danger to your health. City traffic and trucks are about 90 decibels. The siren of a car alarm is about 120 decibels, about the same as a plane taking off.

Children in her neighborhood will be living in an environment where the noise of cars, trucks, and buses is enough to increase stress hormones. But we don't know what the studies about car alarms will show.

The parents here are sick and tired of listening to the shrill siren of car alarms. However, it's for their children that they are most concerned. They've started a group called Parents to Silence Car Alarms. They don't think that making the owner of a car pay a fine is enough. These parents have started a campaign to have car alarms banned.

This is Jonathan Dworsky reporting from the noisy streets of Manhattan.

1.3

Catherine Abate: The streets are much noisier than they were 20 years ago . . . even 10 years ago.

Neal Rauch: New York State Senator Catherine Abate represents Manhattan.

Catherine Abate: The noise affects not only their ability to sleep at night, but for the most part their ability to work during the day. And even parents have come to me and said, "What is the impact on children?" And there are more and more studies that show that young people in particular, that are exposed to a sustained amount of loud noise, have hearing loss. So it's a health issue, it's a quality of life issue.

Neal Rauch: Enforcement of existing laws, along with new regulations, may be cutting down noise in some neighborhoods. It's now illegal for alarms to run for more than three minutes. After that police can break into a car to disable the alarm or even tow away a wailing vehicle. It's hoped these actions will motivate car owners to adjust their alarms, making them less sensitive so vibrations from passing trucks and the like don't set them off.

Achievement Tests Answer Key

UNIT 1

1.1
C

1.2
1. C   2. A   3. B   4. D   5. B   6. B

1.3
People on the news program: E, F
Mr. Tucker: C

2.1
1. catch the news
2. addicted to
3. newsworthy
4. plugged in
5. make a connection

2.2
1. D   2. F   3. G   4. B   5. E

3.1
1. was saved
2. had been made
3. was trapped
4. was rewarded

3.2
1. əz   2. ər   3. əv

3.3
1. C
2. C
3. D

4.1
Answers will vary. Possible answer:
The news is too superficial.

4.2
Answers will vary. Possible answer:
I couldn't agree more.

4.3
Answers will vary. See the scoring rubric on page T-77.

UNIT 2

1.1
C

1.2
1. D   2. A   3. D   4. C   5. D   6. B

1.3
1. B   2. F   3. E

2.1
1. learning disability
2. overcome
3. tough
4. in store for
5. determined

2.2
1. B   2. A   3. C   4. C   5. A

3.1
1. to impress
2. talking
3. hearing
4. finishing

3.2
1. 3   2. 2   3. 3

3.3
1. B   2. E   3. F

4.1
Answers will vary. Possible answer:
There is a lot of discrimination in John's neighborhood.

4.2
Answers will vary. Possible answer:
John realized that a college education could change his life.

4.3
Answers will vary. See the scoring rubric on page T-77.

UNIT 3

1.1
A

1.2
1. D   2. D   3. C   4. D   5. B   6. C

1.3
1. B   2. C   3. D

2.1
1. insomnia
2. surge
3. chronically
4. sleep-deprived
5. fatigue
6. alertness
7. do without
8. snoring
9. irritable
10. priority

3.1

1. If I sleep . . . slept
2. . . . I can get to work . . . could
3. At work, I won't . . . wouldn't
4. . . . if I stop drinking . . . stopped

3.2

1. B   2. A   3. A

3.3

1. A   2. B   3. C

4.1

Answers will vary. Possible answer:
Your eyes move rapidly.

4.2

Answers will vary. Possible answer:
Could you say that another way?

4.3

Answers will vary. See the scoring rubric on page T-77.

UNIT 4

1.1

C

1.2

1. B   2. D   3. B   4. D   5. A   6. B

1.3

(The order of answers is not important.)

1. A   2. C   3. E

2.1

1. intriguing   4. vocalize
2. socialized   5. superior
3. rote memorization   6. unethical

2.2

1. F   2. D   3. E   4. B

3.1

1. C   2. A   3. B   4. B

3.2

1. A   2. B   3. B

3.3

1. for instance
2. Such as?
3. Could you give me some more details?

4.1

Answers will vary. Possible answer:
Koko had a vocabulary of more than 1,000 words.

4.2

Answers will vary. Possible answer:
The professor said (that) Koko had a vocabulary of more than 1,000 words.

4.3

Answers will vary. See the scoring rubric on page T-77.

UNIT 5

1.1

B

1.2

1. A   2. D   3. B   4. B   5. A   6. C

1.3

Susie Potter Gibbs: F
Asención Cantez: C, D

2.1

1. get together
2. generations
3. it's a different story
4. seniors
5. assisted living facilities

2.2

1. D   2. C   3. B   4. F   5. E

3.1

1. isn't it   3. can't it
2. didn't she   4. does it

3.2

1. A   2. A   3. A

3.3

1. how about
2. Why don't you
3. could consider

4.1

Answers will vary. Possible answer:
She eats fresh fruits.

4.2

Answers will vary. Possible answer:
You could stop worrying.

4.3

Answers will vary. See the scoring rubric on page T-77.

UNIT 6

1.1

   B

1.2

1. D   2. D   3. B   4. A   5. A   6. C

1.3

Donor: last priority—E
Recipient:
          top priority—F
          last priority—A

2.1

1. contributions   4. charitable
2. donors   5. cause
3. anonymous

2.2

1. catastrophic   4. rewarding
2. generosity   5. wealth
3. inherit

3.1

1. whose   3. when
2. that or which   4. where

3.2

1. U   2. F   3. F

3.3

1. of least concern
2. the top priority
3. above all

4.1

Answers will vary. Possible answer:

The woman had to decide whether to spend her money on milk. She decided that milk was the top priority.

4.2

Answers will vary. Possible answer:
My top priority would be to pay the gas bill.

4.3

Answers will vary. See the scoring rubric on page T-77.

UNIT 7

1.1

   C

1.2

1. A   2. C   3. A   4. C   5. C   6. A

1.3

(The order of answers is not important.)
National Association of Educational Progress: Joyce Epstein
University of Michigan: Robert Martino, Steven Russo

2.1

1. demanding   4. way over the top
2. distraught   5. monitor
3. pays off

2.2

1. C   2. F   3. G   4. H   5. A

3.1

1. help me (to) do   3. get him to do
2. let their children decide   4. have her come

3.2

1. the first two *es* in *self-esteem*
2. the *a* in *mental*
3. the *a* in *amount*

3.3

1. To put it another way,
2. no phrase
3. What this means is

4.1

Answers will vary. Possible answer:

Junior high and high school students who did more homework performed better.

4.2

Answers will vary. Possible answer:

What this means is that if students do more homework, they will do better on standardized tests.

4.3

Answers will vary. See the scoring rubric on page T-77.

UNIT 8

1.1
D

1.2
1. C   2. C   3. B   4. C   5. D   6. B

1.3
French: more men have white collar jobs
American: more workers who don't work directly for a company, offices are more casual

2.1
1. phenomenon
2. take with a grain of salt
3. overrun
4. shift
5. workforce
6. put it on the back burner
7. witnessed
8. core
9. stacked
10. delicacy

3.1
1. B   2. B   3. A   4. B

3.2
1. D   2. A   3. B

3.3
1. See this
2. Watch how I
3. Notice what I'm doing

4.1
Answers will vary. Possible answer:
The atmosphere of the business world has changed.

4.2
Answers will vary. Possible answer:
People order lattes.

4.3
Answers will vary. See the scoring rubric on page T-77.

UNIT 9

1.1
B

1.2
1. B   2. C   3. A   4. D   5. B   6. D

1.3
C, D, F

2.1
1. assimilate   4. tight-knit
2. native tongues   5. support
3. mainstream

2.2
1. A   2. B   3. B   4. C   5. B

3.1
1. was going   3. has changed
2. didn't fit in   4. am taking

3.2
1. A   2. D   3. B

3.3
D, E, G

4.1
Answers will vary. Possible answer:
Mainstream classes make students feel that they belong.

4.2
Answers will vary. Possible answer:
Students are comfortable around other students who are in the same situation.

4.3
Answers will vary. See the scoring rubric on page T-77.

UNIT 10

1.1
A

1.2
1. C   2. A   3. D   4. A   5. A   6. B

1.3
Senator Catherine Abate: F
Jonathan Dworsky: A, E

2.1

1. fed up with
2. Sick and tired
3. jolted
4. wail
5. sirens
6. irritated
7. pay a fine
8. shrill
9. banned
10. drive you crazy

3.1

1. will have been
2. will be studying
3. will have invented
4. will (still) be using

3.2

1. A   2. B   3. B

3.3

C, D, F

4.1

Answers will vary. Possible answer:
Car alarms bother people.

4.2

Answers will vary. Possible answer:
Car alarms really drive me crazy.

4.3

Answers will vary. See the scoring rubric on page T-77.

NorthStar 4 Achievement Test Scoring Rubric: Speaking

Score	Description
4	A response at this level demonstrates clear and automatic speech, with no awkward pauses and hesitations, and pronunciation is such that the listener has no difficulty with the message; a response at this level is also marked by: • accurate information with logical connections to listening • consistent use of complex grammatical features such as relative clauses, infinitives, and compound sentences • use of variety of vocabulary words relevant to unit • minor mistakes with grammar and vocabulary use
3	A response at this level demonstrates generally clear and automatic speech, with one or two short pauses and hesitations, and typically correct pronunciation of words; a response at this level is also marked by: • mostly accurate information with logical connections to listening • consistent use of complex grammatical features such as relative clauses, adverb phrases, and extended longer formulaic expressions • use of multiple vocabulary words from and related to unit • mostly accurate grammar and vocabulary use
2	A response at this level demonstrates generally clear and automatic speech, with one or two short pauses and hesitations, and generally correct pronunciation of words; a response at this level is also marked by: • mostly accurate information with logical connections to listening • somewhat consistent use of complex grammatical features such as relative clauses, adverb phrases, and longer formulaic expressions • use of some vocabulary words from unit • generally accurate grammar and vocabulary use
I	A response at this level demonstrates somewhat clear and automatic speech, with some short pauses and hesitations, and generally correct pronunciation of words; a response at this level is also marked by: • generally accurate information with somewhat logical connection to listening • consistent use of grammatical features such as prepositional phrases, modals, simple verb tenses, and direct objects; little or no attempt to use complex grammatical structures is made • use of multiple vocabulary words from unit • generally accurate grammar and vocabulary use
0	A response at this level attempts to address the prompt in English, and is marked by multiple long pauses, very slow speech, and limited correct pronunciation of words; a response at this level is also marked by: • general information needs to be more connected to listening; information needs to be accurate • use of few basic formulaic expressions • reliance on one or two vocabulary words from prompt; language is often recycled • frequent errors in grammar and vocabulary use A response at this level could also include no attempt to respond.

Notes

Notes

Notes

Notes

CD Tracking Guide
Achievement Tests